Remote Sensing

in

ArcGIS® Pro

Tammy E. Parece

John A. McGee

James B. Campbell

These educational materials were developed with support from the Geospatial Technician Education-Unmanned Aircraft Systems (GeoTEd-UAS) project funded through the National Science Foundation's Advanced Technological Education program (DUE 1601614).

Remote Sensing in ArcGIS® Pro

Credits

This tutorial was supported by:	In partnership with:
NSF Division of Undergraduate Education 1601614 GeoTEd-UAS	VT COLLEGE OF NATURAL RESOURCES AND ENVIRONMENT VIRGINIA TECH. Virginia Cooperative Extension Virginia Tech Virginia State University www.ext.vt.edu COLORADO MESA UNIVERSITY VIRGINIA VIEW VirginiaView.net

Originated by: James Campbell & John McGee	Chapters by: Tammy Parece	Video design and recording by: Cherie Aukland	Funded by: The National Science Foundation through GeoTed-UAS www.geoted-uas.org

This educational resource (and a broader collection of educational resources) is available either as a hardcopy version or an ePublication (Kindle) from Amazon.com.

Videos designed to accompany this document are available through the Virginia Geospatial Extension Program YouTube Channel: https://www.youtube.com/channel/UCoWJFK0sT5fgN-nYTZrQY3Q

For additional information, please contact:
Tammy Parece
tparece@coloradomesa.edu

Cover design:
    John McGee (Virginia Tech Dept. of Forest Resources and Environmental Conservation)
Cover image acknowledgements:
    Front cover – James Campbell (Virginia Tech Dept. of Geography), Daniel Cross (Virginia Tech
        Conservation Management Institute), and Tammy Parece (Colorado Mesa University Dept. of
        Social and Behavioral Sciences)
    Back cover - *Making Waves in Marlborough Sounds*, Part of the Landsat Image Gallery, available
        from https://landsat.visibleearth.nasa.gov

Remote Sensing in ArcGIS® Pro

BASICS

ADDING DATA

SAVING
&
DISPLAYING
DATA

**ANALYZING
LANDSAT
IMAGERY**

Introduction to this Manual

This manual introduces users to using remote sensing with ArcGIS® Pro. While many examples in this text are associated with satellite imagery, the techniques and examples provided are also applicable to other imagery sources as well, including multispectral image mosaics collected by small unmanned aircraft systems (sUAS; sometimes referred to as drones, UAV's. etc.).

Although the processes discussed in this book are available in most versions of ArcGIS® Pro, many of the tools and shortcut icons introduced in this book are only available with version 2.2 and above. Prior knowledge of ArcGIS® Pro is encouraged, but not required, as an introduction to the basics is provided. This manual was designed to be an introductory text and can be used as a lab manual. This document is not intended to be a comprehensive, theoretical or practical for image analysis manual, or a comprehensive ArcGIS® Pro user manual.

The goal of this book is to expand student access to remote sensing analysis by introducing students to use of ArcGIS® Pro capabilities, thereby facilitating access to additional remote sensing software. This manual does not cover remote sensing fundamentals and users of the manual should refer to remote sensing textbooks, such as suggested in the list of potential references below. Furthermore, users of this manual should remain aware of the distinctions between GIS analysis and the practice of remote sensing, which often use similar software, but require mastery of much different knowledge bases.

The chapters within this book are designed to be completed in sequence. In most cases, each chapter builds on knowledge acquired from preceding chapters. The first nine chapters introduce the user to some of the basics of ArcGIS® Pro. Chapters 10 - 23 assume that readers have knowledge of these basics. The introductory chapters do not include information on how to download basic GIS files but users may use any point, line or polygon vector files, any elevation raster file, and any map document completed in another GIS software to complete these tutorials.

If shapefiles are needed by the user of this book, they can be acquired from the U.S. Census Bureau's Tigerline data base - http://www.census.gov/geo/maps-data/data/tiger-line.html for the mid-Atlantic States as boundary files. Point, line, and polygons files can be downloaded from many U.S. municipalities, such as Roanoke, Virginia (ftp://ftp.roanokeva.gov/GIS/Shapefiles/), Richmond, Virginia (ftp://ftp.ci.richmond.va.us/GIS), or Chicago, Illinois (https://data.cityofchicago.org/browse?tags=gis). You can locate and access many other municipalities' GIS files from the web by using the search terms:

- downloadable GIS files for *name of municipality*, or
- *name of municipality* FTP site.

Most GIS files are downloaded as .zip files. The raster files used in the first six tutorials were downloaded from the United States Geologic Survey (USGS) Seamless Server at http://viewer.nationalmap.gov/viewer/.

If you have a working knowledge of ArcGIS® Pro, then you can start with Chapter 10 in which we introduce remotely sensed imagery principles. If you are familiar with Landsat and EarthExplorer, you can skip most of Chapter 11 (searching and downloading Landsat 8 imagery). However, you should peruse this chapter to identify the image used in most of the other chapters. Chapter 12 revises the metadata for this image. We recommend that you review this chapter as metadata does vary from image to image.

Even if you are familiar with Landsat scenes and downloading the scenes from the web, you will need to complete Chapters 13 through 16. These chapters cover displaying Landsat 8 Imagery and additional processing of the downloaded image for use in Chapters 17 – 19 and Chapters 21 – 23.

Chapters 13 – 19 and Chapters 21 - 23 use a single Landsat 8 scene which covers part of central and western Virginia. Chapter 20 Change Detection, uses two Landsat 8 scenes from southwestern Colorado. This chapter can be completed independently if you already know how to use EarthExplorer. However, we recommend completing Chapters 17 – 19 on image enhancement as these techniques will be useful in identifying the changes that occur between the two Colorado images.

Chapters 13 through 16 must be completed before doing Chapters 17 through 19 and 21 through 23. It is recommended that you complete Chapters 17 through 19 as image enhancement techniques will assist with image classification. You must complete Chapters 21 and 22 before the final chapter – Chapter 23 Accuracy Assessment. While our main purpose is to focus upon use of Landsat 8 imagery in ArcGIS® Pro. These chapters do introduce techniques that prepare you to complete similar analyses using images from other sensors such as Sentinel, AVHRR, and multispectral sensors onboard sUAS platforms. Landsat 8 imagery is used in this text because it is readily available online for most of the Earth's land surface area; it is well documented, consistent, and free.

Again, this book merely serves as an introduction to using ArcGIS® Pro in remote sensing analyses. These chapters do not cover all the tools and methods available within any software program but throughout the book, in specific sections, we acknowledge other techniques/processes and point the readers to other references for additional information. This book is not a substitute for remote sensing textbooks, which present the concepts and context that support application of the techniques covered here. We encourage use of this book in the context of a more complete program to cover the information and concepts that support the applications presented here.

Additional remote sensing resources:

Landsat:

- http://landsat.usgs.gov/
- http://landsat.gsfc.nasa.gov/about/technical-information/
- https://landsat.usgs.gov/what-are-band-designations-landsat-satellites
- http://landsat.usgs.gov/about_landsat5.php
- https://landsat.usgs.gov/landsat-8
- https://www.usgs.gov/media/images/landsat-8-band-designations
- https://landsat.gsfc.nasa.gov/landsat-9/landsat-9-mission-details/
- https://pubs.usgs.gov/fs/2012/3072/fs2012-3072.pdf
- http://landsat.usgs.gov/Landsat_Processing_Details.php

- https://landsat.usgs.gov/igs-networkhttps://landsat.usgs.gov/landsat-surface-reflectance-high-level-data-products

Sentinel:

- http://www.esa.int/Our_Activities/Observing_the_Earth/Copernicus/Overview4
- https://earth.esa.int/web/sentinel/user-guides/sentinel-2-msi/resolutions/spatial
- https://sentinel.esa.int/web/sentinel/missions/sentinel-2/instrument-payload/resolution-and-swath

Other images resources from the USGS:

- USGS Earth Resources Observation and Science (EROS) Center Science Processing Architecture (ESPA) on Demand Interface https://espa.cr.usgs.gov/

Unmanned Aircraft Systems

- Geospatial Technician Education – Unmanned Aircraft Systems http://www.geoted-uas.org

The USDA NAIP Program:

- https://www.fsa.usda.gov/Assets/USDA-FSA-Public/usdafiles/APFO/geospatial-services/pdfs/2017_apfo_webservice_10.pdf

Additional Printed or online Resources for ArcGIS®Pro:

- Toolbox: **Error! Hyperlink reference not valid.**
- Geodatabases: https://pro.arcgis.com/en/pro-app/help/data/geodatabases/overview/types-of-geodatabases.htm
- Symbolization methods: http://pro.arcgis.com/en/pro-app/help/mapping/layer-properties/data-classification-methods.htm
- Resampling methods: http://pro.arcgis.com/en/pro-app/help/data/imagery/resample-function.htm
- Spatial Analyst tools: http://pro.arcgis.com/en/pro-app/tool-reference/spatial-analyst/complete-listing-of-spatial-analyst-tools.htm
- Raster functions: http://pro.arcgis.com/en/pro-app/help/data/imagery/band-arithmetic-function.htm
- Image classification wizard: https://pro.arcgis.com/en/pro-app/help/analysis/image-analyst/the-image-classification-wizard.htm

Geodetic datums

- National Geodetic Survey https://www.ngs.noaa.gov/datums/index.shtml

Map projections:

- NASA Landsat Science Worldwide Reference System
  https://landsat.gsfc.nasa.gov/the-worldwide-reference-system/
- The Geographers Craft
  https://www.colorado.edu/geography/gcraft/notes/mapproj/mapproj_f.html
- USGS map projections
  https://egsc.usgs.gov/isb//pubs/MapProjections/projections.html
- National Geographic's *Investigating Map Projections*
  https://www.nationalgeographic.org/activity/investigating-map-projections/
- Penn State University's *What are Map Projections?*
  https://www.e-education.psu.edu/geog160/node/1918
- ArcGIS.com's *About Map Projections*
  http://desktop.arcgis.com/en/arcmap/10.3/guide-books/map-projections/about-map-projections.htm

Metadata standards

- The Federal Geographic Data Committee Content Standard for Digital Geospatial Metadata: https://www.fgdc.gov/metadata/csdgm-standard

Additional resources for remote sensing and geospatial technologies:

- Remote sensing theory (and application):
  - Campbell, James B. and Randolph H. Wynne. 2011. *Introduction to Remote Sensing* - 5th Edition. The Guilford Press. New York, NY. 677 p. (6th edition forthcoming).
  - Jensen, John R. 2015.Introductory Digital Image Processing: A Remote Sensing Perspective (4th Edition)– *3rd Edition.* Pearson. Upper Saddle River, NJ. 656 p.
- Hands-on Remote Sensing Tutorial
  - Keranen, Kathryn and Robert Kolvoord. 2017. *Making Spatial Decisions Using ArcGIS Pro: A Workbook.* Esri Press. 376 p.

Shellito, Bradley. 2017. *Introduction to Geospatial Technologies.* W. H. Freeman. New York. 560 p.

Additional On-line Resources for Remote Sensing:

- NASA's Astronomer's Toolbox:
  https://imagine.gsfc.nasa.gov/science/toolbox/emspectrum1.html
- Nicholas Faust's (no date) manuscript on Spatial Enhancement Georgia Institute of Technology
  http://knightlab.org/rscc/legacy/RSCC_Spatial_Enhancement.pdf
- Natural Resources Canada - Remote Sensing Tutorial:
  http://www.nrcan.gc.ca/node/9309

- Common band indices:
  https://landsat.usgs.gov/sites/default/files/documents/si_product_guide.pdf

These tutorials cover analysis of remotely sensed imagery using ESRI's ArcGIS® Pro software. The first nine chapters review ArcGIS® Pro basics. If you know ArcGIS® Pro, then you can skip these chapters and start with Chapter 10: Remotely Sensed Imagery available from the United States Geological Survey – the chapter that provides a review about remotely sensed imagery, and accessing free imagery from the United States Geological Survey (USGS).

Once ArcGIS® Pro has been installed on your computer, a shortcut can be added to your desktop or taskbar. The shortcut icon looks like this:

Open ArcGIS® Pro by left-clicking on the icon. When ArcGIS® Pro starts each time, the following screen (figure below) appears. You will need to use your ArcGIS® Online account login in order to use ArcGIS® Pro. If you do not have an ArcGIS® Online account, then you will need to contact your institution's GIS Administrator. If you do have a login, enter your credentials and check the box in front of *Sign me in automatically* (black box below), then you will not need to sign in each time you open ArcGIS® Pro.

The very first time ArcGIS® Pro opens, the following screen appears – please note that sign-in information is shown in the upper right hand corner. If this is the first time, you have used ArcGIS® Pro, the next step is to choose an option -- *Create a new project* (blank, Global, Local). We will cover these in more detail below.

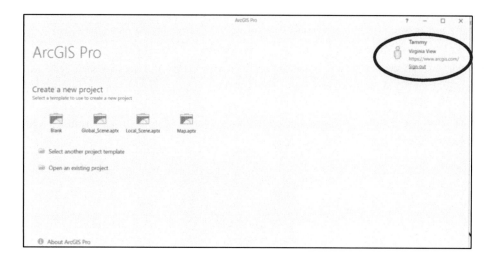

If you have created at least one project before, when ArcGIS® Pro opens, it looks like the figure below -- the last few projects completed are listed on the left.

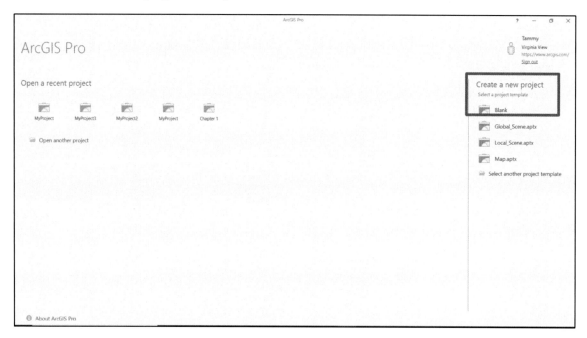

Now from the above figure, make a selection - either *Open a recent project* (on the left) or *Create a new project* (on the right).

Create a New Project

We start with *Create a New Project* – click on *Blank* (red box in prior figure). The following dialog box will appear:

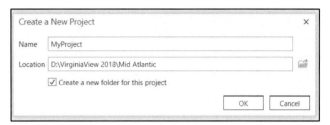

When creating a new project, it does not matter which type of project is chosen – *Blank*, *Global* or *Local*, the same dialog box opens. *Name* the project and save it (under *Location*) where it is stored on the computer. Completing this step, creates a file folder for the project. In the following figure, the *My Project* folder is displayed (from a Windows point of view):

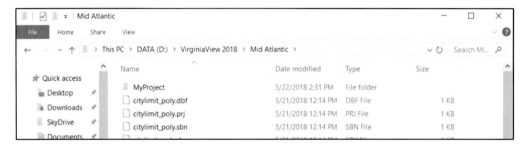

In ArcGIS® Pro, after clicking on *OK*, the following screen appears:

Where is the *Blank Project*? Click on the word *Folders* (indicated by the red arrow in the above figure).

And the project is revealed (named *MyProject*). Please note when naming files, maps or project in ArcGIS® Pro, do not use spaces. If you need a space use an underscore " _ ".

Left-double-click on *My Project*, and multiple files will display under *MyProject* in the *Catalog* window (red box in the following figure) -- this is why ArcGIS® Pro calls these projects and not map documents. Within the newly created project's file folder is a toolbox and a geodatabase. A toolbox for a project is a "container" for the project's geoprocessing tools. The project's toolbox will not be used in this book, although we will use individual tools from the ArcGIS® Pro general toolbox. (For more details on toolboxes, go to http://pro.arcgis.com/en/pro-app/help/projects/connect-to-a-toolbox.htm). A geodatabase is basically a "canister" for data files used in ArcGIS® Pro. Geodatabases are discussed in further detail in in Chapter 5 (Adding Shapefiles to the Project's Geodatabase) and in many subsequent chapters. (For more details on geodatabases, go to https://pro.arcgis.com/en/pro-app/help/data/geodatabases/overview/types-of-geodatabases.htm).

Nothing else is in the project folder because it is a new blank project.

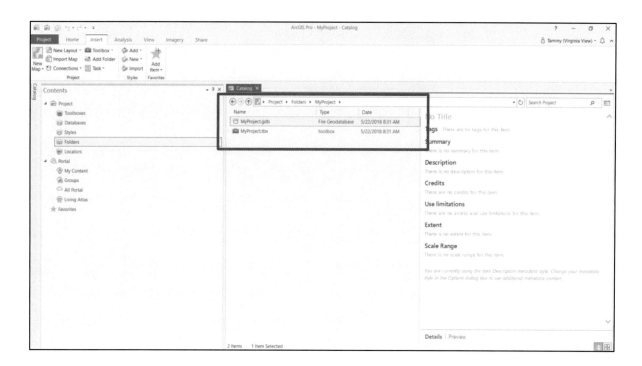

Recall, we chose *Blank* when creating a new project. What happens when *Global* is chosen instead? *Global* opens a basemap of the world:

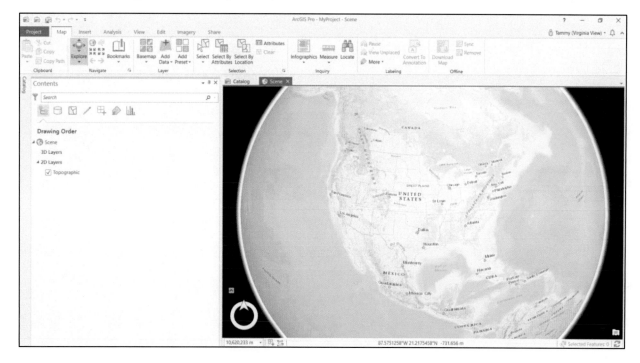

Local was defined when your organization set up their ESRI Organizational Account. As seen in the next figure, for this book, *Local* is the United States.

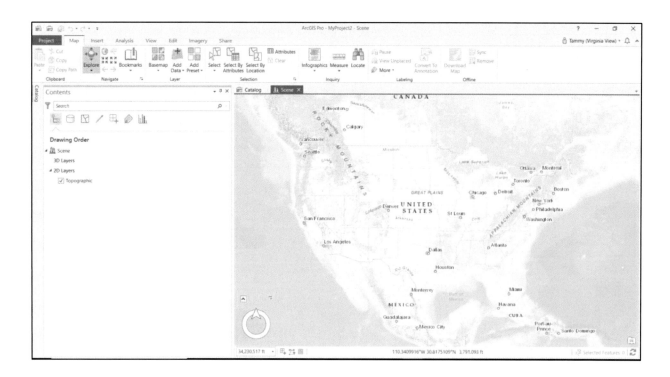

Opening an Existing Project

Now let's *Open a recent project*. Left-click on the desired project and it opens that project. Or, click on *Open another project* (red box in the figure below).

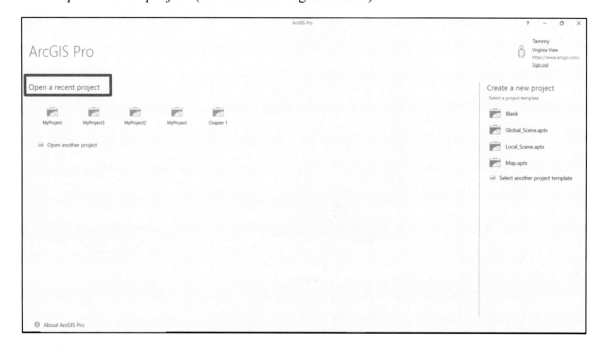

If *Open another project* is chosen, this screen displays. Select *Browse* to navigate to the folder where the desired project is located on the computer.

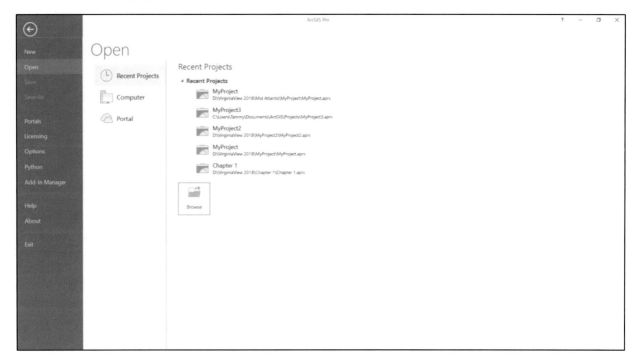

As seen from the figure below, navigation connects to an already established project (*APRX or PPKX*) for ArcGIS® Pro. This process is only for projects created in ArcGIS® Pro. ArcGIS® Pro can open maps created in ArcGIS® (file extensions such as mxd, sxd, mapx), but those maps cannot be opened with this procedure (please see Chapter 2: Using ArcGIS® Pro to Open a Map Created in ArcGIS® Desktop).

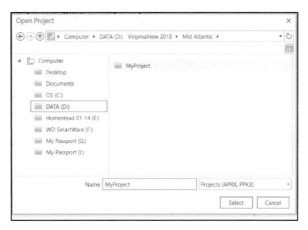

Once the desired project is located, click on the name so it populates in the *Name* field and then click on *Select*.   The following dialog box opens:

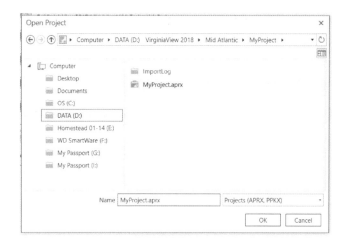

Click on the map name and be sure that it populates in the *Name* field, click *OK* and the project opens. The map displays in the map document window on the right and the layers related to the map in the *Contents* on the left[1].

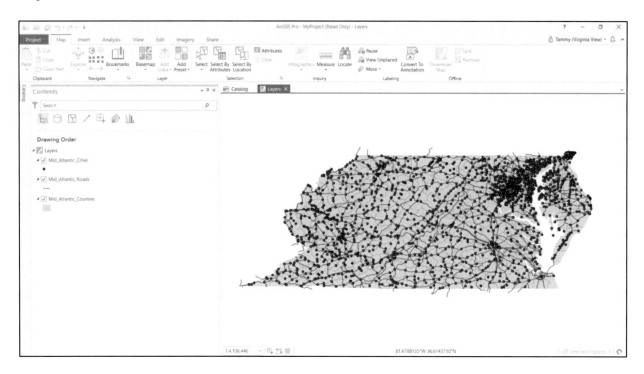

This chapter introduced ArcGIS® Pro with instructions on opening an existing map project and creating a new map project. To learn how to open a Map document created in ArcGIS® Desktop, proceed to the next chapter.

---

[1] What if the layers are listed in the *Contents*, but no map is displayed? Look in the *Contents* window, do the layers have a red exclamation point in front of them? If so, please proceed to Chapter 3: Repairing a Broken Data Link before continuing with this book.

In the prior chapter, we demonstrated creating a new map project and opening an existing map project. Map projects are specific to ArcGIS® Pro. ArcGIS® Pro can open maps created in other GIS programs, such as .mxd files created by ArcGIS® Desktop. In this chapter, we will demonstrate how to open a map document created in ArcGIS® Desktop using ArcGIS® Pro.

Once ArcGIS® Pro is opened, if this dialog box displayed, you will need to sign in to your organizational account (i.e., if you do not already have an organizational account, please see your organization's GIS Administrator). Checking the box in front of *sign me in automatically* (black box below) eliminates the need to sign in each time ArcGIS® Pro is opened.

Opening a Map (.mxd) Created in ArcGIS® Desktop

To open a map created in ArcGIS® Desktop using ArcGIS® Pro, first select *Create a New Project* and, for this chapter, we recommend *Create a New Blank* project (do not choose a basemep). A basemap can be added at a later date – covered in Chapter 4: Connecting to a Folder or an Online GIS Server.

The following figure is a reminder of the display when ArcGIS® Pro first opens:

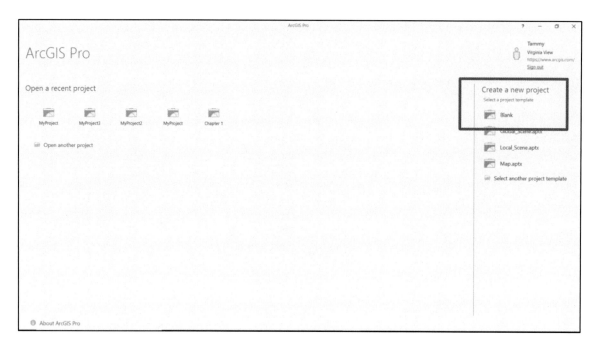

If prompted, name the project and save the project in an appropriate location on the computer. Note – even though you are opening a map document created in ArcGIS® Desktop, ArcGIS® Pro is a project based GIS program, so you will need to set up a project before opening an .mxd map.

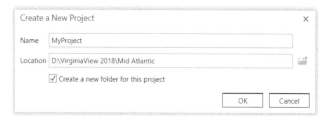

Click *OK* and a blank project opens:

We can now add data to create a new map project, or open maps created in another GIS program (e.g., from ArcGIS® Desktop, etc.). These maps are imported into an ArcGIS® Pro project. We will discuss how to add data in Chapter 6: Adding Data to a Map Project.

To open an .mxd file (map documents created in ArcGIS® Desktop have an .mxd extension), select the *Insert Tab* (red box below) and then select *Import Map* (green box below). Please take note of the message that *the data frames and layout are converted to ArcGIS® Pro format, but these changes do not affect the original document.*

Once *Import Map* is selected, this dialog box opens to prompt navigation to the location of the desired .mxd file. Select the desired map document by clicking on the name, and it will populate in the *Name* box. Click *OK*.

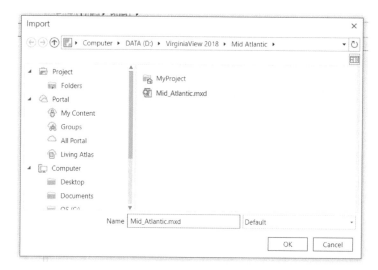

The map opens, signifying that the .mxd map document has successfully imported into ArcGIS® Pro and into the project.

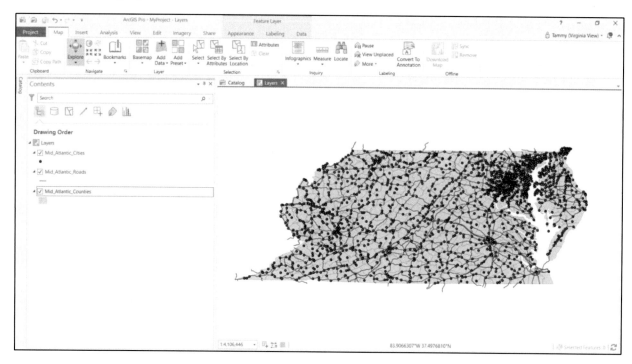

Now the map needs to be save. Click on the *Project* tab (red box in figure below).

The following window opens so that the map can be saved to the current project. Just click *Save* and it saves to the previously created project (the one created at the beginning of this chapter).

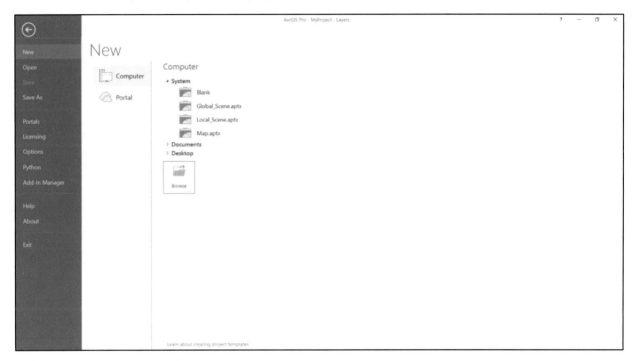

To see if the project was saved, close ArcGIS® Pro. When prompted to open a recent project, select and open the name of the newly converted map project.

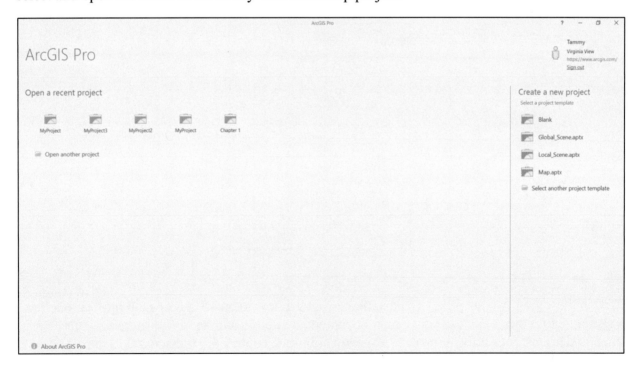

Click on the project name – in this case, we named it *MyProject* - and the map project opens:

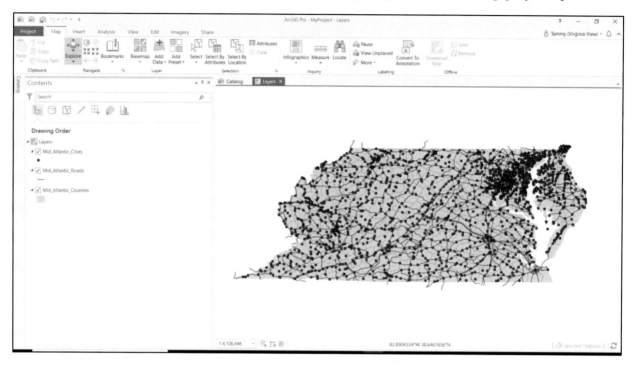

PLEASE NOTE - If the layers do not display in the map window and the layers have the red exclamation points at the beginning of the layer names (see example below) – proceed to Chapter 3: Repairing a Broken Data Link.

Within these first two chapters, we have demonstrated how to create a new map project, open an existing map project, and opening a map document created in another GIS program. Our next chapter demonstrates how to repair a broken data link. Chapters 4 – 9 discuss GIS data, adding it to the project, symbology, metadata, and exporting a map to use in a non-GIS platform.

ArcGIS® Pro is just like ArcGIS® Desktop − the data (or layers) shown in the *Contents* window merely point to the actual data files. This means that the data files (layers, etc.) are not physically saved within the map document (ArcGIS® Desktop) or map project (ArcGIS® Pro). As such, if the project was moved to another folder, to a different drive on the computer, or opened from a renamed drive, then the data address may have changed. When this happens, the link between the data files and the project may be broken.

In this chapter, we demonstrate how to repair a broken data link.

After opening a project or after importing an .mxd file (from ArcGIS® Desktop), if red exclamation points are displayed beside the layer name in the *Contents* (as seen on the right), the link to the data is broken.

Repairing a link on an individual layer in Properties

Right click on the name of one individual layer listed in the *Contents* window.

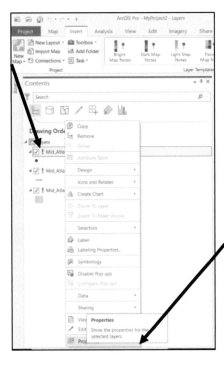

Click on *Properties* at the bottom.

The *Layer Properties* dialog box will appear.

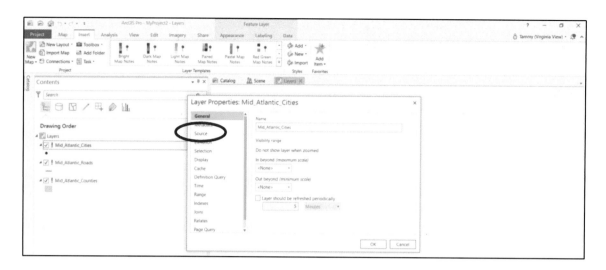

Click on the word *Source* (red oval in the above figure).

In the *Layer Properties* box, click on *Set Data Source* (black box in figure below)

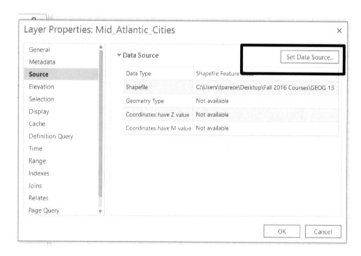

The *Change Data Source* dialog box will appear.

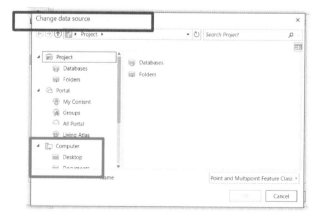

Navigate by clicking on the down arrow, or by finding the specific location in the drive list (green box on the left in the prior figure) to the specific folder on the computer where that specific shapefile is stored.

As shown in the figure below, we used the folders on the left to highlight the D drive, then the file folder under the D drive where the *MidAtlantic Shapefiles* are stored. Once the folder is located, highlight it and it is populated under *Name*, click *Open*.

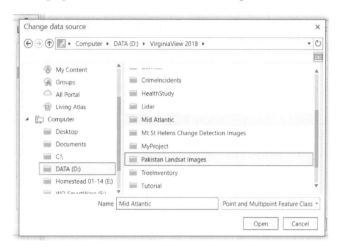

This step opens the file folder where all MidAtlantic Shapefiles are located, but since we choose a point shapefile for which to repair the data link, the only shapefiles visible in the folder are point shapefiles. Choose the correct file (make sure it is the same file as the one selected in *Contents*). Make sure the layer name is populated under *Name* and click *OK*. Return to the *Source* tab, by selecting *OK* a second time.

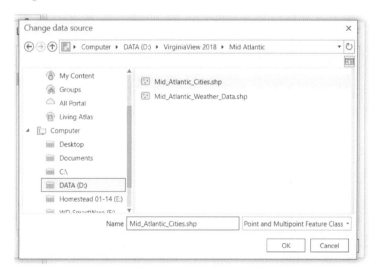

As demonstrated in the next figure, the link to the point shapefile is now repaired, so the data is displayed in the map window on the right.

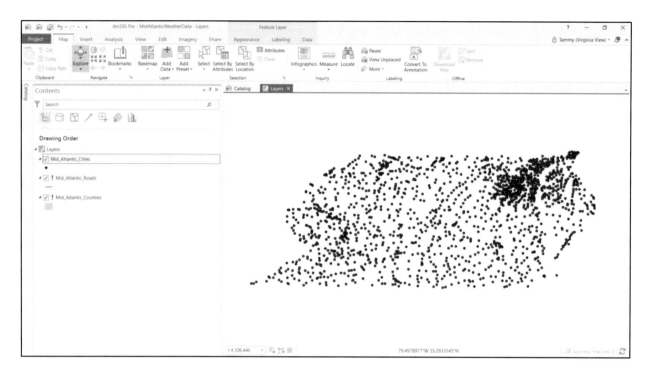

If there are multiple point shapefiles and they are all located in the same folder, then the broken links should be repaired for all point layers. To repair the line and polygon files, the procedure must be repeated for each layer type.

Repairing a link on an individual layer using the Red Exclamation Point

There is another technique to repair broken data links. Instead of going into *Properties*, left-click on one of the red exclamation marks (not the layer name but the actual red exclamation point – as seen in the black box below).

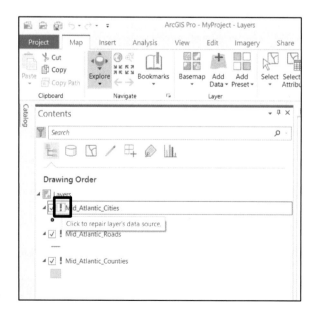

The *Change data source* dialog box automatically appears:

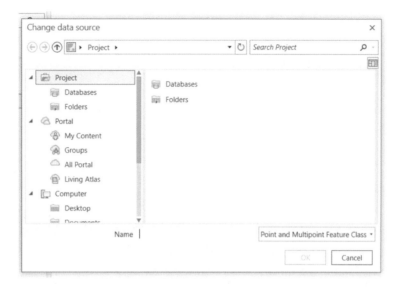

Navigate to the file folder containing the layers by clicking on the drive at the left side of the box - black box in figure below), and find the folder containing the layers. Click on the correct shapefile for that layer, populating it in the *Name* field (red box below).

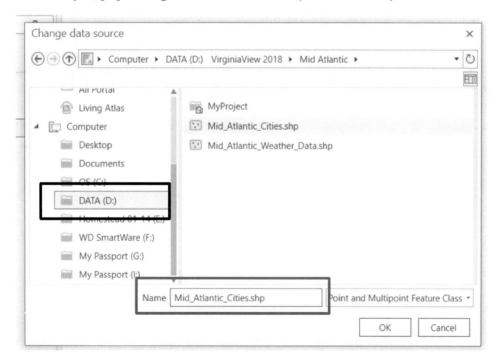

Repeating the procedure for each layer, repairs the broken link for each.

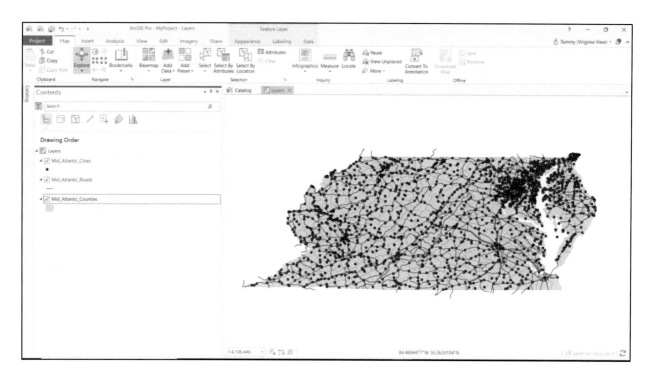

If the map project contains a large number of layers, some of which have a broken data link and some which do not, the list of layers in the *Contents* window can be changed so that only those with a broken data link are visible.

This action can be done by selecting the *Filter* icon (red circle below) and then selecting *Broken data link* (red rectangle below). This step changes the display so only those layers with broken data links are listed, thus allowing more easy identification of the data layers with broken links.

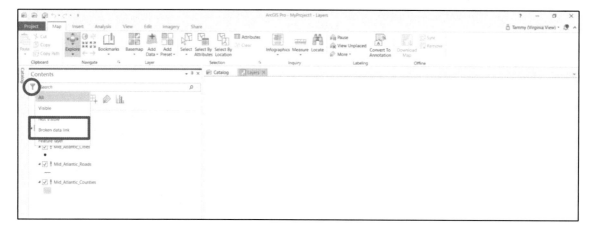

Now we have demonstrated, in the first three chapters setting up projects, in the next chapter, we discuss adding data.

Introduction:

In the prior chapters, we demonstrated how to open a new map project, open an existing map project, import a map created in another GIS program, and how to repair a broken data link. This chapter begins the instruction on adding data to a map project. This specific chapter covers two different topics: (a) connecting to a folder, which will allow you to add data from a local computer; and (b) connecting to a GIS server, which enables you to add data from an outside source with an internet connection ('on the cloud'). The next two chapters also covers adding data.

Connecting to a Folder: In ArcGIS® Pro, you can access data, projects and map documents by navigating to the folder, just like any Windows-based environment. However, ArcGIS® Pro has an option to connect directly to that folder within a map project. Essentially, this creates a shortcut to the data, and, therefore, enables access to data files much quicker. The first part of this chapter explains how to connect to any folder on a local network.

GIS Server Connections: Large amounts of spatial data assets have become freely available to use in GIS programs. However, some of these data may be proprietary, are extremely large files, may be updated frequently, or are data files that are not readily (easily) downloaded. In these situations, data files are often provided via a distributed data system.

Accessing GIS data servers has benefits. One benefit, is that these data assets can be centrally managed. This is critical for more complex data assets that may require frequent updating (for example, parcel data or road networks). This ensures that end users are accessing the most up to date version of the data (as opposed to using a locally downloaded version that may well be outdated). Another benefit, is that GIS data services provide an efficient mechanism to disseminate large data files (which might include orthoimage mosaics/aerial photography). These spatial data files can be streamed to multiple users in formats that are 'software ready'. Therefore, these data sets are easily and seamlessly used by the data layers.

Many entities (including: local governments, state agencies, federal agencies, other nonprofits, and private companies) make their data assets available via a GIS server connection. ESRI's ArcGIS® Pro was designed to communicate with these services and ingest their data into map projects connected to these servers. The second part of this chapter covers how to connect to such servers.

Connecting to ArcGIS® Online Server: You can access data, projects and map documents made publically available from a variety of entities through the online portal to ESRI.

Connecting to a Folder

Open ArcGIS® Pro, open a project, choose the *Insert* tab and then click *Add Folder:*

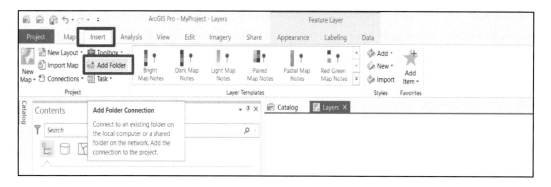

The *Add Folder Connection* dialog box appears.

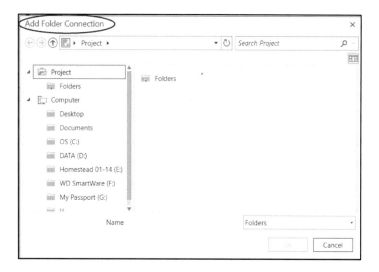

Navigate to the folder that contains the spatial data, using the drives visible on the left of the dialogue box.   Once the folder is found, make sure that it populates in the *Name* field. Then click *OK*.

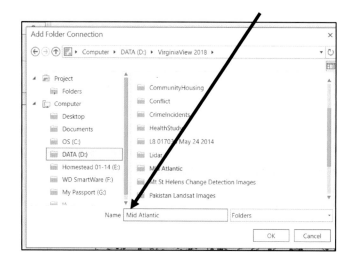

It may look like nothing happened, but select *Catalog* (red box in the figure below). Click on *Folders* (green box) and the folders to which the project is connected displays in the window on the right.

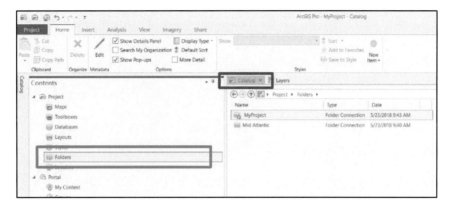

Save your project. By connecting to this folder, a shortcut to the data folder is established. Now, when adding data from this folder, it can be done much more efficiently.

Connecting to a GIS Server

To connect to an on-line GIS Server, go to *Insert* tab (black box) and then click on *Connections* (red box).

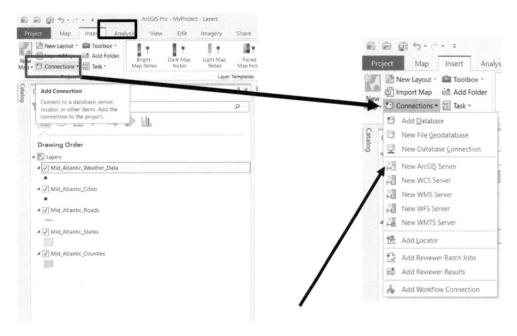

From the dropdown menu, choose *New ArcGIS Server*.

The *Add ArcGIS Server User Connection* dialog box opens.

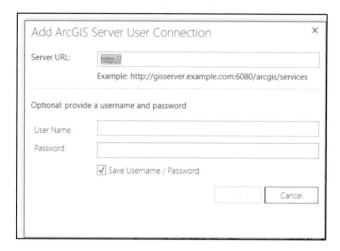

For this example, select the Virginia Base Map Program[1] GIS data streaming service (http://gismaps.vita.virginia.gov/arcgis/rest/services). If you are interested in another GIS Service, conduct an internet search or contact the imagery's owner for the appropriate URL (or you can search for data services via ArcGIS Online. This process is provided in the *Connecting to ArcGIS Online* section of this chapter.

Enter the URL in the *Server URL* box as shown below and click OK:

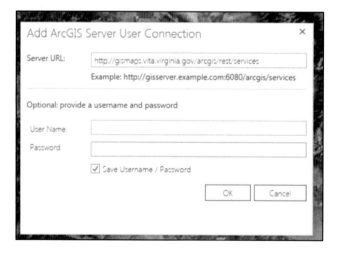

A *Connecting* message displays and then automatically disappears.

---

[1] For more information about the Virginia Geographic Information Network data services, go to: https://www.vita.virginia.gov/integrated-services/vgin-geospatial-services/vgin-geospatial-data-services/

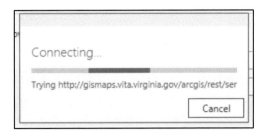

Although, it may look like nothing happened, but go to the *Catalog* tab; click on *Servers* (black box in figure below) and the server connection is now showing. Nothing is showing in the *Layers* display because no images have been added.

To add an image, first, left double-click on the server name -- a list of available options (Broadband, VBMP 2002, etc.) displays:

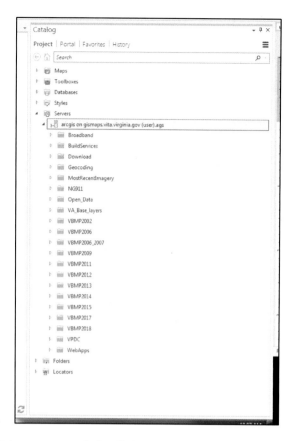

We are going to add 2002 imagery, so left click on VBMP 2002 folder, and an image name displays. Right click on the image name to get a list of options.

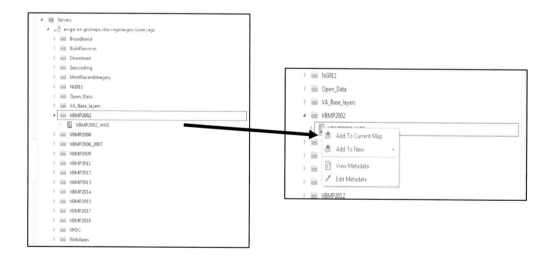

In the following figure, it was added to the current map in the Contents and the Map window:

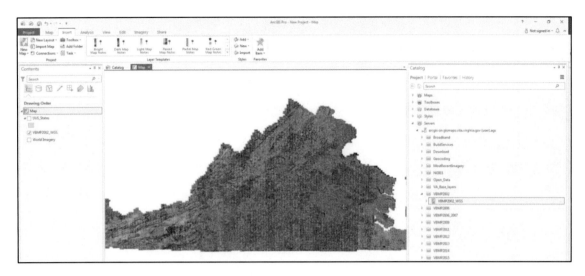

The project is now connected to data that is streaming from an online server. Is it possible to conduct analysis with on-line servers? This depends on the specific server configuration -- refer to the metadata associated the server connection.

Connecting to ArcGIS® Online

ArcGIS® Online is a cloud-based geospatial data sharing portal that is maintained by Esri. ArcGIS® Online can be accessed in two ways. When you first opened ArcGIS® Pro, you had to sign into your organization's account. This process connected to ArcGIS® Online servers. If no basemap was chosen when the project was first set up, it can now be added it under the *Map* tab (red box) and by clicking on Basemap (purple box) or at any later date. Many basemap options are available. Merely click on a basemap option to add it to the map project.

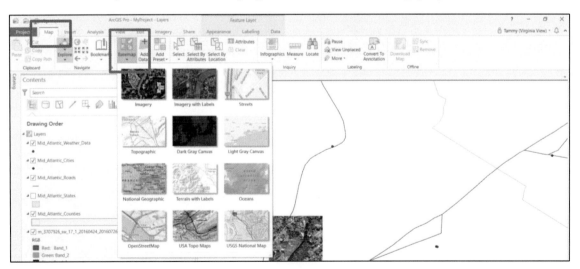

The second way to access ArcGIS® Online is through the ArcGIS® Online portal. Again, you need to be signed in to an Esri Organizational Account in order to connect to the portal. While in the map project, click on the *Catalog* tab (red box in figure below).

Click on *Portal* (green box in figure above) and the *All Portal* opens on the right side.

This connection allows access to any content you have added to your organization's online content (*My Content* – highlighted in blue in the previous figure). *Groups* (listed below *My Content* in prior figure) provides access to any Groups to which you belong. *All Portal* provides access to public ArcGIS® Online content.

To search for data, left double click on *All Portal* and the *Search* box opens on the right.

In the example below, we searched for Virginia Weather Data on the ArcGIS® Online Portal. To get metadata (information about the data), just highlight the layer name and it displays on the right). In the below figure, we clicked on *Traffic Weather Related* to highlight it.

Some items in ArcGIS® Online can be added directly to the map project, some items can only be opened as a stand-alone project. In the following figure, we selected *Bike Fairfax* and obtained a window with options – *Add to layers, Add to new map, Add to Scene.* These data can be added to an existing map or opened as a new map:

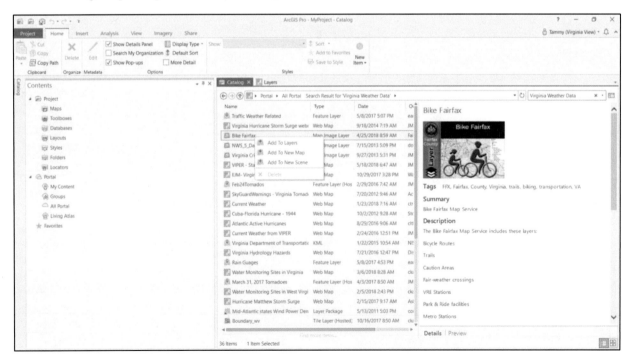

In the next figure, we selected current weather. This provided only one option – *Add and Open*.

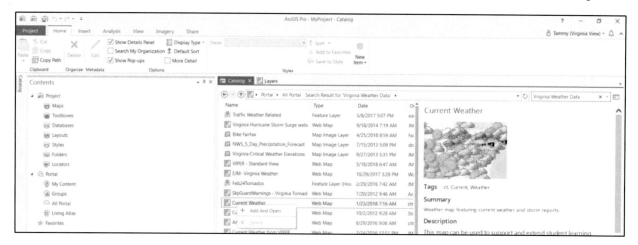

This option opened a new map with the layer displayed.

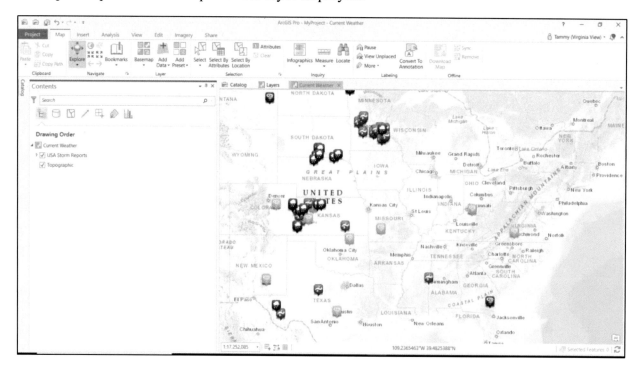

The image below provides an example of an 'imagery' search in ArcGIS Online (on All Portals). Note that you can connect to the National Agricultural Imagery Program (NAIP). There are three options for NAIP imagery: true color, color infrared, or NDVI. NAIP products cover the U.S., however, there are also several imagery sources available for other geographic regions of the globe as well. Of course, the advantages of these services are that they are being served and maintained by someone else. But these layers are being seamlessly shared with users across the globe.

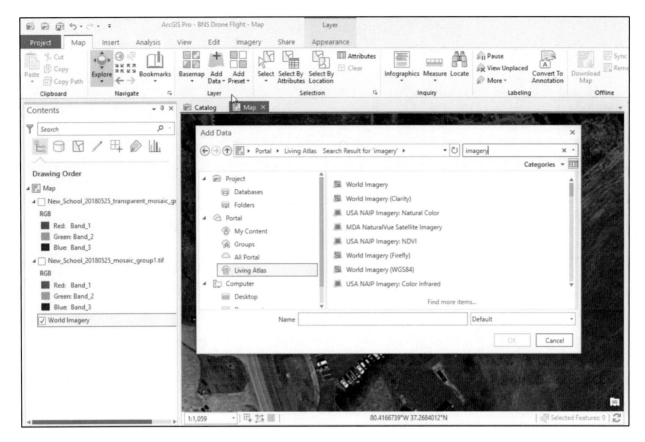

If you cannot find *Portals* within the project, click on the *Project* tab (black box):

Then, click on *Portals* (red box below). This will show the *Portal* connections. If no portals are visible, then you probably need to sign in to ArcGIS® (see Chapter 1).

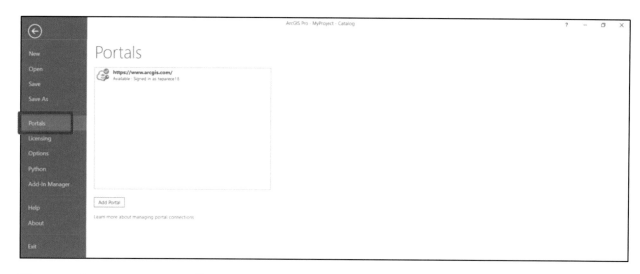

You can also access ArcGIS® Online Content before a map project is opened.

When ArcGIS® Pro first opens, click on *Open another project* (red box in figure below):

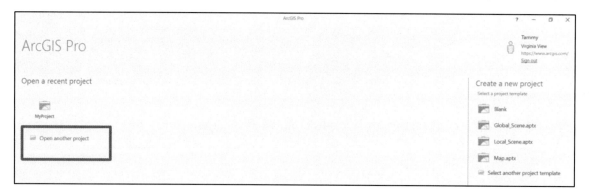

Click on *Portal* (blue box in figure below) and then *Browse* (within the black box).

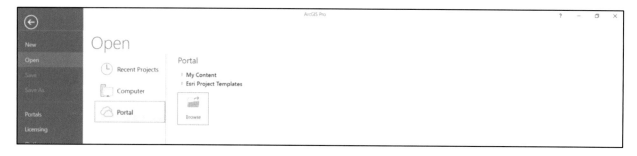

This accesses the *Search* function:

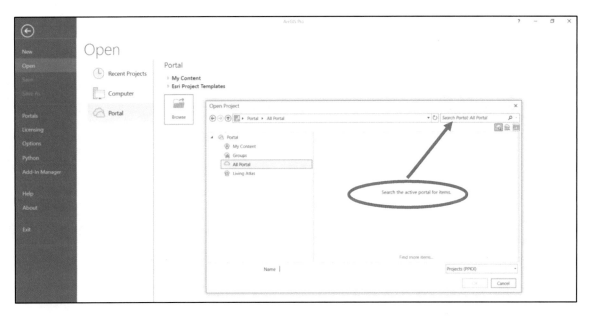

Start by entering search parameters to help narrow the search for the data.

Be sure to search in the correct directory, as this access point has two search options – the first option is to *Search the Active Portal*, the second to *Search My Organization*. When limiting the search to *My Organization*, the search will be limited to data assets that are published only by individuals associated with the organization (your agency, your university, etc.). This may severely restrict search options.

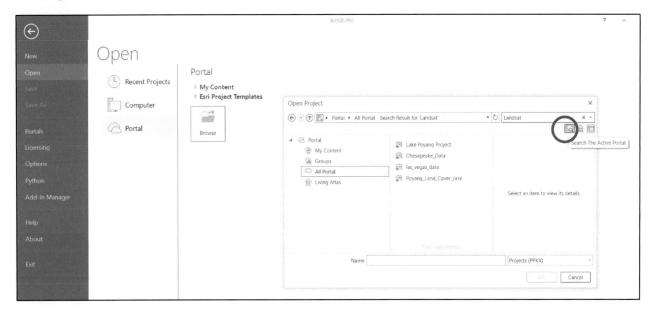

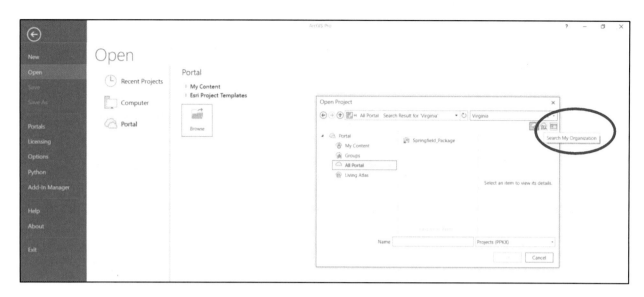

We have now demonstrated how to access data with a hard drive connection and an internet connection. In the next chapter, we discuss the project's geodatabase and how to add data to it.

ArcGIS® Pro is a project-based GIS. As discussed in prior chapters, when setting up a new project, a geodatabase is automatically created up in the project's file folder. This chapter provides instruction of how to add shapefiles to the geodatabase directly.

What is a geodatabase? A geodatabase is a "container" in which GIS data files (vector, raster, and spreadsheets) are stored. A geodatabase is a convenient place to store all data related to one particular project. In some cases, using geoprocessing tools are quite intensive and fail to process the data (particularly with large files). Using a geodatabase as the processing workspace helps facilitate a successful process. Geodatabases can be "set-up" with specific parameters, for example if a particular projection is needed for the project. For more information, please reference documentation provided on Esri's website:
http://desktop.arcgis.com/en/arcmap/10.3/manage-data/geodatabases/what-is-a-geodatabase.htm.

Should you add the shapefiles that you plan use to the project folder's geodatabase? We recommend this step for multiple reasons. Importing a shapefile into the project's geodatabase, imports a copy of the shapefile. The original shapefile stays in its original folder. Should you run into an error and the shapefile in use becomes corrupted, the unaltered original shapefile is still available. Secondly, because ArcGIS® Pro is a project-oriented GIS, using the project folder places the actual shapefiles used within that project, keeping all of the data assets together.

Open ArcGIS® Pro and the project. As seen in this window, a tab called *Catalog* (black box) is located at the top of the map document.

Select the *Catalog* tab. A list of items – *Maps, Toolboxes, Databases*, etc. appear in the *Catalog* window.

Double left-click on the word *Folders*. A list of project folders appears – in the figure below, only one project is listed – *MyProject*. If the desired project is not listed, then refer back to Chapter 4 on how to connect to a folder.

Double left-click on the project folder to expand the folder. Three items are listed in the window below it – ImportLog, MyProject.gdb and MyProject.tbx. If the project displayed only shows the last two items, don't worry, the log might not yet appear. It will show up after you start processing data. The .gdb is the geodatabase. The .tbx is the toolbox for this particular project. As discussed in Chapter 1, we will not be covering the toolbox within this book.

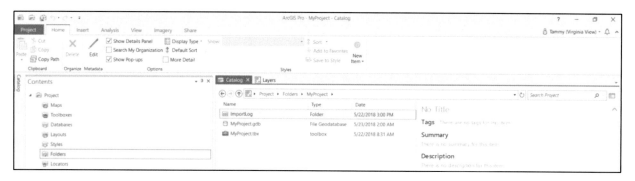

Double-click on the geodatabase and a message displays that the container is empty.

This container is empty.

Now we are going to demonstrate how to import data files into the geodatabase.

Right-click on the geodatabase and click on the word *Import* and choose either *Feature Class* (1 vector shapefile) or *Feature Classes* (2 or more vector shapefiles). In this case, we chose *Feature Classes* because we are going to import all files related to Mid-Atlantic. Please note that some of the files that we are importing into this geodatabase have yet to be added to our map document. We will cover adding new files to the map project in Chapter 6: Adding Data to a Project in ArcGIS® Pro.

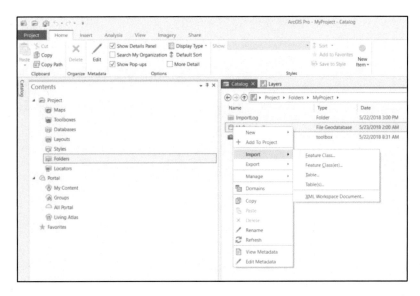

A dialog box called *Geoprocessing* opens on the left side of the screen.

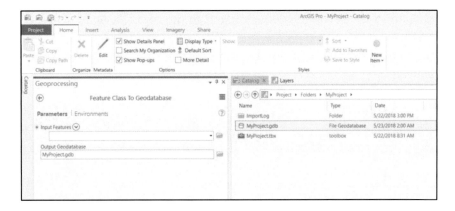

Use the file folder at the end of the *Input Features* box to navigate to the folder where the original files are located.

Since we are adding all files named Mid-Atlantic, we highlighted them all:

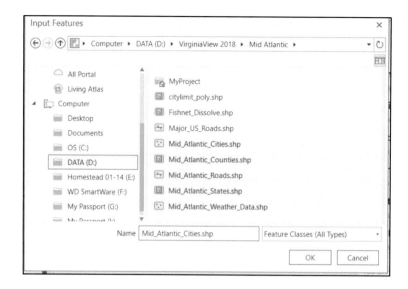

Then select *OK*.

In the figure below, all of the selected files are listed in the *Input Features* box within the *Geoprocessing* window, each on a separate line. When importing multiple feature classes, names do not need to be individually assigned, ArcGIS® Pro will retain the original names.

Select *Run* in the lower right of the dialog box.

This action initiates a geoprocessing tool — view the status bar in the bottom of the geoprocessing window that shows the procedure in process.

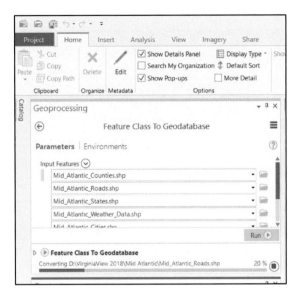

A message will appear when the tool has finished processing – note the green highlighted section at the bottom of the *Geoprocessing* dialog box.

The shapefiles are now located in the project's geodatabase. If they are not visible in the Catalog window on the right, click on the geodatabase to show its contents. The files are not in the map document or *Contents* window, they have only been added to the geodatabase.

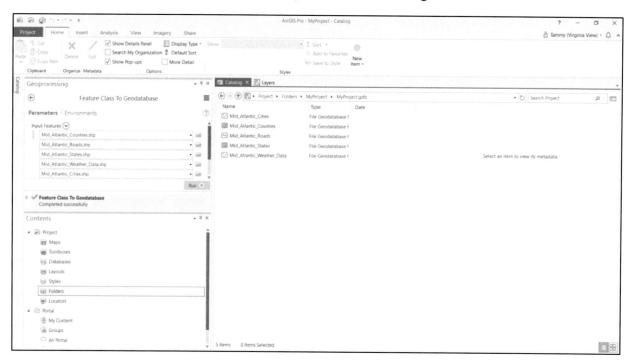

Close the *Geoprocessing* window by clicking on the *X* in the upper right corner.

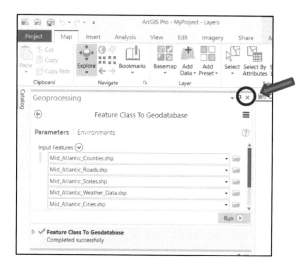

Recall from right clicking on the geodatabase, options other than *Import* were present:

New is used for creating a new data file (beyond the scope of this book)

Import can also be used to add a table (spreadsheet) to the geodatabase:

Export is used when data files are already present in the geodatabase and these files are also needed in a separate project's geodatabase (or another file folder).

Geodatabases can be extremely helpful when working on a map project, but covering each options in detail is beyond the scope of this book. Reference Esri's website. There is extensive information on geodatabases. We recommend that this information be read in detail.

In the next chapter (Chapter 6), we demonstrate adding data to the map project. Chapter 7 provides instructions on displaying the data.

This chapter covers how to add data to a map project and it briefly discusses the differences between vector and raster data files.

Introduction: Types of Data

A GIS supports two basic types of files - vector and raster files. All vector files and some raster files can be used in analyses. JPEG, BMP (also raster files), spreadsheets, word processing documents, PDFs and other file types can be added to the map layout view – but only for display – GIS analyses cannot be performed with these file types.

Vector files represent discrete data and display in GIS as points, lines or polygons.

A point represents a location with only one specific latitude and longitude – points have neither length nor area. In a GIS, points can be displayed with many types of symbols (other than a dot) and at any size but, in actuality, they are just dimensionless points.

Lines have length but no width, and represent features such as transects, streams or roads. (Note – when a river is represented as a line, it does not have area so it does not accurately represent the actual river.)

Polygons are any shape with area, e.g., water bodies such as lakes and oceans, country boundaries, etc., but depending on the map scale, some features with area might only be represented as points (such as cities on a map of the world). A polygon can be any shape with area – square, circle, decagon, or an irregular shape. As an example of an irregular shape, see the image at the top of the next page. The shapes for the different states are the political boundaries. But when listed in the *Contents* window, the shape under the layer name is always displayed as a square.

Points, lines and polygon files are listed in the *Contents* window and displayed in the map document window. In most instances, a GIS will automatically layer polygons on the bottom, next on top are lines and then on top of lines are points.   Why? It's because polygons will automatically cover points and lines (of the same location), so they are displayed automatically so all of the data is visible. The order of display can be manually changed.

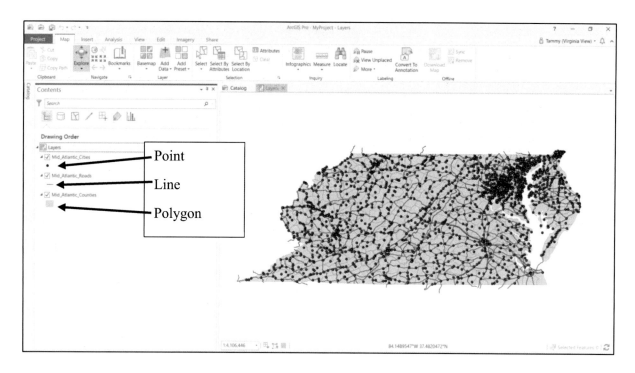

Raster files represent continuous data, such as elevation or weather data, across the surface of the Earth. Raster data can also include imagery, such as aerial imagery (photographs or imagery captured from a drone, a plane, a balloon, or a satellite). Raster data is displayed as grids – columns and rows of square pixels. The size of the pixel, e.g., the ground area each pixel represents varies (both according to the sensor and a decision made by the data's owner). For instance, each pixel of Landsat 8 imagery (with the exception of the thermal channel) represents a 30 meter by 30 meter area (and therefore has a resolution of 30 meters). Imagery captured by the United States Department of Agriculture National Agriculture Imagery Program (NAIP) supports pixel sizes that are typically 1 meter by 1 meter, but their actual sizes can vary depending on the federal imagery contract and the sensor used to capture the data.

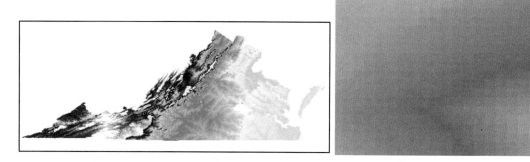

The above figure represents a portion of the 2002 Digital Elevation Model (DEM) for Virginia, pixel size – 30 meters by 30 meters – The entire state is illustrated on the left, while the right image shows a zoomed in area of Virginia's DEM right, and depicts individual pixels.

These figures are a Landsat 8 image (Band 4) projected over a portion of Virginia and West Virginia. On the left – the entire scene. On the right - zoomed in to depict individual pixels. Each pixel represents a specific 900 meter^2 (30 meter resolution) area on the surface of the Earth

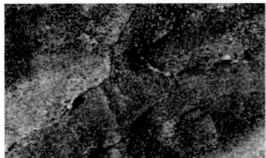

NAIP Aerial Photo (via a GIS Server connection – see Chapter 4: Connecting to a Folder or an Online GIS Server). On the right, zoomed in to show individual pixels (0.8 meter resolution)

Because raster data represents continous phenomena across the surface of the Earth, GIS automatically adds raster data to the bottom of the *Content* window – displayed underneath all vector files. This display can be changed by manually dragging and reodering the layers.

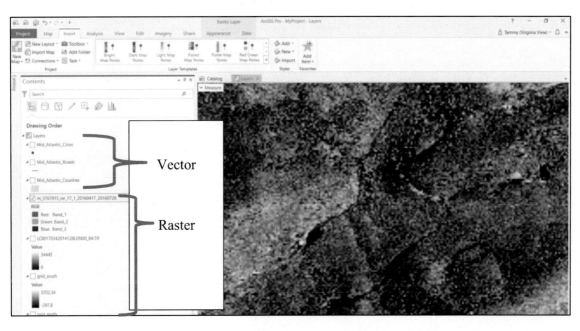

Again, in addition to raster and vector spatial data, GIS software supports an array of other 'nontraditional' GIS data formats, including JPEG, BMP, spreadsheets, word processing documents, PDFs and other file types. These other formats can be added to the map layout view -- but are only available for display. These formats do not support GIS analyses.

Adding Data to a Map Project

On the tool bar, click on the *Map* tab (black box) and then *Add Data* and *Add data to the map*.

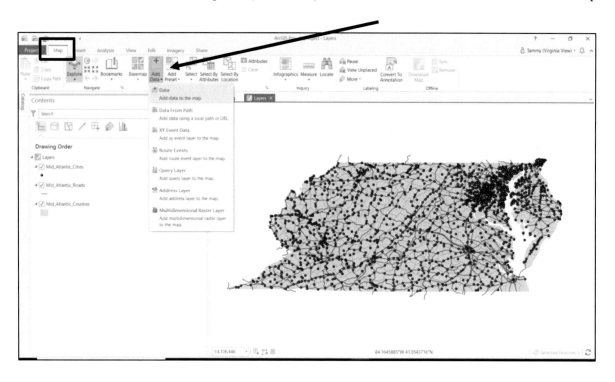

If the project's geodatabase already has data (red box) (see Chapter 5 if the geodatabase is empty), it is easy to find (or if a folder is already connected to the project, see Chapter 4).

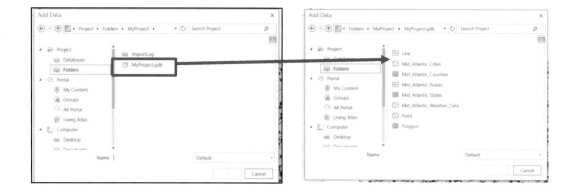

Otherwise, navigate to the project folder by using the computer drive and folders list on the bottom left (blue highlighted area in the figure below).

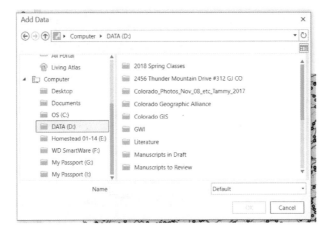

Once the files have been located, click on the file(s) to be added. (If adding multiple files, including vector and raster, hold the control button and click each file until they are all highlighted). In the example below, two additional files are being added to the *Contents* window – *Mid_Atlantic_States and Mid-Atlantic_Weather_Data*.

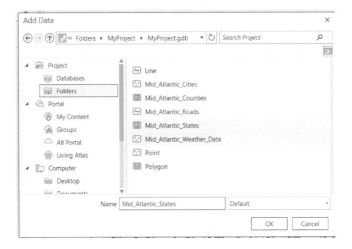

Once the files are selected, click *OK*. The data is added to the *Contents* window so that point layers are displayed on top of line layers, which are displayed on top of polygon layers (see figure at the top of the next page).

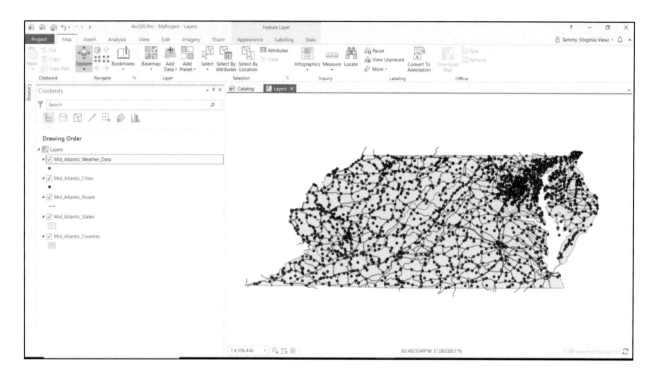

A raster file is added in the same manner. And -- keep in mind that data can be added from different file folders on the computer; they are added separately, navigating to the individual file folder housing the data file. In the screenshot below, we are adding a single band (Band 5) from a Landsat 8 image. (Don't worry now about what Landsat, or Band 5, is -- we discuss these in future chapters. For now, just understand that this satellite image is a raster, not a vector file, and those have different properties and are displayed differently from vector files as discussed above.)

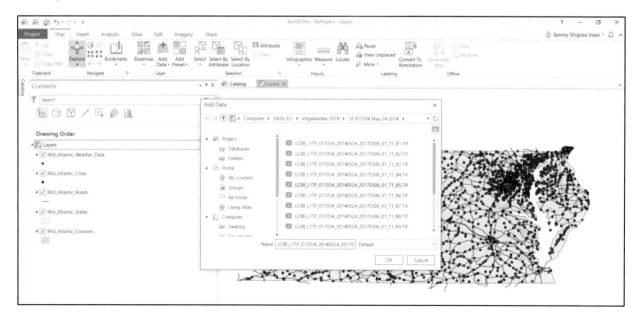

ArcGIS® Pro added the Landsat Band to the bottom of the *Contents,* and is displayed in the map window, but underneath all the other layers (it is partially seen where it extends beyond the boundaries of the state and county vector layers – see red arrow).

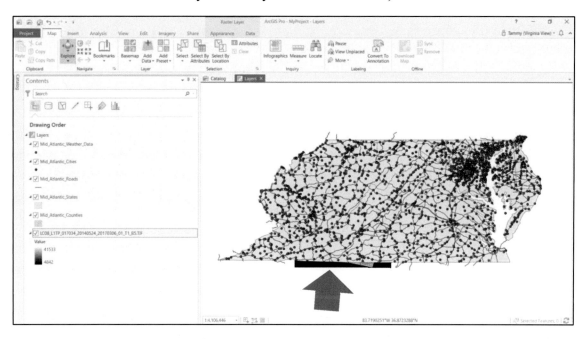

That is all that is required to add vector and raster files to the map project.

Please note that our files have different coordinate systems and datums. We will discuss displaying data and coordinate systems in the next chapter.

Introduction

With the power of GIS and remote sensing, you have the ability to change how data is displayed in the map document. This capability allows display of multiple layers, all at the same time, such as multiple files of the same type. For example -- many different point files, files of many different types (several points, several lines, and several polygons), and multiple copies of the exact same file – all can be displayed with each one being visually distinguished.

Datums and Coordinate Systems

We first need to discuss coordinate systems because, as GIS files are created, they must be referenced to the surface of the Earth. So, as the data is generated by the data base developer, the data are assigned a datum and coordinate system. How and why a specific system is chosen is beyond the scope of this chapter and book and usually involves a choice by the data developer or the data's owner. Additionally, datums and coordinate systems can vary based on the location (country, state or even local municipal government) and spatial scale (large scale vs. small scale maps). This chapter provides a brief example as to how this will change the data, analysis and map display. For more information, see https://support.esri.com/en/technical-article/000007924 or https://www.e-education.psu.edu/geog486/book/export/html/1750 or https://education.usgs.gov/lessons/coordinatesystems.pdf.

We are using the project and data added in the last chapter. First, check the assigned coordinate system under the word *Layers*. Right-click *Layers* and chose *Properties* (red box).

The *Map Properties Layers* dialog box shows the datum and coordinate system associated with each layer and identifies the datum and coordinate system that is used in the map display. In this example, the map is being displayed using datum GCS North American 1983 (red box in the figure below). But, we have layers with 3 different coordinate systems. Click on the triangle symbol in front of the coordinate system name -- it provides information on which layer(s) is/are associated with that coordinate system. For example, USA Contiguous Albers Equal Area

Conic (USGS Version) is assigned to Mid_Atlantic_Weather_Data, Mid_Atlantic_States and Mid_Atlantic_Counties.

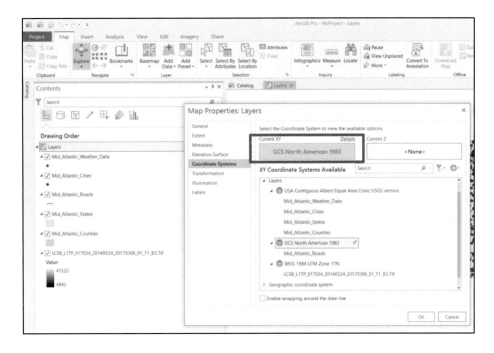

As a default, ArcGIS® Pro assigns the datum and coordinate system to the map project from the first shapefile or raster file that is added to the project. But, this assignment can be changed using this dialog box.

To change the coordinate system, highlight the one desired (in this case, we are changing it to USA Contiguous Albers Equal Area Conic USGS version). Clicking on this coordinate system name, it becomes highlighted, then click on *OK*. The *Map Properties Layer/Coordinate Systems* dialog box reflects this change.

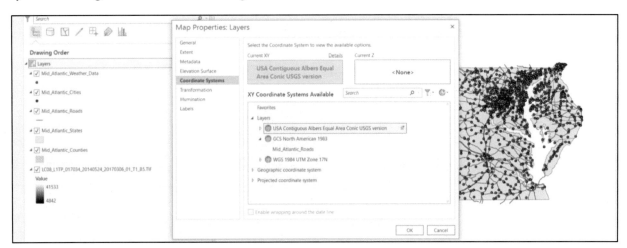

And the map display changes.

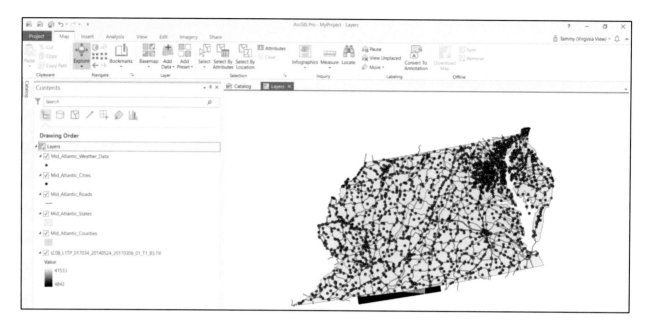

We end our discussion here, but also need to provide a word of caution. Completing analyses using data files with different geographic and projected coordinate systems can introduce error into the results. But, if a geographic coordinate system is changed on a dataset, the results will also be affected. Please understand the different systems available and used, the appropriate applications associated with their use, and how the results may vary between different systems. Using an inappropriate projection can greatly enhance errors. Additionally, such discrepancies must be reported in any analysis.

Data Display and Default Settings

When adding vector or raster datasets to a map project, ArcGIS® Pro selects symbology to display the data. Points are always displayed as *colored dots*, lines as *colored lines*, and polygons as *solid colors outlined with different colors*. Most raster data is displayed as stretched *gray scale*. An exception is aerial photos, such as those displayed using the NAIP GIS Server connection – the default display is red – green – blue (RGB) format. All of these types of display symbology can be modified.

The following figures provide examples of default symbology.

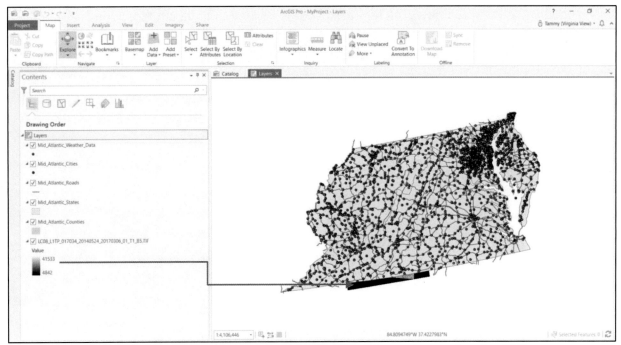

Points, lines and polygons displayed in random colors by GIS

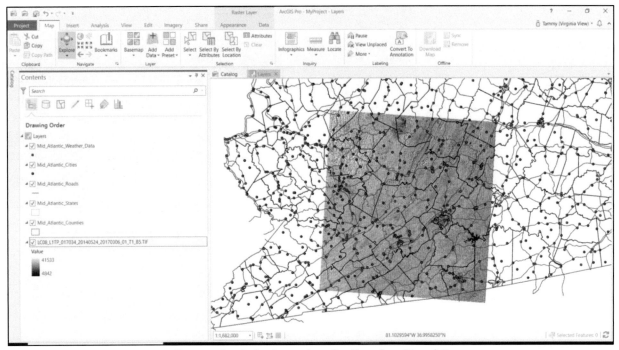

Grayscale default setting for Landsat Band 5

The figure above shows the same map, as displayed in the previous figure, but the polygon files are hollow and the map is zoomed in to show Landsat 8 Band 5 (raster file) displayed in stretched gray scale. (Note, the image displayed in the points, lines and polygons map above also contains the satellite image, but the raster data is located underneath those files – a small slice can be seen at the southern border of Virginia, as indicated by the red arrow.)

In the next figure, the NAIP aerial image is displayed as R-G-B format (red, green, blue) and is overlaid on top of the satellite image.

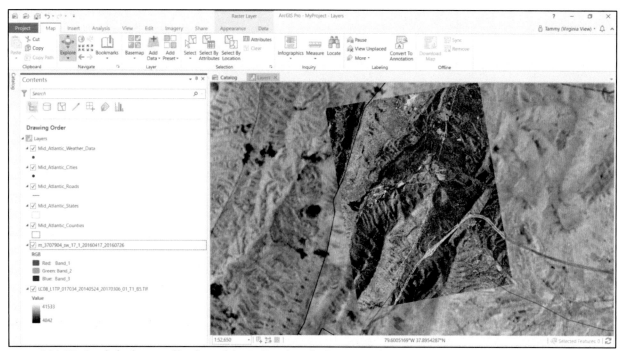

NAIP Aerial photos displayed in RGB (Red, Green, Blue) via the USDA online server connection and overlaid on Landsat 8 Band 5

Changing Symbology on Vector Files

We will first address how to change the symbology associated with one of the point layers. In the following figure, we have turned off all the layers except the two point shapefiles and one polygon shapefile (allowing general locational information to be seen).

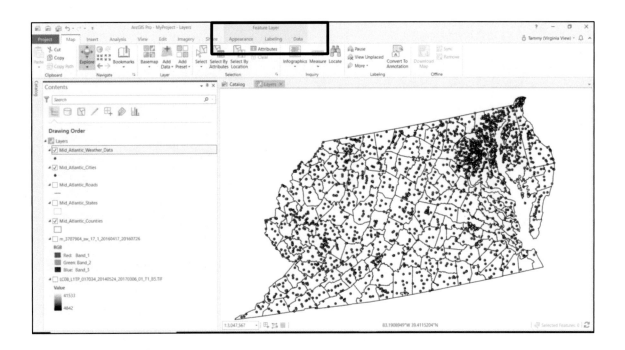

To change the symbology of a point data layer, highlight one of the point layers in the *Contents* window. In this example, the Mid Atlantic Cities has been highlighted. Once a data layer has been highlighted, a new tab appears the *Feature Layer* (black box in the image above). Clicking on *Feature Layer*, in the top of the toolbar, the tools available for this specific layer are displayed – *Appearance*, *Labeling*, and *Data*. This chapter is only addressing symbology, aka *Appearance*.

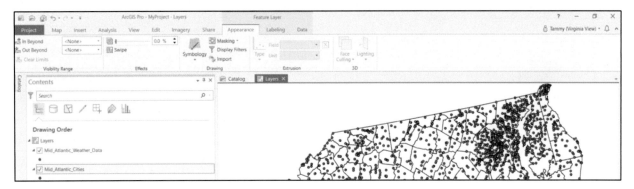

Click on *Appearance* and then click on the down arrow under *Symbology* (the file folder with the paint brush).

We will not discuss all of these options, just the first two options – *Single Symbol* and *Unique Values*.

Click on *Single Symbol* and another dialog box opens in the top of the *Contents* window:

Click on the symbol (black box in the figure on the left) and options appear (right figure below).

Use the scroll bar on the right to see many other options.

Additional options can be added by clicking on *Project Styles* and change to *All Styles*:

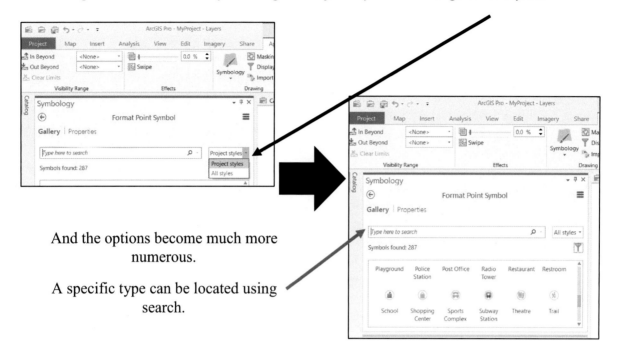

And the options become much more numerous.

A specific type can be located using search.

In the figure below, we searched for symbols associated with "hospital" and 11 symbols were identified. Use the scroll bar on the right to explore all of the potential symbols.

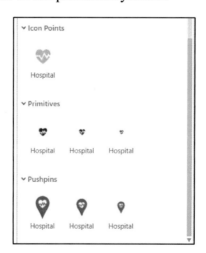

In this chapter's project, we are using Mid-Atlantic Cities and Mid-Atlantic Weather Data -- both are point files and both were originally symbolized as green dots. In the illustration below, symbols for both layers were changed. Can you find the symbols? The symbols used are called *Radio Tower* and *City Hall*.

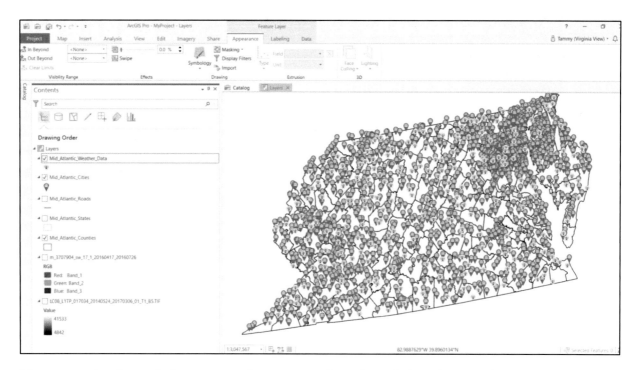

The reason for these choices was to demonstrate the value of choosing wisely when doing symbology. These symbols, while pertinent, make the map difficult to read.

We are going to change the symbols again, but will demonstrate a different technique. In the *Contents* window, left-click on the radio tower symbol and the *Symbology* box opens:

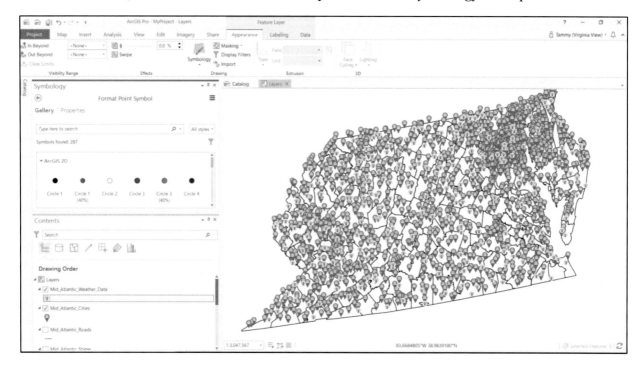

In the following figure, we changed the single symbols for each using this method.

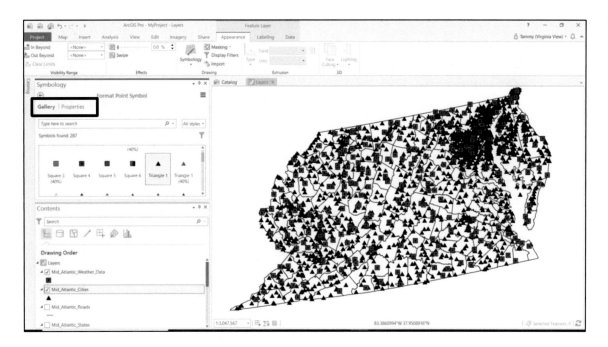

To change the size of symbols, click on *Properties* (next to *Gallery* – black box in above figure).

Use the scroll bar on the right to scroll down finding more options, including *Size*.

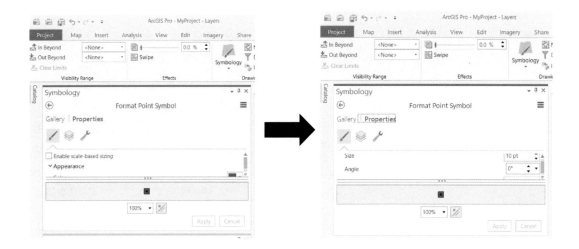

In the figure below, we reduced the symbol *Size* to 7, then clicked on *Apply*. In many instances, with a large number of data points in a shapefile, a symbol is just too large and overwhelms the map display. In the figure below, we turned off the counties file so only the city symbols are displayed.

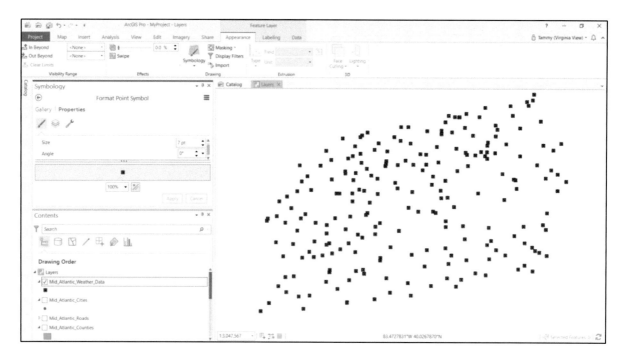

Now, let's go back and explore *Unique Values* for the cities file. Click on the arrow under *Symbology* (under the *Appearance* tab) and then choose *Unique Values*:

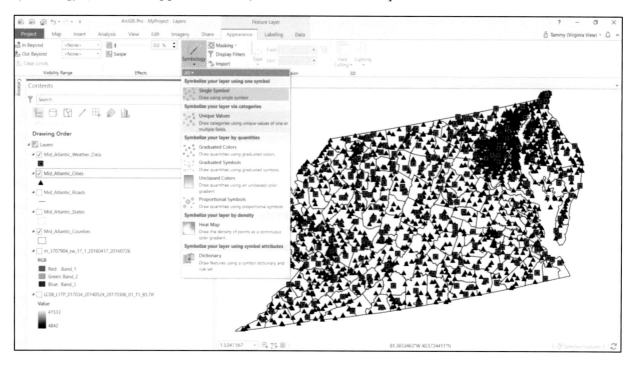

The following dialogue box appears:

This is the procedure to use when symbolizing features based on field values (black box above) from the attribute table. What is an attribute table? An attribute table is a table of the attributes of each feature in a shapefile. So what is an attribute? Attributes are characteristics for each one of the features in the specific layer that were assigned by the data's creator. How do you find them?

Right-click on the layer's name and choose *Attribute Table*.

The *Attribute Table* opens at the bottom of the map document.

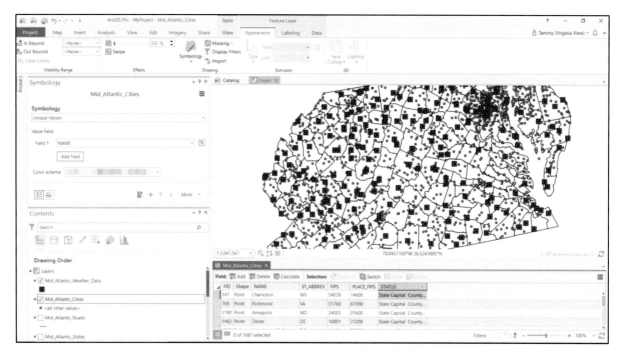

Look at this closer. Most of the columns (aka fields) can be used to display a characteristic of the feature (in this case, cities). We will demonstrate the two available – those cities that are located within a specific state and for the second – the *Status* column.

Go back to *Symbology, Unique Values* and under the *Value Field*, click on the down arrow and choose State Abbreviation (*ST_ABBREV*) – each point is now colored by the state where it is located:

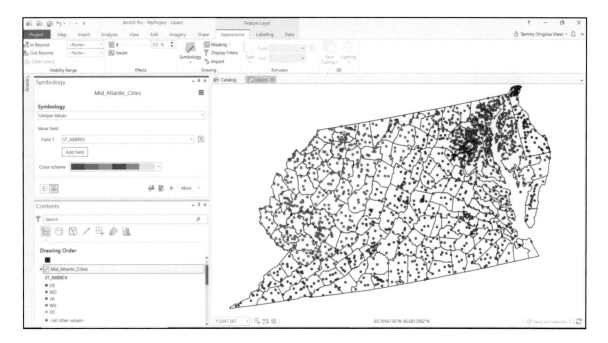

Now change the *Value Field* to *STATUS*:

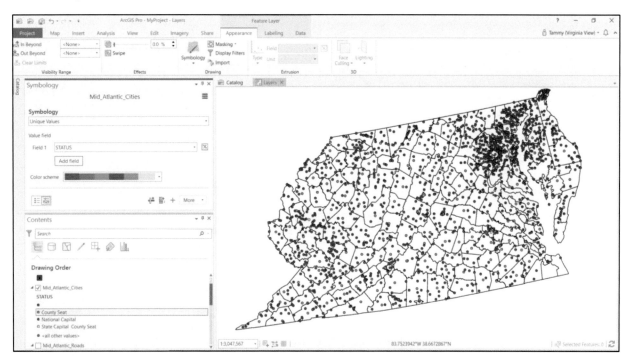

In each instance, the symbology icons, in *Contents* under the layer name, have expanded to explain the color coding. The color coding has been randomly chosen.

But, using *STATUS*, the field without a name is most prominent, so using the other options under symbology, we can to make it a softer color with the National Capital, the State Capitals and the County Seats in decreasing importance. But we will do this using the *Symbology* selection under the layer. Right click on the layer's name and then choose *Symbology* from the list.

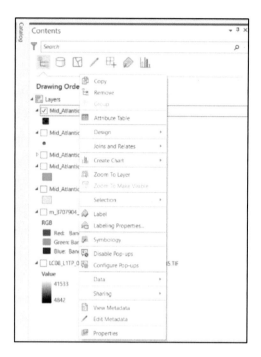

Once the *Symbology* dialog box opens, click on the down arrow at the end of the Symbology line to get the different symbology choices – single symbol, unique values, etc. from a dropdown list.

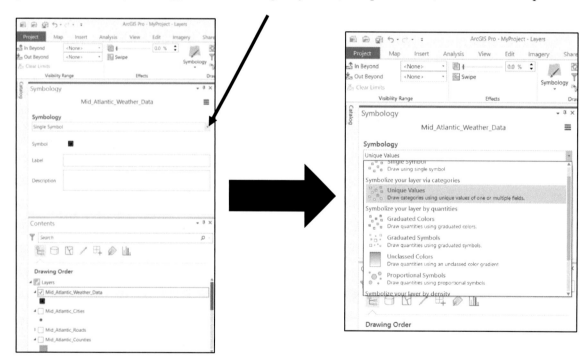

An individual symbol's color can be changed by right clicking on the symbol itself under the layer's name and next to the description – for example below, we right clicked on the red point next to the cities with no status:

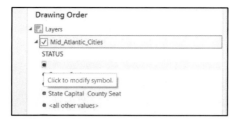

Symbology options for that single symbol opens.

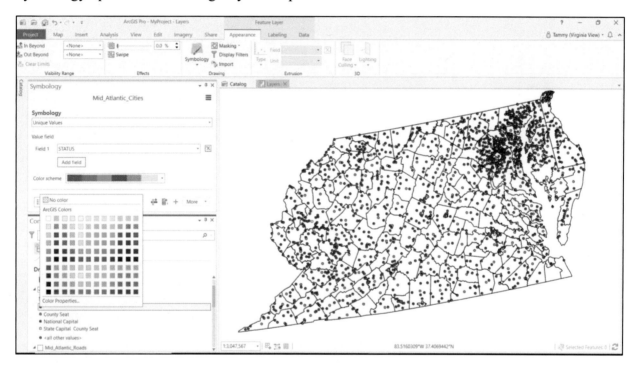

Or, to change the order of the features' status from default (alphabetical) – click on *More*, then *Reverse Order*:

These demonstrated symbology options reflect a very small portion of options. Please practice and explore all the different buttons with options, indicated with the black arrows below. Don't worry, changing symbology does not change the data within the shapefiles.

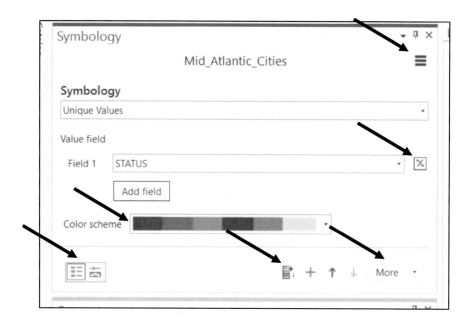

Let's move on to a line layer – Roads. Symbology is changed using the same techniques – as is demonstrated by the following figures.

Single Symbol example:

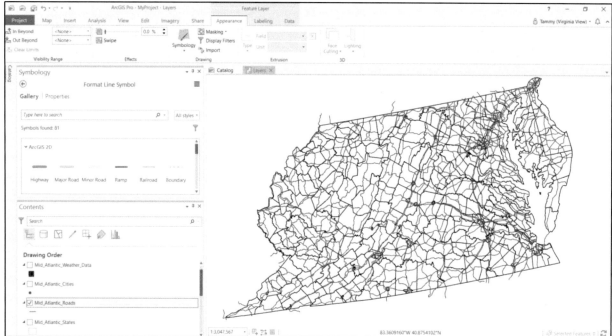

Unique Values Example:

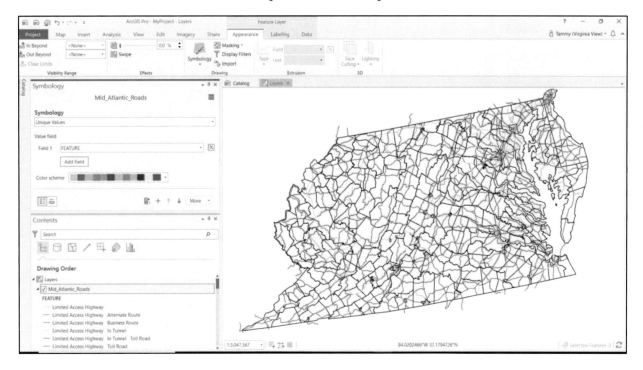

Please note, again, as symbology is changed, it is reflected under the layer's name in the *Contents* window.

Changing the symbology of polygon data is very similar to point data and line data, the main difference is that polygons have area. In the figure below, we moved the polygons on top, just so they can be seen next to the symbology dialog box. To move the layer, just click on the name, hold the left mouse button down and drag it to the top of the *Contents* window. We have both *States* and *Counties* turned on, but only *States* are seen because that shapefile is on the top. Polygons are solid, so the polygon shapefile - *Counties* - cannot be seen underneath *States*.

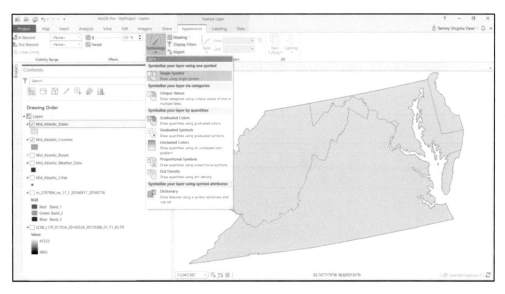

Polygons have very similar choices to points and lines. The major difference is that choices exist to change the fill color, to change both the fill and an outline color (and outline width), or to change the symbology of just the outline. Symbolize can also occur with *Unique Values*.

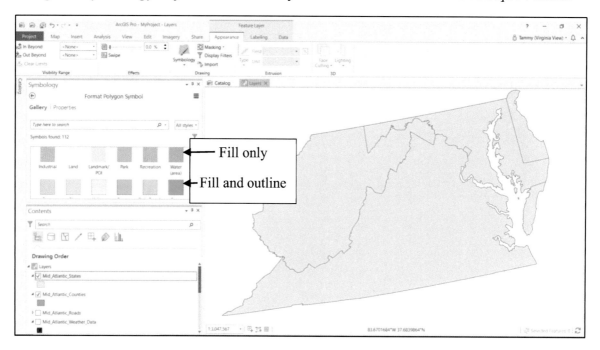

Use the scroll bar on the right to exam all options:

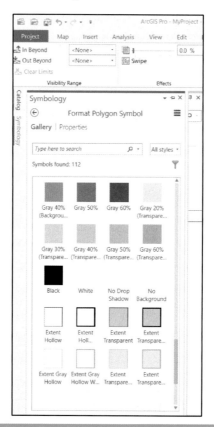

Look at the map in the figure below, and re-create it. We have only used the symbology as discussed above – *Single Symbol* and *Unique Values*.

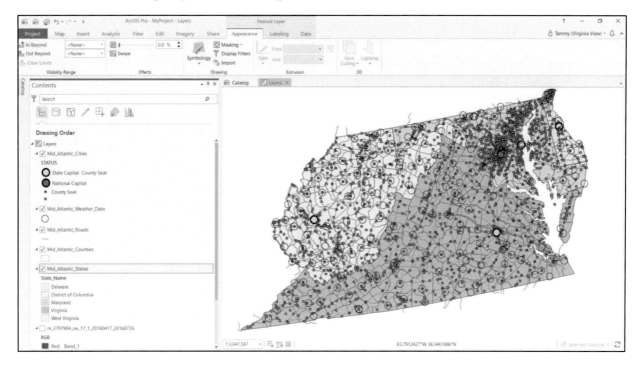

The ultimate display in the map document needs to address multiple layers, their visual representation in the map and the needs of the audience or customer.

Changing Symbology on Raster Datasets

Changing the symbology on a raster dataset (such as a digital elevation model) is accomplished in a similar manner. Highlight the layer's name in the *Contents* window and a *Raster Layer* tab displays. Please note in the figure below, we have the northern part of Virginia's digital elevation model (2002). Remember, the default symbology for most raster files is grayscale.

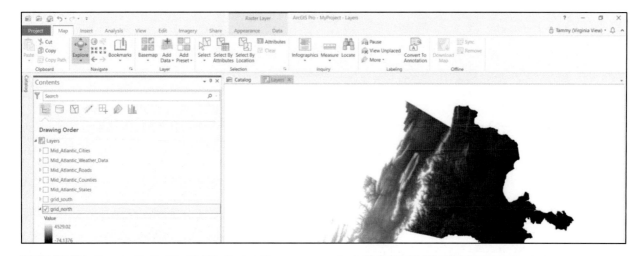

Click on the name *Raster Layer* > *Appearance* tab and options appear – including *Symbology*:

Please note that we are only going to discuss symbology in this chapter. Many of these other options are related to enhancing the image on display and are discussed in later chapters of this book.

The first option is *Stretch* – click on this option.

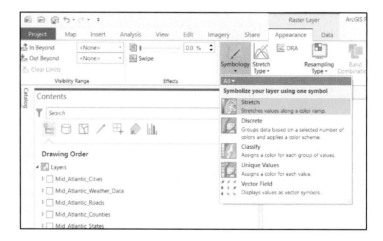

The Symbology dialog box opened in the top of the *Contents* window. Hover the mouse over the grayscale color scheme and it informs us that this is a *Continuous Color Scheme*.

The down arrow at the end of the grayscale scheme, gives many options for color.

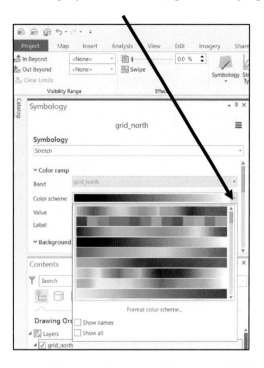

Hovering the mouse over each of these colors provides a verbal description of the scheme. Why is this important? This particular raster file is elevation data, so it is likely most appropriate to use an elevation color scheme. Once chosen, give it some time -- raster files process a bit slower than vector files, because of their size.

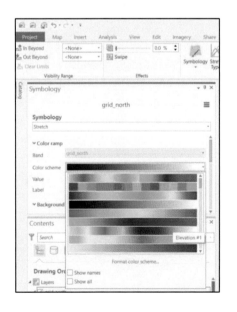

These 3 bars indicate that the program is processing the change (clocking).

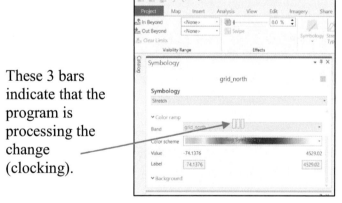

Results of changing the *Stretch* symbology to Elevation #1 – a more appropriate display for elevations – higher elevations appear white (highest elevations many times are snow covered), lowest elevations are blue (many times areas of water).

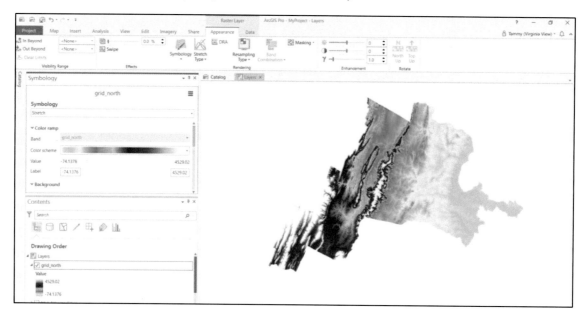

Discrete symbology is a symbology scheme chosen by GIS, which includes GIS automatically grouping the raster values.

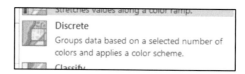

The results of using a *Discrete* symbology are below. The color scheme is Elevation #1 but it is no longer stretched over the range of values within the raster file -- each range of values is assigned a specific color. This scheme looks similar to stretched but has distinct boundaries for each elevation range.

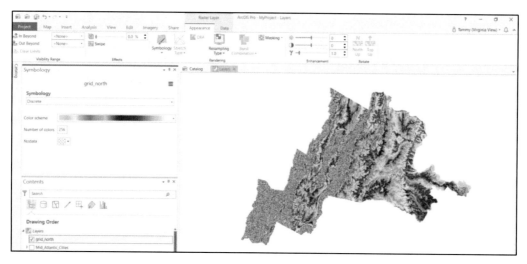

With *Classify*, options are chosen by the user for symbolization – some are discussed in more detail later. When this option is chosen, a message appears – yes, compute the histogram:

GIS is computing the *Histogram* for this raster dataset – a histogram is a graph of the individual raster grid-cell values and the number of grid cells that correspond to each specific value.

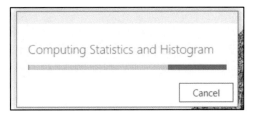

The options are now enabled.

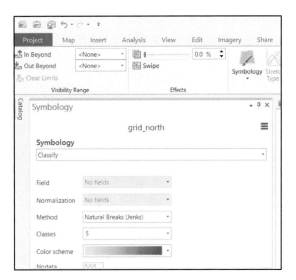

First choice is the *Method* of classification. Default is always *Natural Break (Jenks)*. For the specifics on the *Method* for the classification – please see http://pro.arcgis.com/en/pro-app/help/mapping/layer-properties/data-classification-methods.htm.

We are going to leave the setting - *Natural Breaks*.

The second choice is the number of *Classes*. GIS chose 5, change this to 8 classes. The next choice is *Color scheme* – change to Elevation #1.

The results appear that it does not look much different from *Stretched*, but look in the *Contents* – it has ranged the symbology by specific values – we no longer have one complete range, but values less than or equal to 359.101122, then the next range is from 359.101123 to 756.236627, etc. This is one major difference between the '*classify*' approach and the '*stretch*' approach.

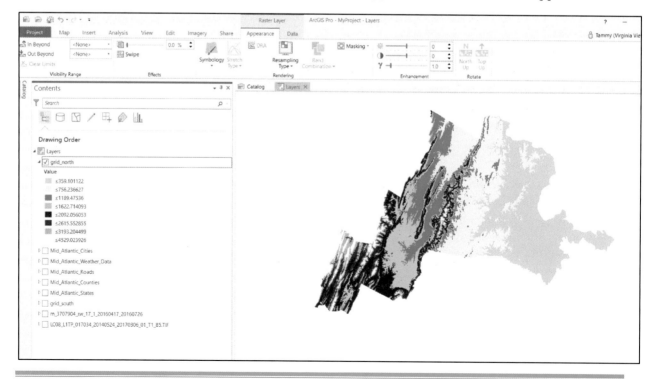

We are not going to explore *Unique Values* and *Vector Field*, and we do caution about using these options. With raster data, each individual cell has a unique real number value, which means that the possibility exists that each one of the cells have a value like no other cell in the data set. Using *Unique Values* on such a large data set could cause ArcGIS® Pro to crash, as the number or unique cell values may exceed the capacity of the computer.

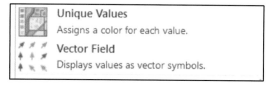

Just like with vector symbology, other options are available within each type of raster symbolization. Please explore these on your own:

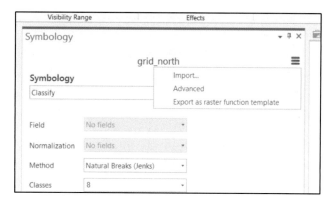

Caution!

As we have demonstrated, using different classification techniques with the same datasets can produce vastly different looking maps. Be sure that you understand what you are trying to communicate to the audience, and integrate an appropriate classification accordingly.

Especially be careful when changing symbology on raster datasets. Know what you want to communicate to the audience. Do you want the display to show distinct differences in colors because of distinct breaks in the data? Or is it more appropriate to display the raster as stretched because there are no distinct borders between values (i.e. on the actual surface of the Earth, elevation changes gradually not with distinct boundaries)? For more information on symbology in raster datasets – please see the *GIS Help*.

With these first 7 chapters, we have demonstrated how to open ArcGIS® Pro, create a map project, open an existing map project, import a map, connect to external data, add data, and symbolize data.

The next chapter (8) will discuss metadata within ArcGIS® Pro, Chapter 9 will demonstrate how to create a map that is usable in a non-GIS based program. Chapter 9 will conclude the introduction to ArcGIS® Pro basics. Chapter 10 introduces remotely sensed images.

Introduction

What is metadata? Metadata is information about data. Your morning bowl of cereal has metadata (information about the product), that is located on the side of the cereal box. This is known as a nutritional label. For datasets, metadata is contained in the form of a metadata file.

In this chapter, we discuss various locations in *ArcGIS® Pro* that contain information about already created vector and raster files, and how to create metadata for the map project. Please note that when a new data file is created (either vector or raster), metadata should also be created for the new file. Creating metadata for a new data file is beyond the scope of this book and chapter.

Finding Metadata in Existing Files

The first place to find metadata is the title of the file. Look at the titles in the *Contents window* (figure below). Some titles are obvious. The *Mid_Atlantic Cities* layer, for example, probably includes cities in the Mid-Atlantic region of the United States. Many of the other data layers listed in the figure are self-explanatory as well. In some instances, names of vector files can help to describe the data.

But if we look at the raster files in the contents (figure), the names are not so revealing. Raster file names are comprised of information pertinent to the file. It just takes some knowledge and a bit of experience to interpret these filenames. The filenames themselves provide some metadata about the imagery.

If you are unfamiliar with raster file names, there are other areas where metadata can be acquired. These areas will be discussed later.

For now, let's look at the second option to examine metadata. Right now, all we know is the title of the file but we really don't know, other than boundaries or locations, what the file contains.

So, the next place to look is the *Attribute Table*. Do you remember how to view the attribute table? Right-click on the layer's name (in *Contents*) and then click on *Attribute Table*. In the figure below, we are examining the attribute table for Mid-Atlantic Counties:

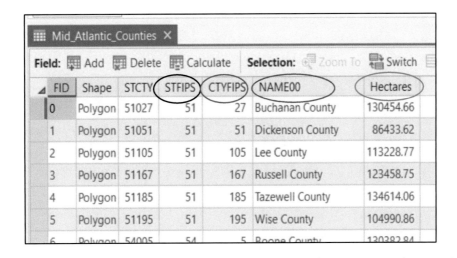

Here we will discover additional information about the file – the state of location (*STFIPS* - U.S. *Federal Information Processing Standard Publication* which lists the unique federal identification number for each US State and Territory) [black oval], the county's name (red oval), the federal identification number (*CTYFIPS*) [blue oval] for each county, the combined FIPS number for state and county (*STCTY*), and the area of the county in *Hectares* (green oval). Additionally, GIS assigned two bits of data – *FID* – a unique identifier for a single feature within this shapefiles, and that it is a *Polygon* type file.

Right-click on any of the raster file names, notice that the *Attribute Table* name is grayed out. Most raster files do not have an attribute table.

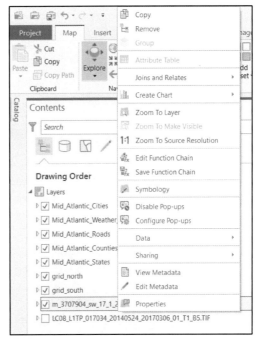

Let's move on to locations of other metadata. Right-click on any of the vector file names and go to *Properties*. Notice that there is a *Metadata* tab, but don't click on it yet!

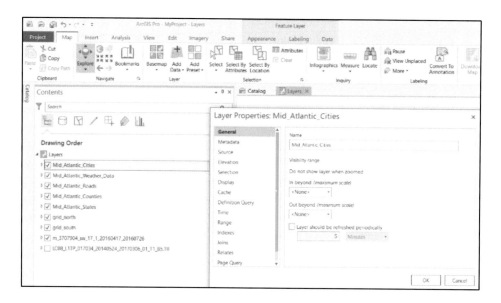

First, click on the *Source* tab – some metadata is located on this tab:

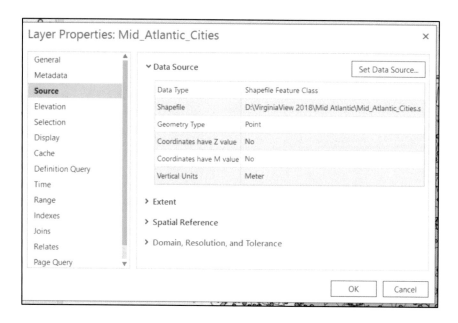

Expand *Extent*:

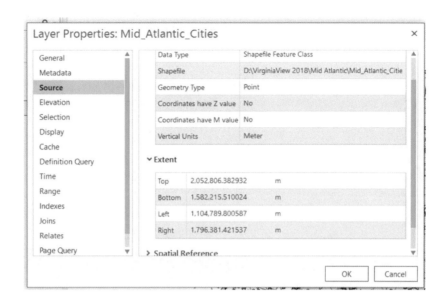

Then expand *Spatial Reference*:

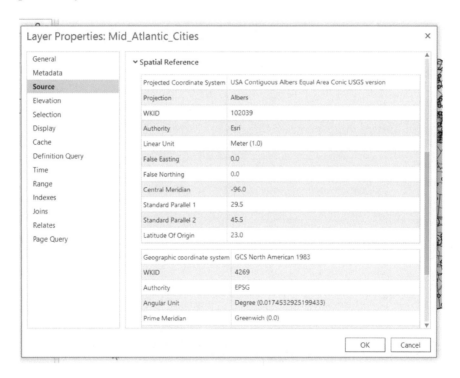

Expand *Domain, Resolution and Tolerance* – Examine all of the information (metadata) about the data file.

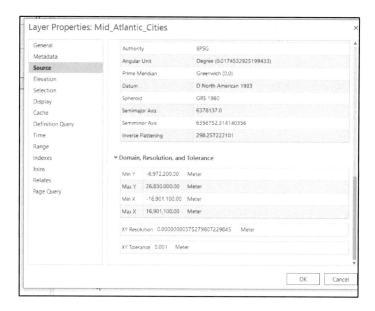

Please note that each one of the dialog boxes associated with the tab's list (on the left) in the *Layer Properties* dialog box can contain metadata – specifics of the metadata depend on the individual data file.

Now let's look at the *Metadata* tab. This tab has additional information that is completed by the data file's creator. If this information associated with a particular metadata element is blank, then it is likely that the creator did not complete the information associated with this metadata element (NAIP and Landsat imagery are examples).

In the prior figures in the Mid-Atlantic Counties' shapefile, we were able to explain the fields of the *Attribute Table*. But, what if the field names are not common, or cannot be deciphered (for example, *CDD* and *HDD* in the Mid-Atlantic Weather Data file – next figure)?

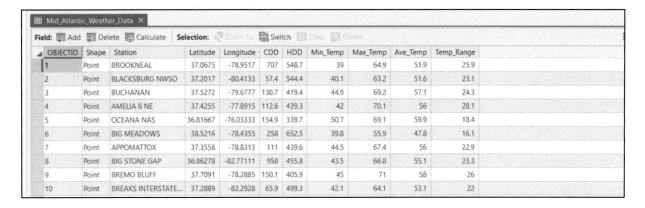

Are the definitions for these field names located on the National Weather Service Website? Are the abbreviations related to weather? Right-click on the layer's name and go to *View Metadata* (red box).

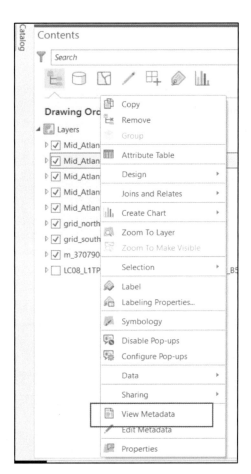

Catalog opens and much more extensive metadata displays in the window on the right.

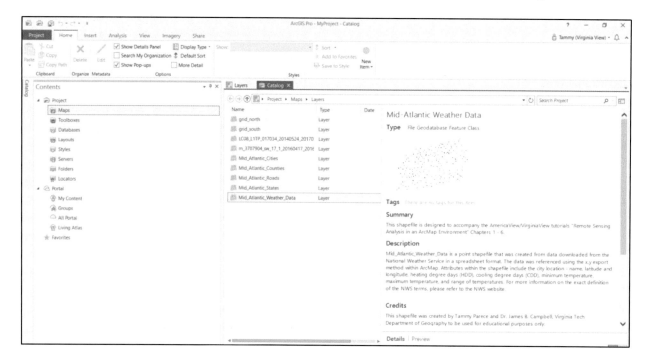

In this display, the metadata data displayed is based on *Item Description metadata style* (look at the very bottom of the box).

This can be changed -- click on the *Project* tab in the upper left corner:

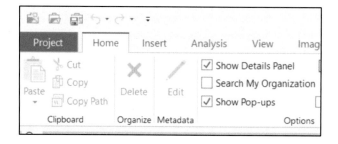

Click on *Options* and the *Options* dialog box opens:

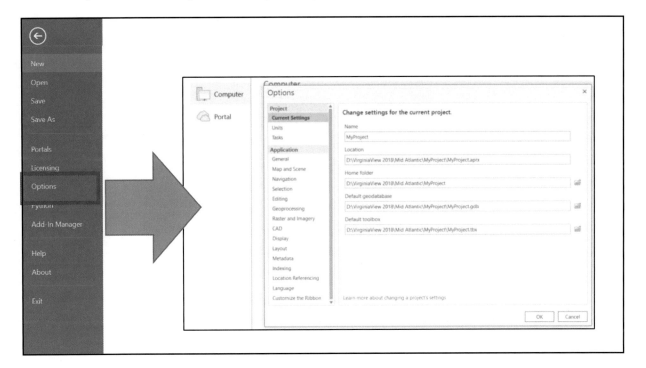

Choose the *Metadata* tab:

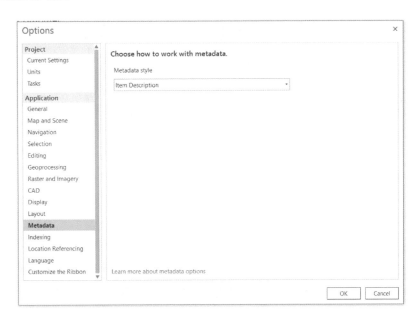

Under *Metadata style*, choose *FGDC CSDGM Metadata*[1] and click *OK*.

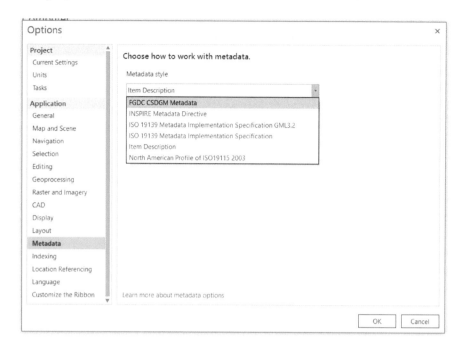

FGDC CSDGM is the abbreviation for Federal Geographic Data Committee Content Standard for Digital Geospatial Metadata: https://www.fgdc.gov/metadata/csdgm-standard

Now go, back to the Project by clicking on the left-pointing arrow in the upper left corner:

Click on the *Refresh* button in the *Catalog* window:

---

[1] Please note that the FGDC is moving to adopt the ISO 19115 as the new metadata standard for the FGDC.

The metadata style is updated – use the scroll bar on the right to see how much additional data is present:

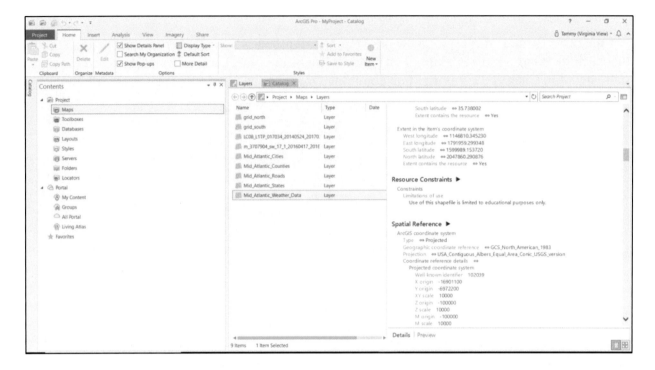

Please note, if the metadata style did not change, even after clicking on *Refresh*, click on the name of any other layer in the *Catalog* window, then click back on the layer and it updates.

With a raster file, metadata may or may not be displayed in this manner. Again, consult the owner's website.

In the below figure, when we clicked on the elevation *Grid North* file, we received a message in the window on the right.

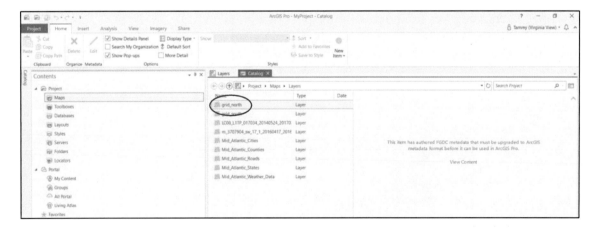

Since this is an older data file, the update can be processed using ArcGIS® Desktop (not ArcGIS® Pro). ESRI online Help provides details on this process. (http://desktop.arcgis.com/en/arcmap/10.3/tools/conversion-toolbox/synchronize-metadata.htm)

For the other two raster files, in the window on the right, messages display in each field stating that each field has no information. For Landsat, we discuss metadata and where to find in in more detail in Chapter 12: Information about the Downloaded Landsat 8 Image.

Remember from Chapter 4: Connecting to a Folder or an Online GIS Server, metadata for NAIP aerial imagery is online.

The final raster file – *LC08_L1TP_0170342014052402170306O_01_T1_B5.TIF* – is a Landsat 8 Band 5 image acquired over Roanoke – Blacksburg, Virginia on May 24, 2014. Some of the metadata is in the name of the file. But, Landsat 8 metadata is covered in Chapter 12: Information about a Downloaded Landsat 8 Image.

Creating Metadata in the Map Project

Metadata can be created for the map project. We have actually seen some metadata in Chapter 7: Displaying Data – remember coordinate system information for the map project?

Right click on the word *Layers* – and choose *View Metadata*:

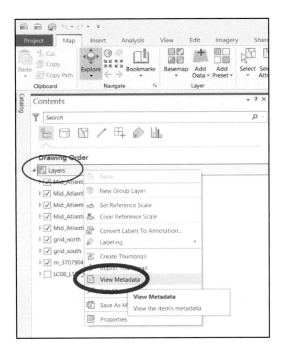

Here are the results:

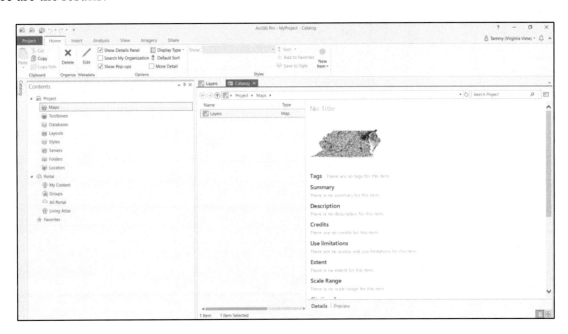

Okay, so currently, the only populated information is a screenshot of the map.

To create metadata, select *Edit Metadata*.

When editing metadata, the window on the right looks substantially different. Let's look closer.

At the top of the screen, messages are displayed:

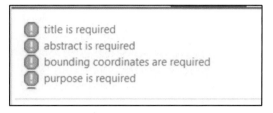

ArcGIS® Pro provides notes for required information and what is missing, according to the FGDC CSDGM. As of the writing of this book, including all this information is not mandatory to work with a map project. But these standards are quite comprehensive and, in many instances, the government, your employer (or future employer) may require use of these standards.

Just click in the box for the missing information and start typing:

Follow the same procedure for filling in the missing data for all fields.

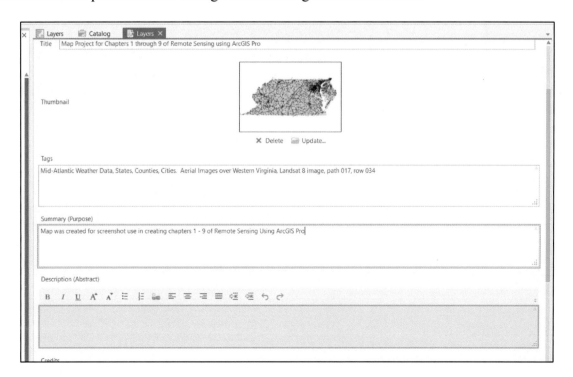

It is recommended that metadata is completed for all projects. Metadata adds value to the datasets that you develop. Metadata may limit future phone calls, can limit liability by providing use limitations. In addition, you can document and receive credit for your work.

Once the metadata entered is complete (or, in order not to lose the information already added before it is entirely complete), click on *Apply* (please note the disclaimer – the map project stills must be saved):

This concludes the chapter on metadata. We did not cover each of the fields and information required. Please see the *FGDC CSDGM* or FGDC ISO 19115 for more specifics and definitions of metadata elements.

Also keep in mind that private employers, federal, state, and local governments often have established guidelines to support the development of geospatial metadata. If you have received funding from an outside source, consult with your funding agency to make sure that you comply with their associated metadata requirements.

The next chapter, Chapter 9: Saving and Explorting Maps will conclude the introduction to ArcGIS® Pro.

Introduction:

While working in ArcGIS®® Pro, map projects, changes made while editing vector and raster files are saved, but some proprietary data formats cannot be used in other applications. For example, an *.mxd, .aprx* or *.pprx* format cannot be inserted within a Word document or data spreadsheet. In order to integrate maps from ArcGIS® Pro in other software programs, the map is exported to an appropriate file type, including jpegs and PDFs. This chapter provides the process for saving a map project and exporting it as a usable format that we can integrate within other media and software programs.

Saving the Map Document

ArcGIS® Pro does not automatically save map projects, so if a map document is closed prior to saving, any work that has not been saved will be lost. When a map project is first created, it was named and saved in a specific location (folder) on the computer, so the project was saved that very first time.

Thereafter, when saving the project, just click on the save file icon at the top of the computer screen. We recommend that the map project be saved frequently.

If the save button is not enabled as seen above (red circle), that means ArcGIS®® Pro did not register any changes.

To save the map to a new project, click on the *Project* tab.

Then click on *Save As*, and navigate to locate the drive on the computer where the project should be saved, name the project and click *Save*.

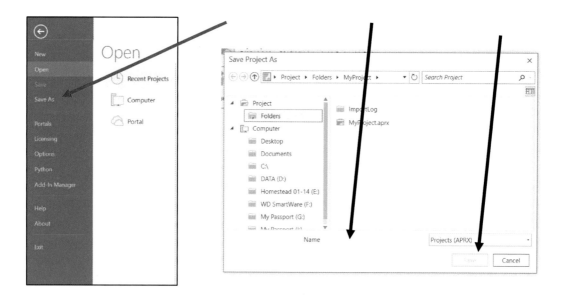

Note: the map project will be saved just as it appears in the map viewer. The symbology, the location of the files listed in the *Contents,* and the extent of the map are all saved. *(Note: this chapter only applies to the map project itself. Editing shapefiles, attribute tables and raster data sets are not covered within this chapter or book.)*

Saving the Map Document to use as a Figure in Another Document

ArcGIS® Pro is the only software program that can read .mxd, .aprx and .pprx files. If map graphics need to be integrated in a different software program (i.e. a word document, a presentation, or a poster), the map needs to be saved as another format option (jpeg, pdf, gif, etc.).

Click on the *Share* tab and *Export Map to File.*

But this step only exports what is currently visible in the map viewer (see next figure). It may not be an appropriate image to use in another document, because important map elements are missing (including a legend, scale bar, north arrow, title, etc.).

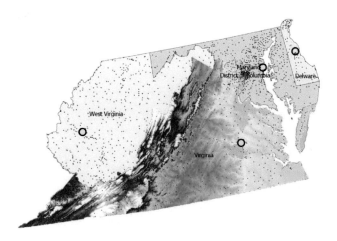

In order to include and export other elements with the map (scale bar, etc.), a map layout must first be generated. To create a map layout, select the *Insert* tab, then select the down arrow next to *New Layout* and choose the appropriate layout for the map. In the example below, we chose *ANSI Landscape Letter* (but any number of options exists, including poster sizes).

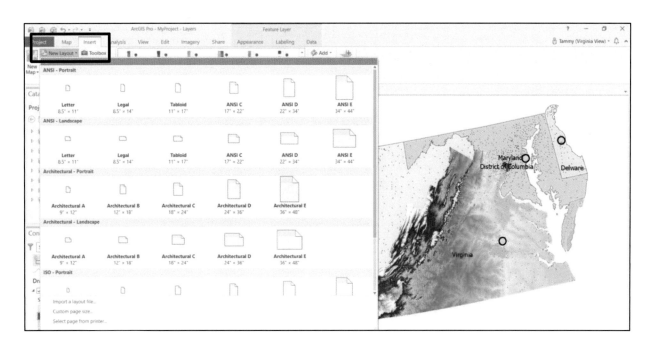

The map viewer changes as shown in the figure below.

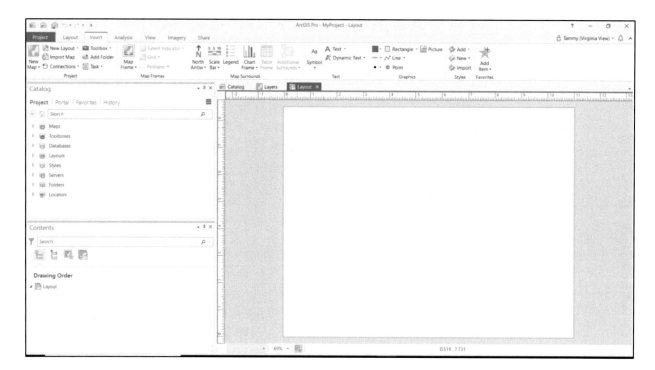

The next step is to choose a *Map Frame* – click the down arrow next to *Map Frame* and choose one.

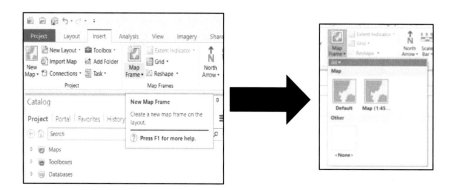

And a frame appears around the map in layout view.

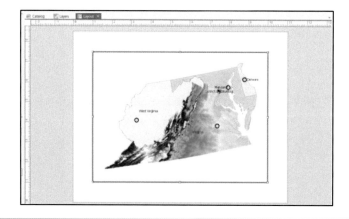

Additionally, all of the elements required to create a map can now be found in the *Layout* toolbar:

Use the tools in the *Layout toolbar* to add a north arrow, scale bar, legend, etc., as seen in the figure below:

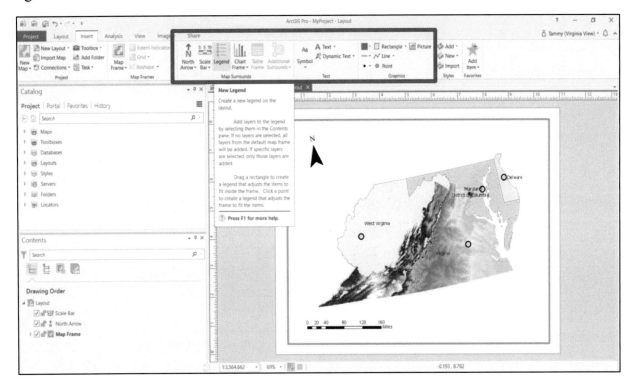

In the following figure, the map now has a north arrow, a legend, a scale bar. While this map is far from finished, this toolbar provides all the elements needed to add text, a title, etc.

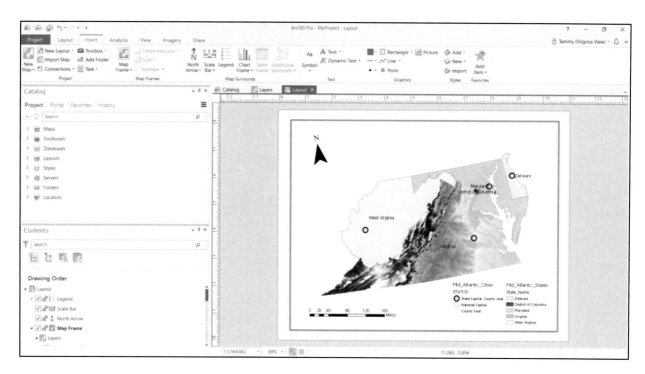

Now let's export the map layout, by selecting *Share* and *Export Layout*.

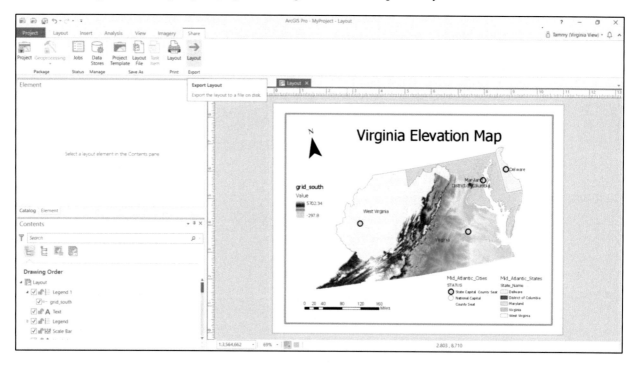

Navigate to a folder and save the exported map layout. Choose the desired type of file format from the dropdown list and then name it.

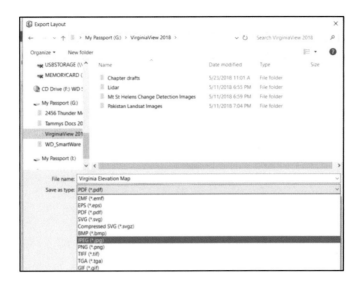

Once named and the appropriate format is chosen, click *Export* to export the layout.

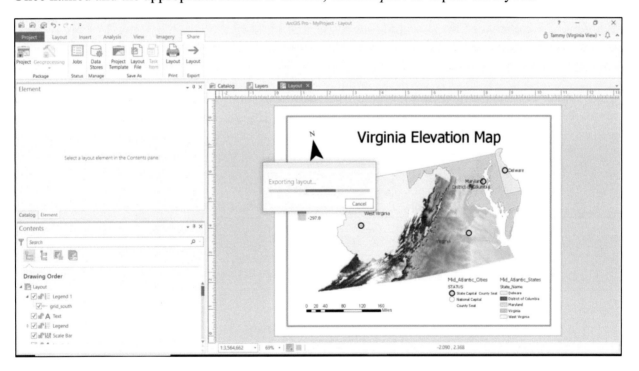

The saved file (jpeg, pdf, etc.) is located in the designated folder as an exported format option that can be integrated with non-GIS software packages.

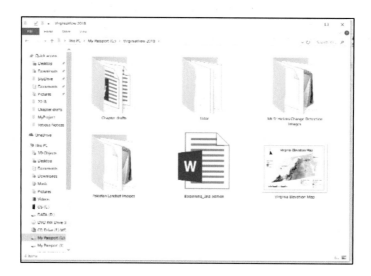

In this case, the file was saved as a jpeg. There are many other file formats and export options available. There are also many techniques associated in designing a professional looking map layout. While we did not cover all of these techniques in this chapter, these additional characteristics are added by using the layout toolbar.

This chapter concludes the introduction to ArcGIS® Pro basics. Chapters 10 – 25 will cover remotely sensed imagery and use of Landsat 8 scenes within ArcGIS® Pro for display and analysis.

Remotely sensed imagery is acquired using various methods (aerial cameras, radar, lidar, satellite sensors, etc.) and aerial platforms (UAVs, aircraft, balloons, satellites, etc.). The United States Geological Survey (USGS) has been designated as a central clearinghouse for much of the imagery collected by the federal government with a mission to organize imagery and facilitates its distribution to the public. The USGS library is searchable using EarthExplorer (www.earthexplorer.usgs.gov) and such images are available to the public for purchase, or for free, depending upon specifics of the acquisition.

Although the USGS collection is very large, it does not have a complete library of all remotely sensed Earth imagery. This chapter briefly discusses some of the images available on the EarthExplorer site. Because the library expands on a regular basis, we recommend that the site be examined on a regular basis.

Remote Sensing Basics

Different forms of remotely sensed imagery are categorized by various characteristics. For example, Landsat and Sentinel satellite imagery, each consist of multiple bands of images. Each image band is characterized by a distinctive region of the electromagnetic spectrum, specific radiometric properties, and a specific spatial resolution.

The electromagnetic spectrum encompasses a range of all types of radiation (energy). Reference the image below from NASA's Goddard Space Flight Center website.

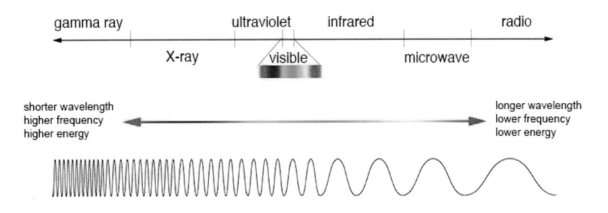

Image from: https://imagine.gsfc.nasa.gov/science/toolbox/emspectrum1.html

Humans can only see radiation in a very small range of the spectrum (*the visible spectrum*), but mechanical sensors can record radiation in those wavelengths outside of the visible spectrum, for display and analysis by computer systems. Why is this important? Features on the Earth's surface (water, soil, plants, snow and all manmade objects, etc.) absorb and re-emit energy (conveying spectral properties that uniquely characterize the Earth's surface and the objects we observe on its surface). Because of these unique spectral properties, we can "see" and analyze Earth's features using remotely sensed imagery using more than just the spectral data that seen visually. We discuss further specifics of spectral analysis in Chapter 19: Spectral Enhancement of Landsat 8 Imagery.

Radiometric properties refers to the "brightness" of the various features, which are defined by range of brightness values used by a specific sensor (for example, an 8-bit image provides 256 brightness values, a 16-bit image provides 65,536 brightness values). We discuss radiometric analysis in Chapter 17: Radiometric Enhancement of Landsat 8 Imagery.

Spatial properties refer to the area of the Earth's surface covered by one pixel of the image. Spatial properties vary from sensor to sensor, but also within one sensor, depending on its sensitivity to a specified region of the electromagnetic spectrum. For example, Landsat 8's red band pixel size measures 30 meters by 30 meters and Sentinel's red band pixel size measures 10 meters × 10 meters. While Landsat 8's red band has a ground resolution of 30 meters × 30 meters, Landsat 8's thermal band has a ground resolution of 100 meters × 100 meters. We discuss spatial resolution in Chapter 18: Spatial Enhancement of Landsat 8 Imagery.

Why is this important? When we compare one image to another, spectral, spatial and radiometric properties are important. When we analyze changes in vegetation, we must compare bands with the same spectral properties.

Landsat Imagery

The U.S. Landsat program consists of a family of Earth imaging satellites, notable as the longest-running system of land-observation satellites in the world. Landsat 1 was launched in 1972 and its most recent (Landsat 8) launched in February, 2013. Landsat 9 is on target to launch in December 2020 (https://landsat.gsfc.nasa.gov/landsat-9/landsat-9-mission-details/).

All Landsat images are available for download, at no cost, from the USGS's EarthExplorer library (image downloads are discussed in the Chapter 11: Downloading Landsat 8 Imagery using EarthExplorer).

As with other remotely sensed imagery, Landsat's spectral bands (sometimes referred to as channels) are defined by a distinctive regions of the electromagnetic spectrum, but not all Landsat sensors cover the same regions. Specifically, Landsat 8 uses band definitions that differ from other Landsat sensors.

See the diagram below and at https://pubs.usgs.gov/fs/2012/3072/fs2012-3072.pdf for a comparison of different Landsat platforms.

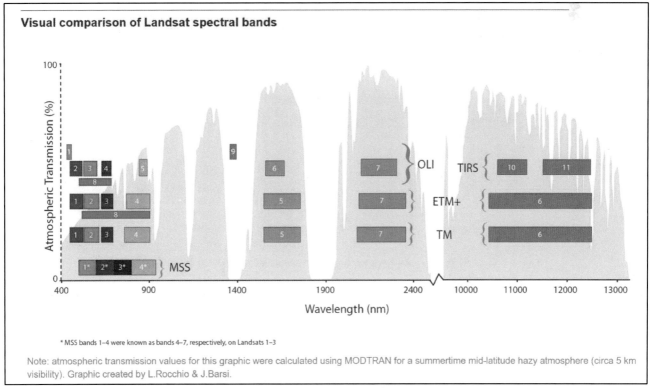

Image from http://landsat.gsfc.nasa.gov/about/technical-information/

For more information and specific details of Landsat satellites, sensors and potential analyses using Landsat images go to: http://landsat.usgs.gov/

Sentinel

Sentinel is also an Earth imaging satellite program. The Sentinel program, is designed, launched, and managed by the European Space Agency. Each Sentinel mission involves two satellites. For example, Sentinels 1-A (launched in 2014) and 1-B (launched in 2016) are radar imaging weather satellites. Sentinels 2-A (launched in 2015) and 2-B (launched in 2017) are multi-spectral high-resolution land-observation satellites (comparable to the US Landsat system).

As with Landsat, some Sentinel images are available to the public without cost from the USGS via the EarthExplorer website. We do not discuss downloading Sentinel imagery in this book, but the image download and analysis procedures are similar to that of Landsat.

Sentinel 2 acquires images in 13 spectral bands and various spatial resolutions (see image below and http://www.esa.int/Our_Activities/Observing_the_Earth/Copernicus/Overview4 or https://lta.cr.usgs.gov/sentinel_2 for more information).

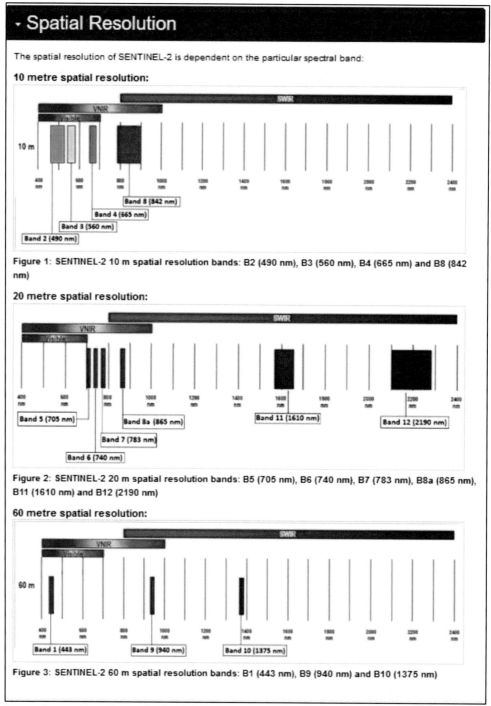

Image from: https://earth.esa.int/web/sentinel/user-guides/sentinel-2-msi/resolutions/spatial

Other Imagery Available from EarthExplorer

Many other remotely sensed image products and data are available from the USGS data library via EarthExplorer.

Image Data Available on EarthExplorer

When entering the EarthExplorer (https://earthexplorer.usgs.gov/) website, this screen displays:

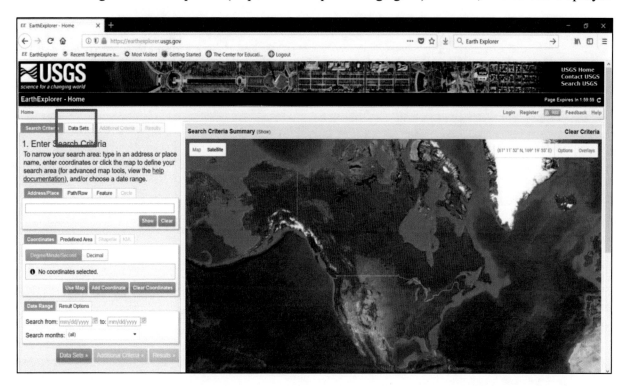

To see what imagery/data is stored in the USGS data clearinghouse, click on the *Data Sets* tab (red box in above figure). To determine the images and/or data available under each category, expand the + sign in front of the category name.

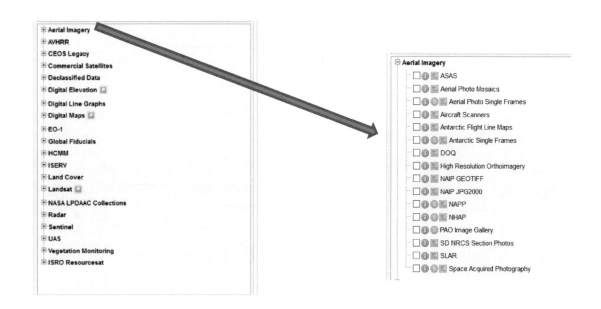

To access metadata associated with a specific image, click the information button next to the image's name (red box).

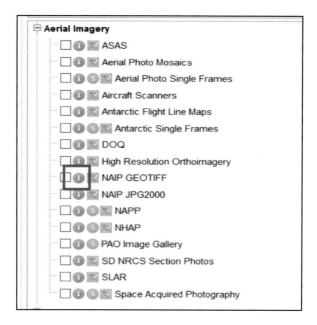

In this specific case, clicking on the *Information* icon took us to the website for the NAIP program (the United States Department of Agriculture National Agriculture Imagery Program).

To determine if a specific image is available as a free download or at a cost, just click on the green dollar icon next to the *Information* button.

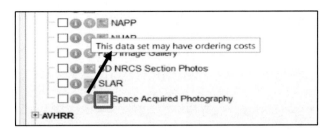

To identify the geographic region covered by an image product, click on the icon right next to the image's name (red box above).

After selecting the icon next to the name of the image product, the map document window will illustrate areas associated with the selected image product – highlighted in green below.

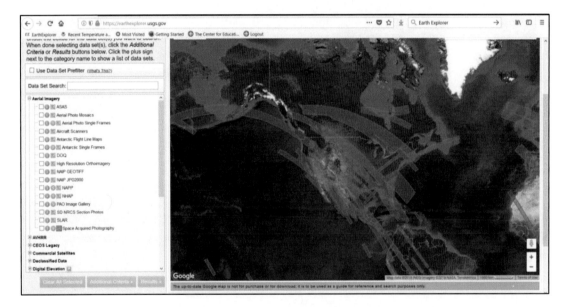

In the next figure, we selected Vegetation Monitoring/Quick DRI and the coverage areas are highlighted in brown.

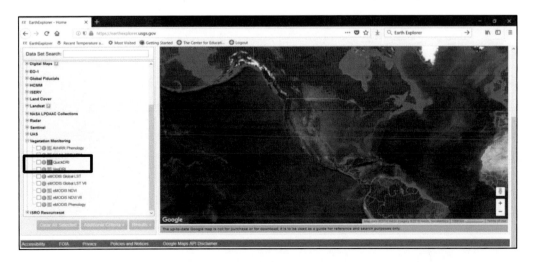

Using different colors to highlight coverage areas, allows display of multiple image locations at the same time and will help determine what images are available for a specific area:

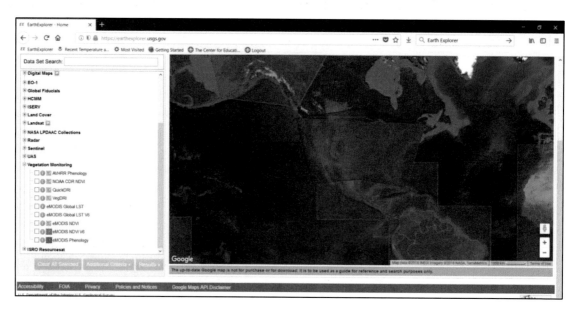

Whether remotely sensed imagery are being used for analysis, or just as a stand-alone image for reference purposes, a decision must be made to choose the most appropriate one. If the image is needed for a specific purpose, coverage area, spatial extent, spectral and radiometric properties and the audience/customer must all be taken into account during the decision process. Such decisions are beyond the scope of this book, and we refer to our introduction for additional literature to assist in this decision making process, and recommend that all metadata be reviewed for all images under consideration.

In the next chapter of this book, we provide a step-by-step instruction on how to download imagery, specifically a Landsat 8 image used in other chapters of this book.

Introduction:

This chapter provides step-by-step instructions to select and download Landsat 8 imagery via the USGS's EarthExplorer website. Landsat 8 imagery will be used in subsequent chapters of this book. This chapter provides download instructions that can be applied to other imagery products also available from EarthExplorer (including NAIP, Sentinel, MODIS, etc.).

For this chapter, you will require a computer with a high-speed internet connection.

Once any imagery is downloaded, you will need to determine if the downloaded imagery requires further processing beyond that already provided by the USGS. This chapter, includes a discussion of some of the processing steps provided by the USGS. This chapter refers the reader to metadata for additional information, and includes a brief discussion of metadata. In other chapters of this book, we cover metadata in more detail, as well as basic image processing capabilities – band combinations, spatial, spectral and radiometric enhancement, and image classification specific to the Landsat 8 image downloaded in this chapter. We do not cover any other imagery in detail in this book. This said, many of the processing and image enhancement procedures that are covered in this text are also relevant to other image products as well. In the interest of conciseness and focus, this resource will not address other forms of processing, but it will direct readers to other resources for additional information.

Downloading Landsat Imagery

EarthExplorer is a repository of imagery products available for ordering and downloading. To access EarthExplorer, go to http://earthexplorer.usgs.gov/.   The website looks like this:

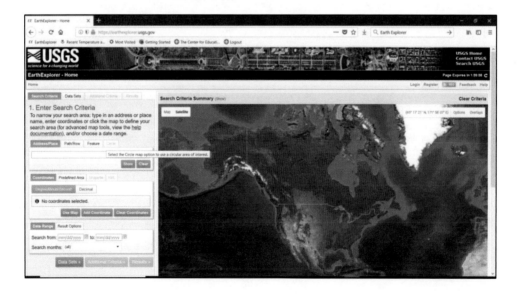

Before starting to navigate the site, *Login* (red box below). Then when the desired image is located, it can be downloaded.

If you have an account, enter the user name and password.

If you do not have an account, select *Create New Account*. Then follow the steps in the *User Registration* area.

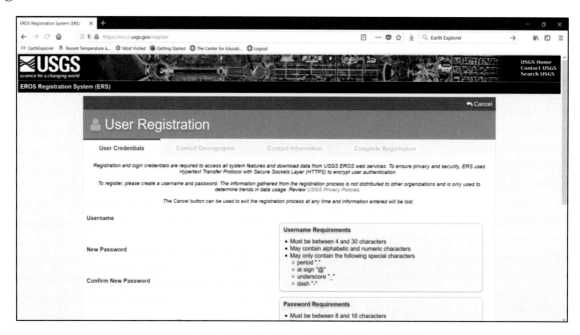

Once you are logged in, the user name will show in the upper right hand corner (red box).

Now let's search for the area of interest (the region for the required image). Under *Search Criteria* on the left side of the website, search is accomplished by using a location address or name (i.e., Roanoke, Virginia), by latitude and longitude, by feature name (i.e., Niagara Falls), or by Path/Row of the specific image (we discuss Path/Row later).

In the figure below, we have used a location name – Roanoke, Virginia. Select the *Show* button and EarthExplorer provides additional detail in the box located under the location name.

Click on the name – Roanoke, VA, USA. EarthExplorer populates the latitude and longitude field and inserts a locational balloon in the map display.

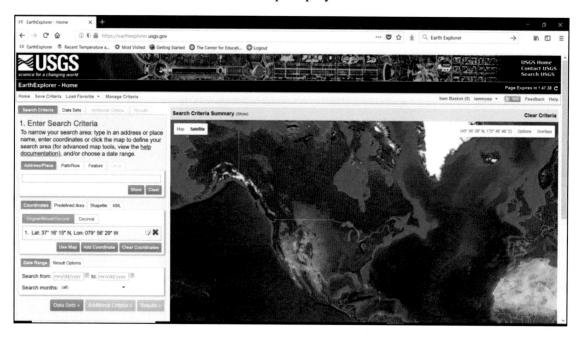

We could now go on to the *Data Sets* tab to identify image data sets available through EarthExplorer that cover the area of interest, but, first, limiting the *Date Range* is essential.

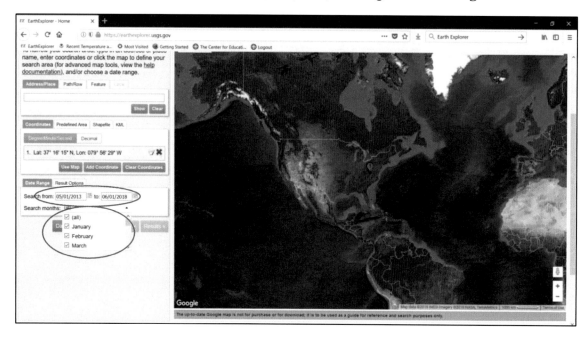

Please recall from the prior chapter that Landsat 8 launched in early 2013, so we are using May 2013 as the start date (and the end date is the date of this writing). You can also choose a specific month (which is necessary to limit the returns to a specific season). For our purposes, we are going to leave the dates as shown to demonstrate what happens when searching a wide range of dates. Including a larger date range will obviously increase the image download options.

Go to the *Data Sets* tab at the top:

Under the *Data Sets* tab, expand the + sign next to Landsat, which provides a list of available Landsat images, some with different types of processing.

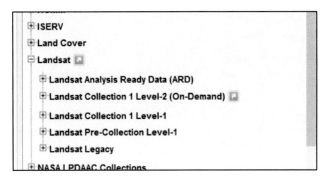

We are now going to discuss these options as they identify different levels of processing by the USGS. Let's start with Landsat Analysis Ready Data (ARD). https://landsat.usgs.gov/ard

This option is used for processing large amounts of data in time-series analyses. This is not the image product that we need for our application.

For Landsat Collection 1, Level 2 (On-Demand), click on the arrow in the orange box. This is the *Related Links* button.

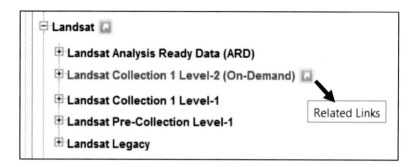

Clicking on *Related Links*, navigates to this website:

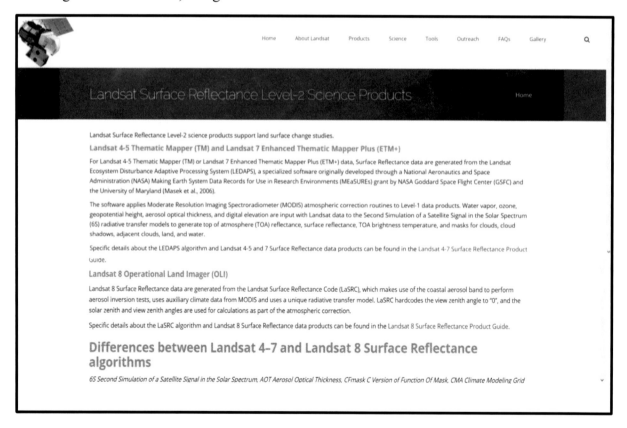

The Collection 1 Level-2 products are associated with Landsat 4, 5, 7 and 8. These products are already processed for Surface Reflectance. What is surface reflectance? Please read the information on the link, which provides specifics on algorithms for atmospheric corrections.

We are not choosing this level of image product because these are image products that must be ordered. Here, we want to find an image that we can directly download to our computer.

Landsat Collection Level-1.

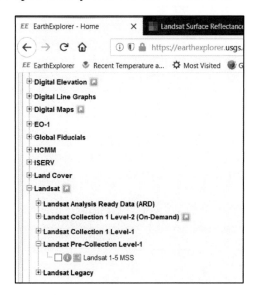

The Collection 1 Level-1 imagery is available for all Landsat imagery, it is downloadable, and it has undergone some processing by the USGS. To determine which specific processing necessary for the project, see the following references:

- https://landsat.usgs.gov/what-are-landsat-collection-1-tiers
- https://lta.cr.usgs.gov/LETMP
- https://landsat.usgs.gov/landsat-level-1-standard-data-products
- https://landsat.usgs.gov/landsat-processing-details

Landsat Pre-Collection Level 1 does not include Landsat 8. This option is not relevant to our image requirements, since we specifically want to use Landsat 8.

Landsat Legacy

Landsat Legacy consists of a series of categories of Landsat data that each meet specific levels of data quality, to allow users to easily find data suitable for specific kinds of analysis. Classes are defined by specific sensors, dates of acquisition, and caliber of processing.

Expand the + sign next to Landsat Legacy to see what images and processing are available.

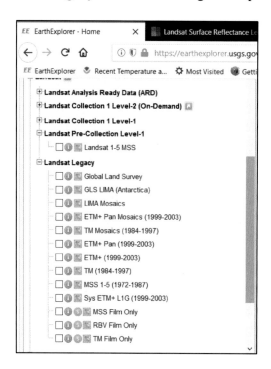

The Legacy framework ensures that Landsat Level-1 products form a consistent archive of known data quality that can support time-series analyses and data "stacking", while simultaneously supporting continuous improvement of the archive and permitting users to access to all data as they are acquired. Specifics are outlined at *(https://landsat.usgs.gov/landsat-collections)*.

Legacy data are not relevant for our current lesson, but make a mental note about the existence of Landsat Legacy products as these may be useful to you in future endeavors.

Landsat Imagery available from Other Sources

The USGS has also processed some images for normalized difference vegetation index (NDVI) and bulk ordering. They are available through on-demand ordering at https://espa.cr.usgs.gov/.

So after looking at the different levels of processing, we really only have one choice if we want to directly download an image - **Collection 1 Level-1**, so select that box in front Landsat 8 - associated with this image product.

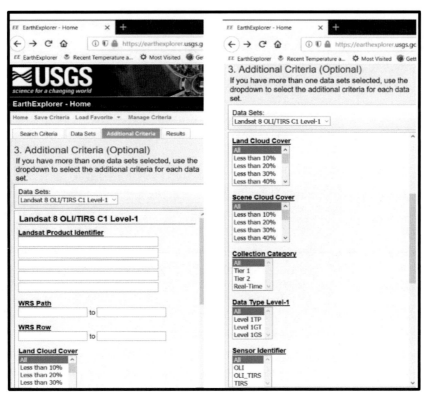

Additional Criteria

Now select the *Additional Criteria* tab at the top. The *Additional Criteria* tab provides additional options to filter the requests of the image data archive. These choices will help focus the number of images that are returned.

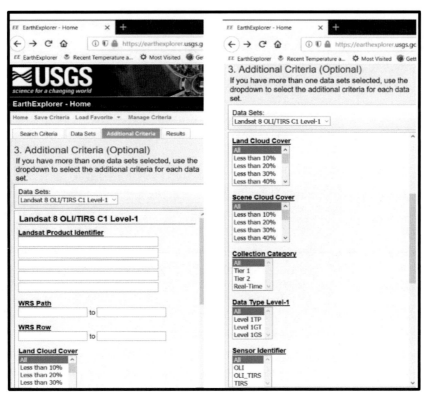

The Landsat Product Identifier (LPI) is a unique number assigned to each image. For this chapter, we don't know any LPI's. We will discuss this number in detail in the next chapter (Chapter 12: Information about the Downloaded Landsat 8 Image).

WRS Path and WRS Row are unique for each location covered by a Landsat Scene. Again, for this chapter, we don't know this information offhand. If you would like to figure that out now, go to: https://landsat.gsfc.nasa.gov/the-worldwide-reference-system/; this topic will also be discussed in the next chapter.

Land Cloud Cover and Scene Cloud Cover.

The Cloud Cover and Scene Cloud Cover variables are very important. Choosing an image with limited to no cloud cover is extremely important for many land analyses. The image on the right is an example of an almost completely cloud-covered Landsat scene over Charleston, South Carolina.

Cloud cover patterns vary over space. Therefore, the difference between land cloud cover and scene cloud cover is important. In some scenes, part of the image may include a large body of water, so, if you are mapping terrestrial components, cloud cover over the open water may not matter. The following screenshot is an example. This scene includes Charleston, South Carolina. But the scene also extends over the Atlantic Ocean. Clouds over the ocean may not matter if the application is focus on terrestrial applications.

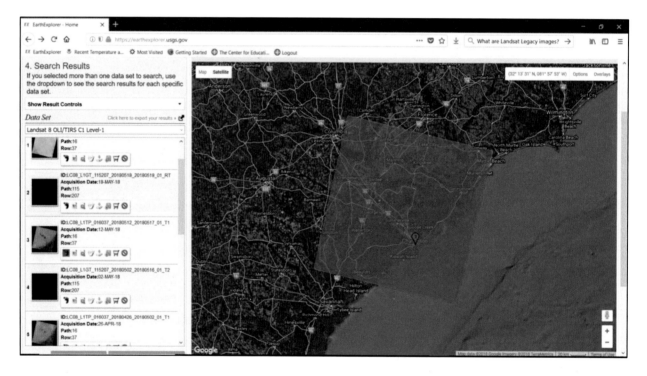

We will be using an image over and Roanoke Virginia is not near any large bodies of water (such as the Great Lakes or Atlantic Ocean). So for terrestrial analyses, the search criteria should be limited to scenes with less than 10% cloud cover.

We are only interested with images captured during the day, so we will choose 'day' (*Day/Night Indicator*). Most Landsat scenes only are daytime images, but the authors of this book know that nighttime images over Roanoke are also available. Use of the nighttime scenes are beyond the scope of this book.

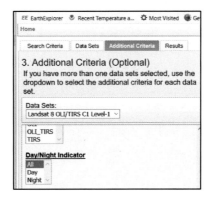

For all of the other parameters, we are going to leave those as *All* (no filtering).

Now select *Results*! We have 48 images returned (red box), displayed 10 at a time in reverse chronological order (the most recent scenes are listed first).

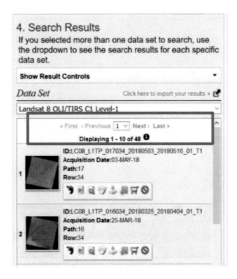

Interpreting the search results

Let's first look at one of the results, so we understand what we have at hand. Each of the images returned has specific information related to that image. The first image was acquired on 03 May 2018. A thumb-nail snapshot of the image is provided (on the left). This image appears to be cloud free (compare it to the image below it, for 25 March 2018, which shows some cloud cover in the southwest corner of the image.)

Remember *Path* and *Row*? All daytime images over this specific region are Path 17 and Row 34. This image does contain Roanoke, Virginia but also extends into West Virginia.

How do we know this? Click on the footprint icon.

In the map window, it shows the region covered by this entire scene.

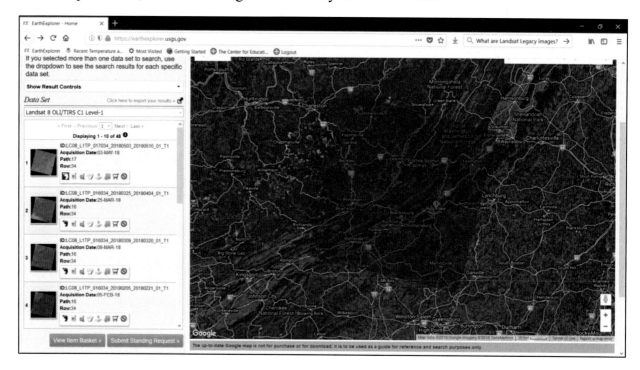

Now click on the *Show Browse Overlay* icon (the very next icon, to the right of the footprint).

That icon is actually a jpeg of the Landsat natural color scene (for more about natural color see Chapter 16: Band Combinations for Landsat 8 Imagery). Notice, this scene is not entirely cloud free (white circle show the locations of clouds).

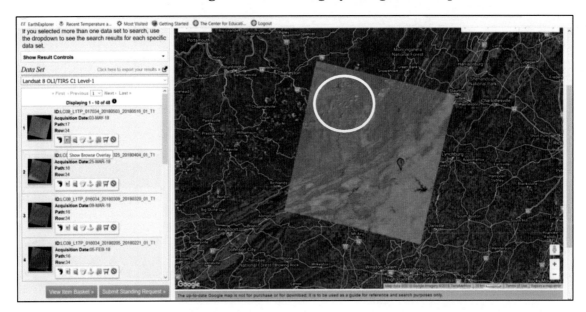

Skip the next icon and click on the one that looks like pen and paper – *Show Metadata and Browse.*

The figure below appears showing the scene in Natural Color:

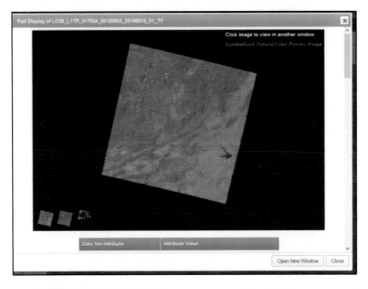

And below it, is *Metadata,* provided as a summary tabulation of key information associated with this scene. (The image below is an accumulation of screenshots while using the scroll bar on the right.) We are not going to discuss metadata –in this chapter. Landsat Metadata is discussed in detail in the next chapter (Chapter 12: Information about the Downloaded Landsat 8 Image).

This scene's Metadata can be downloaded by selecting *Click here to export the results* (red box) in figure below (at the top of the *Search Results* box in EarthExplorer), which then allows you to select the format of your Metadata.

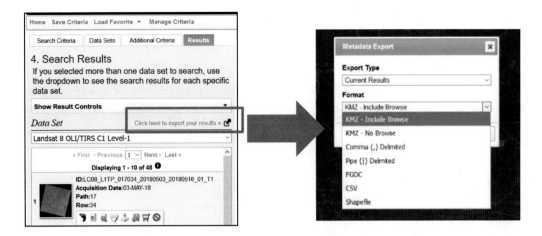

Why would you just need metadata? Perhaps you lost the metadata from a scene that you downloaded previously, or perhaps you are just reviewing metadata for prospective scenes you might use, and don't need the Landsat scenes until you have reviewed all the options.

The next button is the *Download* icon. Do not select this image to download. We will choose another image to download later. At this point, we are just looking at the imagery options.

However, if the download icon is not enabled, then the scene is not available for direct download -- the image is ordered using the shopping cart icon.   We will discuss imagery to be ordered before we proceed to download.

A scene that is downloadable, can also be ordered. Why would you want to order versus downloading. When downloading, it is one scene at a time. Want multiple scenes? Order them using the shopping cart icon.

Ordering a Landsat Scene

EarthExplorer is a very user friendly site, so if you want to order the image via the shopping cart, the site will walk you through the process (see details below).

Ordering a scene can be completed in multiple ways – the shopping cart and the bulk download option, which can be accessed through the yellow floppy disc icon (*Add to Bulk Download*).

What is the advantage of a bulk download? It may be necessary to download multiple scenes at one time, through a single transaction.

Some scenes can be eliminated from the established search criteria by clicking on the *Exclude Scene from Results* icon – the very last icon in the list:

When performing a bulk download, the images are placed in the item basket (red box).

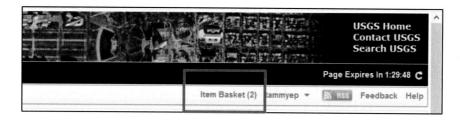

Select the *Item Basket* option to view the items that have been chosen for ordering.

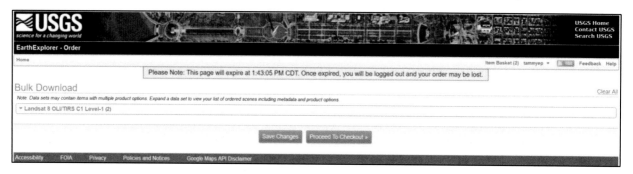

Select *Proceed to Checkout*:

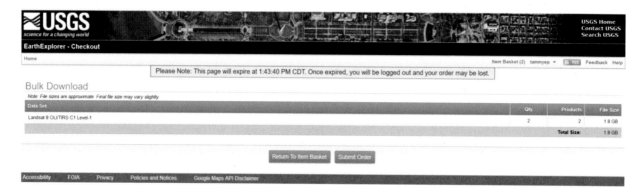

Then select the *Submit Order.*

EarthExplorer displays the following confirmation message.

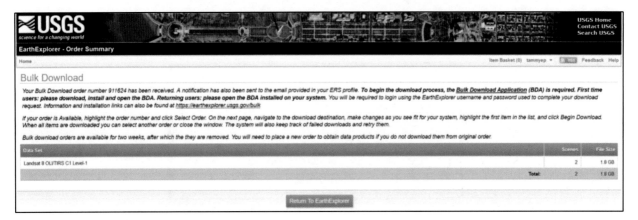

You will also get an email acknowledging the order, which provides specific instructions on how to download the order (red box).

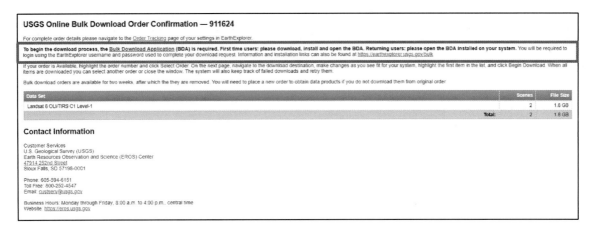

Directly Downloading a Landsat Scene

Search and download (using the direct download option) the image for Roanoke, Virginia dated June 14, 2016 (see figure below). We will use this scene in other chapters of this book.

After clicking on the *Download* icon, the following window will appear:

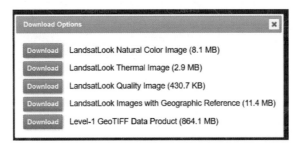

Select the Level-1 GeoTIFF Data Product (notice that it is almost 1 GB of data) by clicking on the Download option for this product. If the button is not enabled, you forgot to login.

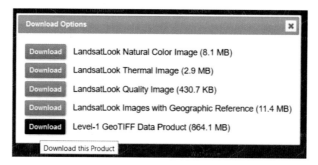

The following dialog box appears:

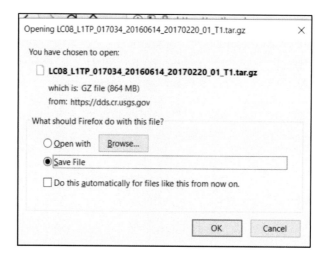

Make sure the radio button for *Save File* is selected, then click *OK*. The file will be saved to the computer's download file folder, or to a specific project folder that you specify. This is a very large file, so it will take a few minutes or more (depending on the WiFi speed). You can watch the progress of the download by looking at the browser icon in the status bar at the bottom of the computer screen.

Once the file has finished downloading, navigate to the folder (either the download folder or a folder that you specified) to find the downloaded Landsat file. Note that this file is compressed, and will need to be extracted – it will be listed as a .tar.gz file.

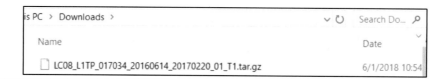

Right click on the file name, click on 7-Zip[1] and select *Extract Files*.

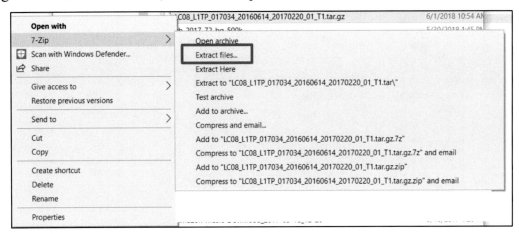

This dialog box opens. Under *Extract to:* make sure this is where the file should be saved. If not, click on the ... at the end of the line and navigate to the folder to store the images (we recommend a project folder).

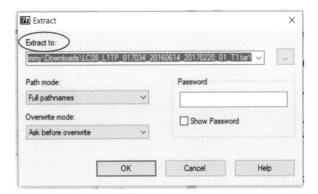

Once the correct folder populates in the *Extract to:* box, click *OK*

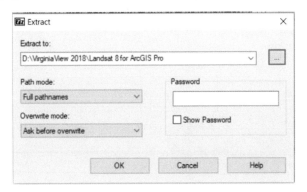

---

[1] 7-Zip is a free software that supports data decompression of large files, including downloaded Landsat Files, and needs to be installed on your computer in order to extract the downloaded Landsat imagery. If the computer does not have 7-Zip installed, please see your IT Administrator or go to https://www.7-zip.org/ and install it yourself.

The dialog box in the figure below opens:

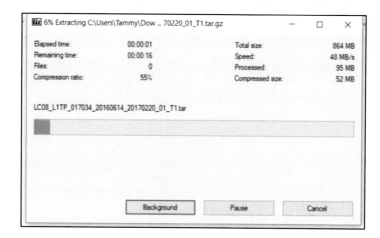

Once the file has been extracted (unzipped), navigate to the folder where it was unzipped. A *.tar* file will be showing. This is another zipped file. (*Note - because of the file size, Landsat scenes are double-zipped, so they are unzipped twice*).

Right click the tar file and unzip it (if prompted, select *Extract to Here*):

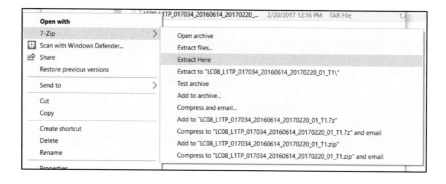

Once the unzipping process has finished, the following files are in the project folder:

Name	Date modified	Type	Size
LC08_L1TP_017034_20160614_20170220_01_T1.tar	2/20/2017 12:16 PM	TAR File	1,760,830
LC08_L1TP_017034_20160614_20170220_01_T1_ANG	2/20/2017 12:14 PM	Text Document	115 KB
LC08_L1TP_017034_20160614_20170220_01_T1_B1	2/20/2017 12:15 PM	TIF File	117,392 KB
LC08_L1TP_017034_20160614_20170220_01_T1_B2	2/20/2017 12:15 PM	TIF File	117,392 KB
LC08_L1TP_017034_20160614_20170220_01_T1_B3	2/20/2017 12:15 PM	TIF File	117,392 KB
LC08_L1TP_017034_20160614_20170220_01_T1_B4	2/20/2017 12:15 PM	TIF File	117,392 KB
LC08_L1TP_017034_20160614_20170220_01_T1_B5	2/20/2017 12:16 PM	TIF File	117,392 KB
LC08_L1TP_017034_20160614_20170220_01_T1_B6	2/20/2017 12:16 PM	TIF File	117,392 KB
LC08_L1TP_017034_20160614_20170220_01_T1_B7	2/20/2017 12:16 PM	TIF File	117,392 KB
LC08_L1TP_017034_20160614_20170220_01_T1_B8	2/20/2017 12:16 PM	TIF File	469,384 KB
LC08_L1TP_017034_20160614_20170220_01_T1_B9	2/20/2017 12:16 PM	TIF File	117,392 KB
LC08_L1TP_017034_20160614_20170220_01_T1_B10	2/20/2017 12:16 PM	TIF File	117,392 KB
LC08_L1TP_017034_20160614_20170220_01_T1_B11	2/20/2017 12:16 PM	TIF File	117,392 KB
LC08_L1TP_017034_20160614_20170220_01_T1_BQA	2/20/2017 12:16 PM	TIF File	117,392 KB
LC08_L1TP_017034_20160614_20170220_01_T1_MTL	2/20/2017 12:16 PM	Text Document	9 KB

Success! You have downloaded the Landsat 8 scene that includes Roanoke, Virginia, dated June 14, 2016. In the next chapter (Chapter 12: Information about the Downloaded Landsat 8 Image), we will discuss these files in more detail. In subsequent chapters, we introduce techniques to analyze this imagery and extract information to support research.

You will need to determine if the downloaded imagery needs further processing beyond that completed by the USGS. For more information about the level and type of USGS processing of Landsat scenes, go to http://landsat.usgs.gov/Landsat_Processing_Details.php. See also Masek, J.G., et al., *A Landsat surface reflectance data set for North America, 1990-2000. Geoscience and Remote Sensing Letters*, 2006. **3**: p. 68-72.

Introduction:

Landsat is the longest continuous operating Earth observation satellite program. The first Landsat Satellite was launched in 1972 and the most recent, Landsat 8, was launched in 2013. Landsat missions continue. Landsat 9 is scheduled to launch in December 2020.   For specific details on Landsat satellites, sensors, and potential analyses go to: http://landsat.usgs.gov/

In the previous chapter, a Landsat 8 scene dated June 14, 2016 was downloaded from the USGS image clearinghouse called EarthExplorer. This chapter provides information about the scene. Decisions on exactly which images are required for specific analyses are beyond the scope of this chapter and this book.

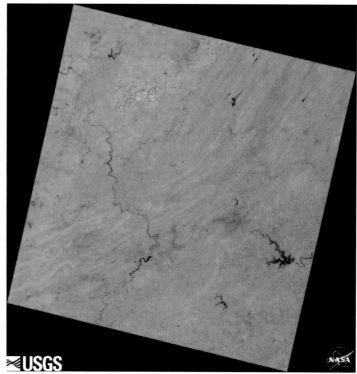

JPEG of the Landsat scene downloaded from the previous chapter

When exploring available images in EarthExplorer, metadata relevant to the image was provided. Metadata provides information about each specific Landsat Scene. In this chapter, we discuss some specific metadata elements, but we will not review each line. Many of these metadata elements are self-explanatory.

On the left side of the table below is the category of metadata and, on the right side is the metadata for the category specific to this Landsat Scene. If unsure what the category means, while in EarthExplorer, left-click on the category name (below, we clicked on "Landsat Product Identifier").

This Landsat Product Identifier link navigates to a webpage describing that specific category – a *Landsat Product Identifier* (figure below). This is the "naming convention of each acquired scene based on acquisition and processing parameters". Additionally, each character associated with the Landsat Product Identifier has meaning.

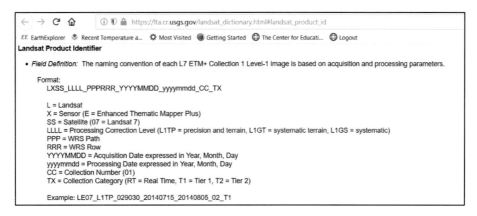

From the metadata, let's examine our scene's product identifier:

LC08_L1TP_017034_ 20160614_20170220_01_T1

- L = Landsat
- C = OLI and TIRS -- these are the sensors aboard Landsat 8 (https://landsat.usgs.gov/landsat-8)
- L1TP = Level 1 precision and terrain
- 017 – path for this scene
- 034 – row for this scene
- 20160614 – date the scene was acquired June 14, 2016
- 20170220 – the date the scene was last processed by the USGS. Please note that this date can change as new processing methods are developed.

- 01 – Collection number
- T1 – a tier one product (please refer to https://landsat.usgs.gov/landsat-collections for more information)

The next item in the metadata list is the *Landsat Scene Identifier* – this number can be used to order this scene again, without the necessity of following all the steps (searching, etc.) demonstrated in Chapter 11: Downloading a Landsat 8 Image using EarthExplorer. This number looks very similar to the Product Identifier. The major difference is the date of acquisition. In the Landsat Scene Identifier, the data of the image is expressed in Julian format – 2016166 – the 166th day of the year 2016. After the date of acquisition, are the characters LGN01. LGN is the ground station identifier (https://landsat.usgs.gov/igs-network) and 01 denotes the version of this scene.

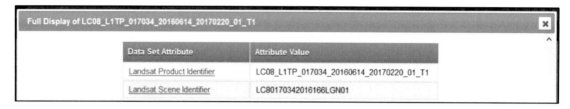

The next few lines of this metadata repeat information within in the Product and Scene identifiers. We used the scroll bar on the right to display this additional metadata.

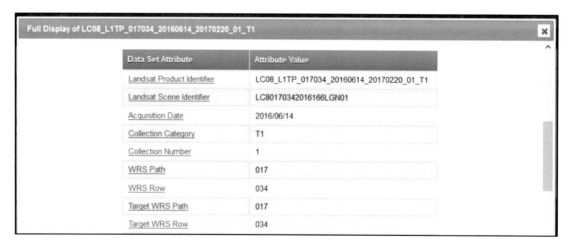

Let's look at *Start Time* and *Stop Time*. This is the time that Landsat 8 acquired this particular scene on June 14, 2016 (i.e. when the satellite was passing over this region). This information is GMT (Greenwich Mean Time).

Another useful element is the Land and Scene Cloud Cover. In this example, both are at 0.66%

Day/Night Indicator	DAY
Land Cloud Cover	.66
Scene Cloud Cover	.66

Use the scroll bar on the right to display and explore additional metadata elements.

Ground control points – a satellite image (or any remotely sensed image) must be referenced to the ground to identify specific features, the number of points used for this scene (Geometric referencing is usually the very 1st processing completed by the USGS). RMSE (root mean square error) is also provided for the georeferencing.

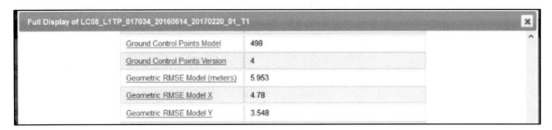

Full Display of LC08_L1TP_017034_20160614_20170220_01_T1	
Ground Control Points Model	498
Ground Control Points Version	4
Geometric RMSE Model (meters)	5.953
Geometric RMSE Model X	4.78
Geometric RMSE Model Y	3.548

Sun Elevation & Azimuth – this is important for areas above and below the Equator; remember, the sun's position changes with the season and, thus, may affect spectral properties of individual features.

Sun Elevation L1	67.2625631
Sun Azimuth L1	122.67683935

Sensor Identifier – this is Landsat 8, so the sensors aboard are OLI and TIRS. A scene just with OLI data can be ordered. This particular platform has both sensors:

Data Type Level-1	OLI_TIRS_L1TP
Sensor Identifier	OLI_TIRS

Scrolling on...

Projection – UTM and provides the Zone and Datum. What is missing on the UTM zone? Because this is above the Equator – North Zone 17. (If the same zone were south of the Equator, the zone would be designated as South Zone 17).

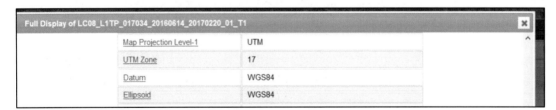

Full Display of LC08_L1TP_017034_20160614_20170220_01_T1	
Map Projection Level-1	UTM
UTM Zone	17
Datum	WGS84
Ellipsoid	WGS84

Grid Cell sizes – note the difference in sizes. Please refer back to previous chapters on cell size for raster data and differing cell sizes for each Landsat band.

Grid Cell Size Panchromatic	15
Grid Cell Size Reflective	30
Grid Cell Size Thermal	30

Moving on down a few lines, latitude and longitude are provided (in degrees, minutes and decimal seconds) for the different corners of the scene, for example – upper left (UL), lower right (LR), etc.

Center Latitude	37°28'28.96"N
Center Longitude	80°22'15.74"W
UL Corner Lat	38°31'36.19"N
UL Corner Long	81°10'36.59"W
UR Corner Lat	38°07'36.52"N
UR Corner Long	79°03'14.69"W

Notice the last of the latitude and longitude coordinates has the abbreviation *dec* – the difference is that the latitude and longitude in this area are written with positive and negative values (for direction) in decimal degrees.

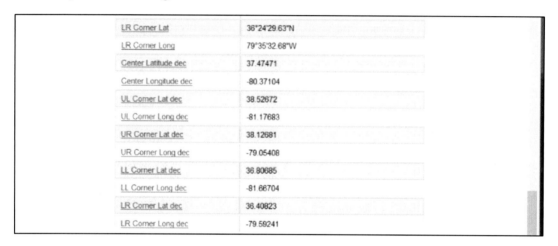

LR Corner Lat	36°24'29.63"N
LR Corner Long	79°35'32.68"W
Center Latitude dec	37.47471
Center Longitude dec	-80.37104
UL Corner Lat dec	38.52672
UL Corner Long dec	-81.17683
UR Corner Lat dec	38.12681
UR Corner Long dec	-79.05408
LL Corner Lat dec	36.80685
LL Corner Long dec	-81.66704
LR Corner Lat dec	36.40823
LR Corner Long dec	-79.59241

So, if when downloading the Landsat scene, you forgot to record the metadata on EarthExplorer, does that mean returning to EarthExplorer? By default, the metadata file is always included with each image, and is included in the downloaded zip folder. When the file download was unzipped, 14 individual files are revealed. All the files have the Landsat Product Identifier (red box in next figure); remember our discussion above – the LPI number contains metadata, since it provides some basic information about each Landsat scene!

LC08_L1TP_017034_20160614_20170220_01_T1	6/4/2018 7:12 AM	JPG File	5,478 KB	
LC08_L1TP_017034_20160614_20170220_01_T1.tar	2/20/2017 12:16 PM	TAR File	1,760,830	
LC08_L1TP_017034_20160614_20170220_01_T1_ANG	2/20/2017 12:14 PM	Text Document	115 KB	
LC08_L1TP_017034_20160614_20170220_01_T1_B1	2/20/2017 12:15 PM	TIF File	117,392 KB	
LC08_L1TP_017034_20160614_20170220_01_T1_B2	2/20/2017 12:15 PM	TIF File	117,392 KB	
LC08_L1TP_017034_20160614_20170220_01_T1_B3	2/20/2017 12:15 PM	TIF File	117,392 KB	
LC08_L1TP_017034_20160614_20170220_01_T1_B4	2/20/2017 12:15 PM	TIF File	117,392 KB	
LC08_L1TP_017034_20160614_20170220_01_T1_B5	2/20/2017 12:16 PM	TIF File	117,392 KB	
LC08_L1TP_017034_20160614_20170220_01_T1_B6	2/20/2017 12:16 PM	TIF File	117,392 KB	
LC08_L1TP_017034_20160614_20170220_01_T1_B7	2/20/2017 12:16 PM	TIF File	117,392 KB	
LC08_L1TP_017034_20160614_20170220_01_T1_B8	2/20/2017 12:16 PM	TIF File	469,384 KB	
LC08_L1TP_017034_20160614_20170220_01_T1_B9	2/20/2017 12:16 PM	TIF File	117,392 KB	
LC08_L1TP_017034_20160614_20170220_01_T1_B10	2/20/2017 12:16 PM	TIF File	117,392 KB	
LC08_L1TP_017034_20160614_20170220_01_T1_B11	2/20/2017 12:16 PM	TIF File	117,392 KB	
LC08_L1TP_017034_20160614_20170220_01_T1_BQA	2/20/2017 12:16 PM	TIF File	117,392 KB	
LC08_L1TP_017034_20160614_20170220_01_T1_MTL	2/20/2017 12:16 PM	Text Document	9 KB	

Most of these files in the downloaded package are in *TIF* format (image files available for analysis). But there are also 2 *Text* Documents.

Right-click on the file name of the text document, click on open, and, in a Windows-based environment, it automatically opens using Notepad or something similar.

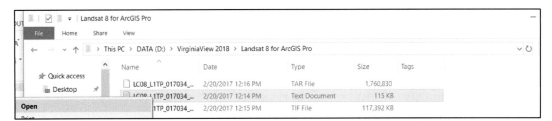

Note that this file is difficult to read in Notepad.

```
LC08_L1TP_017034_20160614_20170220_01_T1_ANG - Notepad                                    —    □    ×

File Edit Format View Help
GROUP = FILE_HEADER    LANDSAT_SCENE_ID = "LC80170342016166LGN01"    SPACECRAFT_ID = "LANDSAT_8"    NUMBER_OF_BANDS = 11  BAND_LIST
                5.000000,    6.000000,    7.000000,    8.000000,    9.000000,              10.000000,   11.000000,   12.00
                956655.449768,    955697.156160,    954737.122352,    953775.266341,    952811.681741,
434805.953634, -5439668.264911, -5444524.361520,                      -5449374.237331, -5454217.816796, -5459055.259372, -54
                -5661086.200154, -5665643.781257, -5670194.909613, -5674739.292873, -5679277.227372)   EPHEMERIS_ECEF_Z = (
4195506.360473,   4189561.036014,   4183610.730724,                   4177655.903372,  4171696.277682,  4165732.065765,   4
000,   36.000000,   37.000000,   38.000000,   39.000000,              40.000000,   41.000000,   42.000000,   43.000000,   44.000
        4.63919502e-01,   4.63861862e-01,   4.63804219e-01,   4.63746575e-01,   4.63688928e-01,              4.63631279e-0
01,               -7.92507347e-01, -7.92541095e-01, -7.92574839e-01, -7.92608578e-01, -7.92642313e-01,
,   3.95529158e-01,               3.95529166e-01,  3.95529174e-01,  3.95529182e-01,  3.95529190e-01,  3.95529198e-01,
1_PIXEL_SIZE = 30.000  BAND01_START_TIME = 10.655433  BAND01_LINE_TIME = 0.004236000  BAND01_MEAN_HEIGHT = 750.000  BAND01_M
908759e-10,   9.427362e-10,  1.357648e-15,  4.395930e-17)  BAND01_SAT_Z_NUM_COEF = ( 3.668600e-03,  2.173574e-07, -1.103439e-0
                2.516170e-12,  2.001155e-11,  1.479797e-11, -4.754700e-18,  4.113370e-19)  BAND01_SUN_Y_DEN_COEF = ( 0
INE_DEN_COEF = ( 1.821269e-07, -7.391128e-06, -7.682866e-11,  1.022867e-12)  BAND01_SCA01_SAMP_NUM_COEF = (-1.216327e+00,  2.
```

The metadata file can also be opened in Excel (or any spreadsheet program), where it can be viewed more clearly.

So, here is how to open it in Excel. Open a blank workbook in Excel:

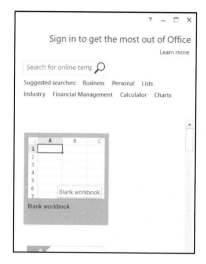

Click on the *Data* tab:

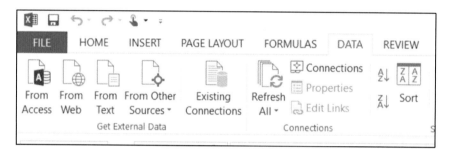

Then click on *Get Data From Text*:

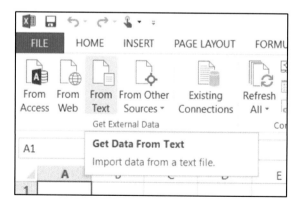

Navigate to the file folder containing the unzipped Landsat files – again, 2 of these file types are text documents:

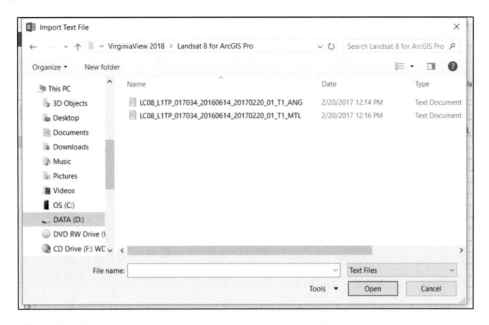

Click on the first file (the one with _ANG at the end of the file name) and once it is populated in the *File Name* box, click on *Import*:

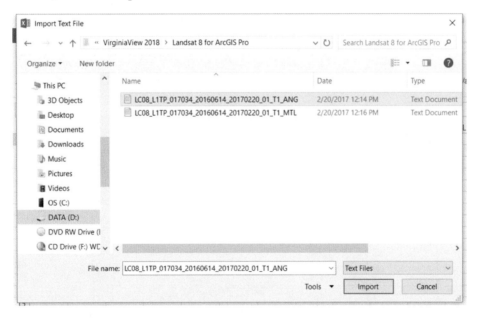

The *Text Import Wizard* opens:

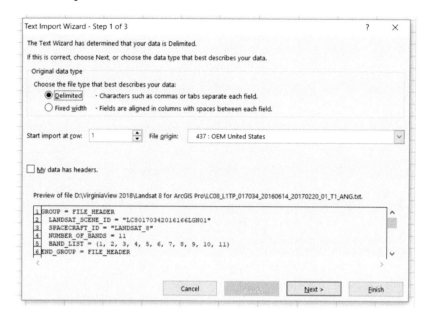

Leave the default settings for this window (*Step 1 of 3*), and click on *Next* (bottom right of dialog box).

In *Step 2 of 3*, the parameters under *Delimiters* (red box in figure below) determines how the data populates the workbook (the default is *Tab*). The *Data Preview* window (green box in figure below) shows what it will look like. Again, for our purposes, leave the defaults, so click *Next*.

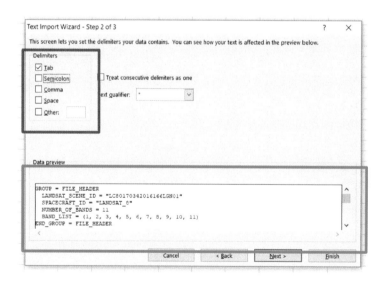

Step 3 of 3, again, for our purposes, leave the defaults and click on *Finish*.

Please note that, for our purposes, the default settings work well. But, if importing data from another source, theses settings may need to be altered.

One final window – reviews the parameters – if settings look correct, click *OK*:

The results are much easier to read in Excel (or another spreadsheet program). This file contains additional metadata elements that are not included in EarthExplorer.

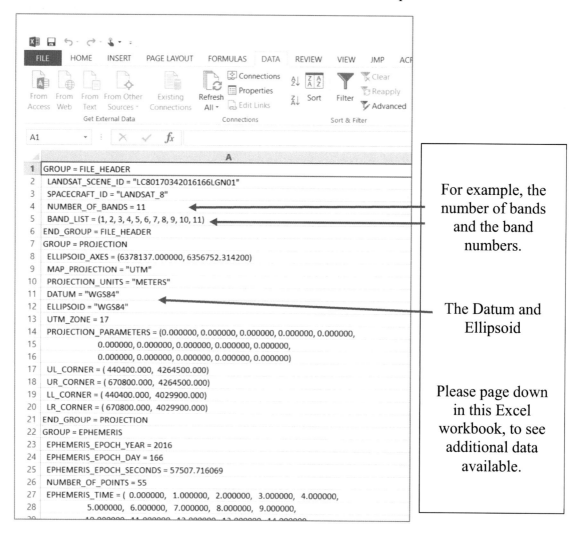

For example, the number of bands and the band numbers.

The Datum and Ellipsoid

Please page down in this Excel workbook, to see additional data available.

For example – much of this information in related to the image processing already completed by the USGS:

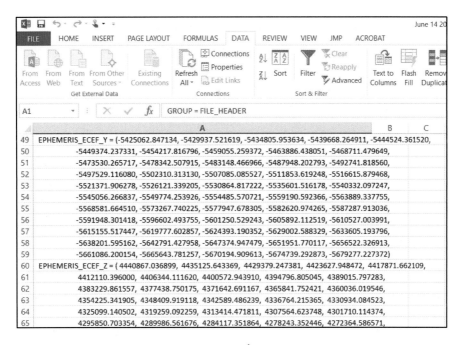

Now, follow the same procedure and import the 2nd Text Document into Excel.

This file is exactly like the metadata in EarthExplorer:

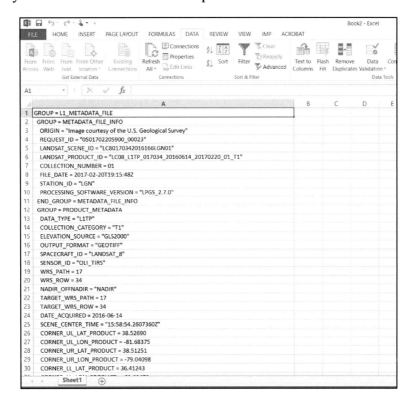

Now, save the Excel workbook, so the import will not need to be redone (*File, Save As*).

June 14 2016 Metadata	6/4/2018 8:15 AM	Microsoft Excel W

What else was provided in the download? Remember we noted TIF files above:

LC08_L1TP_017034_20160614_20170220_01_T1_ANG	2/20/2017 12:14 PM	Text Document	115 KB
LC08_L1TP_017034_20160614_20170220_01_T1_B1	2/20/2017 12:15 PM	TIF File	117,392 KB
LC08_L1TP_017034_20160614_20170220_01_T1_B2	2/20/2017 12:15 PM	TIF File	117,392 KB
LC08_L1TP_017034_20160614_20170220_01_T1_B3	2/20/2017 12:15 PM	TIF File	117,392 KB
LC08_L1TP_017034_20160614_20170220_01_T1_B4	2/20/2017 12:15 PM	TIF File	117,392 KB
LC08_L1TP_017034_20160614_20170220_01_T1_B5	2/20/2017 12:16 PM	TIF File	117,392 KB
LC08_L1TP_017034_20160614_20170220_01_T1_B6	2/20/2017 12:16 PM	TIF File	117,392 KB
LC08_L1TP_017034_20160614_20170220_01_T1_B7	2/20/2017 12:16 PM	TIF File	117,392 KB
LC08_L1TP_017034_20160614_20170220_01_T1_B8	2/20/2017 12:16 PM	TIF File	469,384 KB
LC08_L1TP_017034_20160614_20170220_01_T1_B9	2/20/2017 12:16 PM	TIF File	117,392 KB
LC08_L1TP_017034_20160614_20170220_01_T1_B10	2/20/2017 12:16 PM	TIF File	117,392 KB
LC08_L1TP_017034_20160614_20170220_01_T1_B11	2/20/2017 12:16 PM	TIF File	117,392 KB
LC08_L1TP_017034_20160614_20170220_01_T1_BQA	2/20/2017 12:16 PM	TIF File	117,392 KB
LC08_L1TP_017034_20160614_20170220_01_T1_MTL	2/20/2017 12:16 PM	Text Document	9 KB

The characters at the end of the Product Identifier for the TIF files are *B1, B2, B3*, etc. These are the individual band numbers and the images used for analysis. Remember in Chapter 10 – Imagery Available from the USGS, we discussed the different areas of the electromagnetic spectrum. Each band number represents a different portion of the electromagnetic spectrum (see figure below). The last column represents the various pixel (cell) sizes for each band.

Landsat 8 band designations

	Bands	Wavelength (micrometers)	Resolution (meters)
Landsat 8 Operational Land Imager (OLI) and Thermal Infrared Sensor (TIRS) Launched February 11, 2013	Band 1 - Coastal aerosol	0.43 - 0.45	30
	Band 2 - Blue	0.45 - 0.51	30
	Band 3 - Green	0.53 - 0.59	30
	Band 4 - Red	0.64 - 0.67	30
	Band 5 - Near Infrared (NIR)	0.85 - 0.88	30
	Band 6 - SWIR 1	1.57 - 1.65	30
	Band 7 - SWIR 2	2.11 - 2.29	30
	Band 8 - Panchromatic	0.50 - 0.68	15
	Band 9 - Cirrus	1.36 - 1.38	30
	Band 10 - Thermal Infrared (TIRS) 1	10.60 - 11.19	100
	Band 11 - Thermal Infrared (TIRS) 2	11.50 - 12.51	100

(Public domain.)

Image from: https://www.usgs.gov/media/images/landsat-8-band-designations

Also, recall-- we cautioned that the different band numbers for different satellites may not correspond to the same region of the electromagnetic spectrum. As an example, for Landsat 5 these are as follows:

- Seven spectral bands, including a thermal band:
  - Band 1 Visible (0.45 - 0.52 µm) 30 m
  - Band 2 Visible (0.52 - 0.60 µm) 30 m
  - Band 3 Visible (0.63 - 0.69 µm) 30 m
  - Band 4 Near-Infrared (0.76 - 0.90 µm) 30 m   Size of the pixel
  - Band 5 Near-Infrared (1.55 - 1.75 µm) 30 m   for the band
  - Band 6 Thermal (10.40 - 12.50 µm) 120 m
  - Band 7 Mid-Infrared (2.08 - 2.35 µm) 30 m

Image from: (http://landsat.usgs.gov/about_landsat5.php)

Specifically, note that Band 4 in Landsat 5 is the near-infrared (covering 0.76 – 0.90 µm) and Band 5 in Landsat 8 is the near-infrared (covering 0.85 – 0.88 µm – a much narrower range).

Is any other pre-processing required before you start using the Landsat Scene? You may wish to consider preprocessing for surface reflectance (see Masek, J.G., et al., *A Landsat surface reflectance data set for North America, 1990-2000.* Geoscience and Remote Sensing Letters, 2006. **3**: p. 68-72.)

For more information about the level and type of USGS processing of Landsat scenes, go to http://landsat.usgs.gov/Landsat_Processing_Details.php.

Please proceed to the next chapter which begins to prepare this downloaded Landsat 8 scene for analysis.

The Landsat 8 scene downloaded in the previous chapter provided 11 different images, each with a different band designation and each covering a specific region of the electromagnetic spectrum. In this chapter, we will add the 11 individual bands (TIF files) into ArcGIS® Pro and examine the properties of each of these files.

Introduction

Landsat images are acquired as grayscale images. When these image bands are added to ArcGIS® Pro, each band is listed separately in the *Contents* window. Familiarity with a Landsat scene is important in order to complete different types of analyses, such as unsupervised classifications, supervised classifications, and different indices (ex: NDVI). Our text will cover differing analyses in subsequent chapters.

Remember, from prior chapters, that each band covers a different spectrum of the electromagnetic spectrum. The wavelengths associated with each band can also vary between Landsat sensors, and differ between alternative satellite image acquisition systems (e.g., Landsat and Sentinel – see tables below).

Reference

Barsi, J.A.; Lee, K.; Kvaran, G.; Markham, B.L.; Pedelty, J.A. The Spectral Response of the Landsat-8 Operational Land Imager. *Remote Sens.* **2014**, *6*, 10232-10251. doi:10.3390/rs61010232

Landsat 8 Operational Land Imager (OLI) and Thermal Infrared Sensor (TIRS)	Bands	Wavelength (micrometers)	Resolution (meters)
	Band 1 - Ultra Blue (coastal/aerosol)	0.435 - 0.451	30
	Band 2 - Blue	0.452 - 0.512	30
	Band 3 - Green	0.533 - 0.590	30
	Band 4 - Red	0.636 - 0.673	30
	Band 5 - Near Infrared (NIR)	0.851 - 0.879	30
	Band 6 - Shortwave Infrared (SWIR) 1	1.566 - 1.651	30
	Band 7 - Shortwave Infrared (SWIR) 2	2.107 - 2.294	30
	Band 8 - Panchromatic	0.503 - 0.676	15
	Band 9 - Cirrus	1.363 - 1.384	30
	Band 10 - Thermal Infrared (TIRS) 1	10.60 - 11.19	100 * (30)
	Band 11 - Thermal Infrared (TIRS) 2	11.50 - 12.51	100 * (30)

* TIRS bands are acquired at 100 meter resolution, but are resampled to 30 meter in delivered data product.

Landsat 7 Enhanced Thematic Mapper Plus (ETM+)	Bands	Wavelength (micrometers)	Resolution (meters)
	Band 1 - Blue	0.45-0.52	30
	Band 2 - Green	0.52-0.60	30
	Band 3 - Red	0.63-0.69	30
	Band 4 - Near Infrared (NIR)	0.77-0.90	30
	Band 5 - Shortwave Infrared (SWIR) 1	1.55-1.75	30
	Band 6 - Thermal	10.40-12.50	60 * (30)
	Band 7 - Shortwave Infrared (SWIR) 2	2.09-2.35	30
	Band 8 - Panchromatic	.52-.90	15

* ETM+ Band 6 is acquired at 60-meter resolution, but products are resampled to 30-meter pixels.

Landsat 4-5 Thematic Mapper (TM)	Bands	Wavelength (micrometers)	Resolution (meters)
	Band 1 - Blue	0.45-0.52	30
	Band 2 - Green	0.52-0.60	30
	Band 3 - Red	0.63-0.69	30
	Band 4 - Near Infrared (NIR)	0.76-0.90	30
	Band 5 - Shortwave Infrared (SWIR) 1	1.55-1.75	30
	Band 6 - Thermal	10.40-12.50	120* (30)
	Band 7 - Shortwave Infrared (SWIR) 2	2.08-2.35	30

* TM Band 6 was acquired at 120-meter resolution, but products are resampled to 30-meter pixels.

Landsat 1-5 Multispectral Scanner (MSS)	Landsat 1-3	Landsat 4-5	Wavelength (micrometers)	Resolution (meters)
	Band 4 - Green	Band 1 - Green	0.5-0.6	60*
	Band 5 - Red	Band 2 - Red	0.6-0.7	60*
	Band 6 - Near Infrared (NIR)	Band 3 - Near Infrared (NIR)	0.7-0.8	60*
	Band 7 - Near Infrared (NIR)	Band 4 - Near Infrared (NIR)	0.8-1.1	60*

* Original MSS pixel size was 79 x 57 meters; production systems now resample the data to 60 meters.

Tables from: https://landsat.usgs.gov/what-are-band-designations-landsat-satellites

Table 1: Wavelengths and Bandwidths of the 3 Spatial Resolutions of the MSI instruments

Spatial Resolution (m)	Band Number	S2A Central Wavelength (nm)	S2A Bandwidth (nm)	S2B Central Wavelength (nm)	S2B Bandwidth (nm)
10	2	496.6	98	492.1	98
	3	560.0	45	559	46
	4	664.5	38	665	39
	8	835.1	145	833	133
20	5	703.9	19	703.8	20
	6	740.2	18	739.1	18
	7	782.5	28	779.7	28
	8a	864.8	33	864	32
	11	1613.7	143	1610.4	141
	12	2202.4	242	2185.7	238
60	1	443.9	27	442.3	45
	9	945.0	26	943.2	27
	10	1373.5	75	1376.9	76

Table from: https://sentinel.esa.int/web/sentinel/missions/sentinel-2/instrument-payload/resolution-and-swath

Adding Landsat 8 TIF files to ArcGIS® Pro

Remember, when the Landsat folder was unzipped, there were 11 individual TIF files. Each file is associated with a separate band (see figure below).

LC08_L1TP_017034_20160614_20170220_01_T1_B1

LC08_L1TP_017034_20160614_20170220_01_T1_B2

LC08_L1TP_017034_20160614_20170220_01_T1_B3

LC08_L1TP_017034_20160614_20170220_01_T1_B4

LC08_L1TP_017034_20160614_20170220_01_T1_B5

LC08_L1TP_017034_20160614_20170220_01_T1_B6

LC08_L1TP_017034_20160614_20170220_01_T1_B7

LC08_L1TP_017034_20160614_20170220_01_T1_B8

LC08_L1TP_017034_20160614_20170220_01_T1_B9

LC08_L1TP_017034_20160614_20170220_01_T1_B10

LC08_L1TP_017034_20160614_20170220_01_T1_B11

Open ArcGIS® Pro and create a *New Project* document, name the project, and navigate to your preferred place on the computer to save it.

Then click on *Insert > New Map*.

Click on the *Add Data* button.

Navigate to the folder where the unzipped Landsat TIF Files are located (your project folder). Click on all the 11 TIF Files to highlight them and then *OK* to add them to the map project.

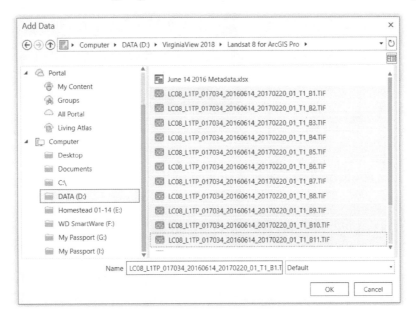

Be patient while the files are added:

The following image will appear in the ArcGIS® Pro map display window.

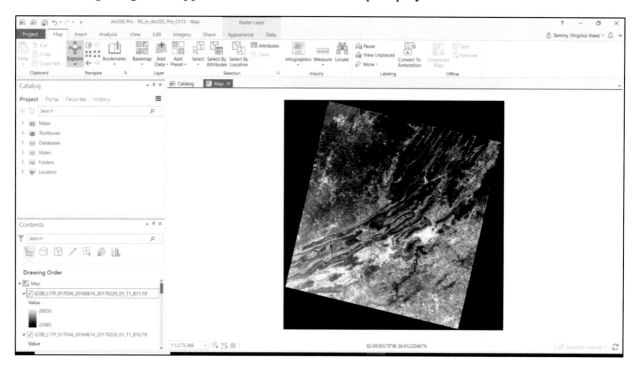

There are actually multiple images (bands) associated with each scene. These image bands are stacked on top of one another. The bands are listed in the *Contents* window (typically left of the map).

Please notice a couple of items. It is difficult to see all the TIF Files in *Contents*, so unpin *Catalog*, by clicking on the pushpin in the upper right corner of the Catalog window:

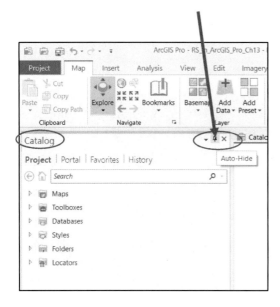

We now see more images in the *Contents* window.

Use the scroll bar on the right to see all of the layers.

If the bands are not in the preferred order in the *Contents* window, then they can be reordered.

To change the order of the layers, simply click a band and drag it above (or below) other bands.

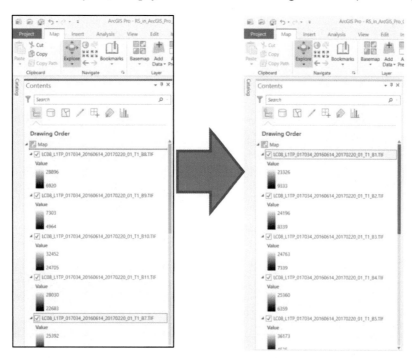

We recommend descending order, B1 through B11.

Notice that the *Landsat Product Identifier* is associated with each image band, and the band number appears at the end. The top file is the one that is drawn last (in the map display window), and is therefore displayed "on top of the others" in the Map window:

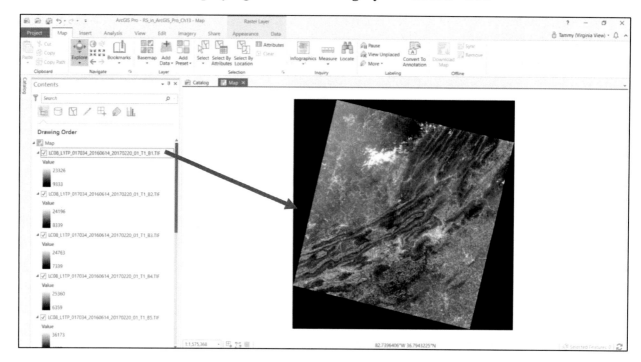

Each band can be turned off, just like vector and other raster files. It is possible to view bands that are displayed below other bands by unchecking the bands towards the top of the *Contents* window.

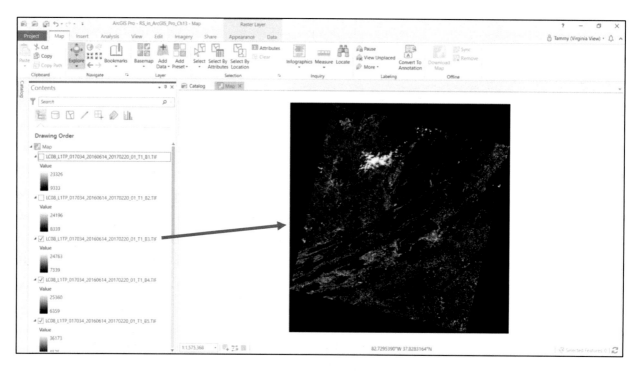

To see all the layers listed in the *Contents* window, just collapse the symbology by clicking on the icon at the beginning of the layer name.

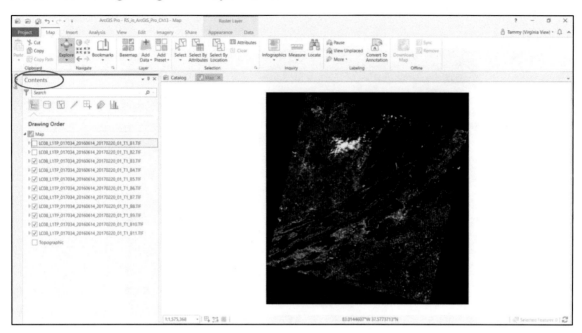

As we have been exploring options, notice that each band is displayed in grayscale.

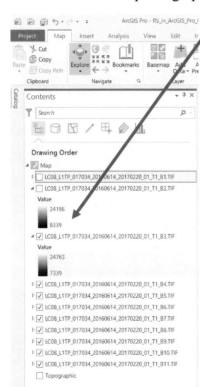

The digital number (DN) next to the grayscale reveals the brightness values within each band.

Landsat 8 scenes are recorded in 16 bits, so each band has a range of 65,536 (2^{16} = 65,536) brightness values. Brightness values refer to the reflectivity of the specific feature, the higher the number – the more reflective. *(For more information – see Introduction to Remote Sensing by Campbell and Wynne, 2011.)*

As each layer is unchecked, starting with Band 1 and down to Band 11, each band is displayed in the map document window. Each band looks different. Individual bands appear slightly different in the map display window because each band contains data from a different region of the electromagnetic spectrum. Each band serves a different purpose.

Metadata has been observed in two areas thus far. The Landsat Product Identifier number remains present in ArcGIS® Pro and within the range of brightness values for each band.

Please note that the dark pixels surrounding the Landsat scene are not brightness values. This is the GIS's attempt to make the image have the same areal extent at its corners. These outer border areas are actually black because the cells have 'no data' associated with them.

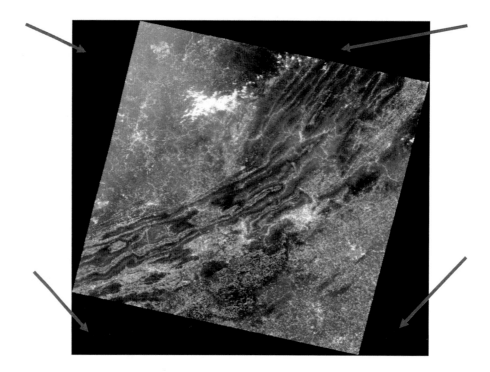

Let's hide these black border areas. To do this, go to the *Raster Layer Appearance* tab and click on the *Symbology* option and then select *Stretch.*

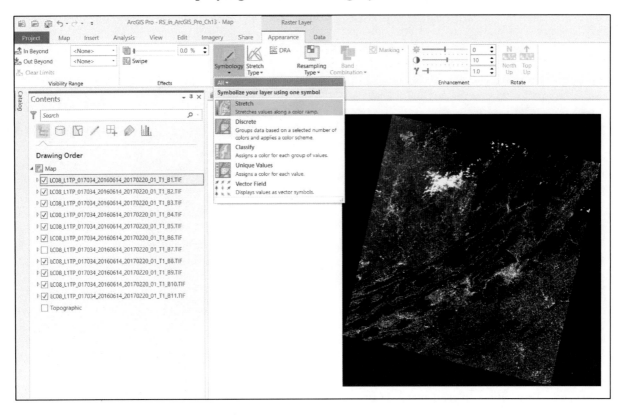

When the Symbology dialog box opens, click in the box next to *Display Background Value*.

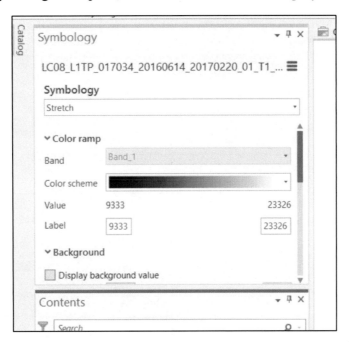

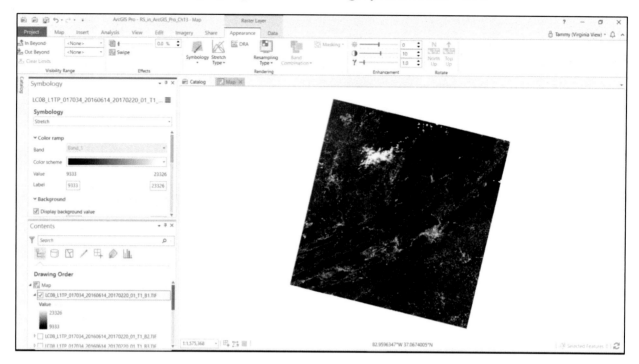

The black border areas associated with all the bands of imagery cannot be changed all at the same time. These black areas must be changed individually. But, but once the *Symbology* window is open, just highlight the next layer name and the *Symbology* window changes to that image, so the change is made quickly. Once finished, close the Symbology window.   All TIF files (the individual bands) are now displayed with only the Landsat image values (the "no data values' have been eliminated).

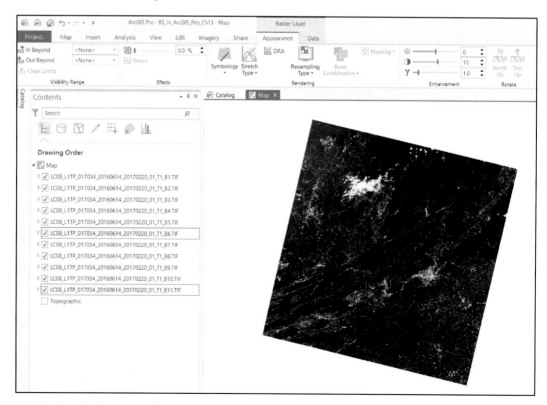

We have all our layers turned on in the above figure. As noted above, we can turn the top layers off to see the next layer. But, we can also leave two layers turned on and "see" beneath the top layer. Turn off all layers except Bands 4 and 5. Be sure to click on the *Raster Layer Appearance* tab (red box in figure below).

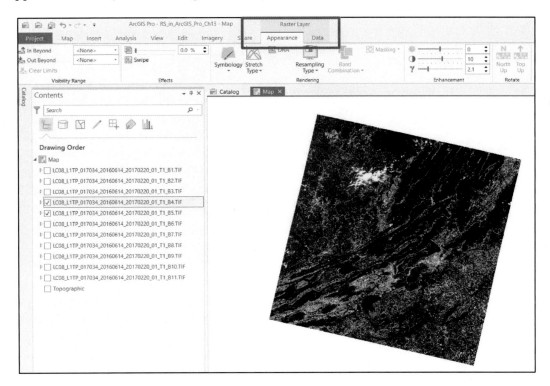

Look at the two icons just to the left of the *Symbology* button. The top one is *Layer Transparency* and the bottom one is *Swipe*.

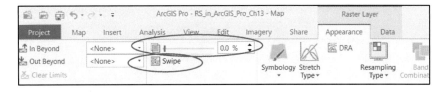

For *Layer Transparency*, move the sliding bar or enter a percentage in the percentage box.

In grayscale, it is difficult to see any difference.

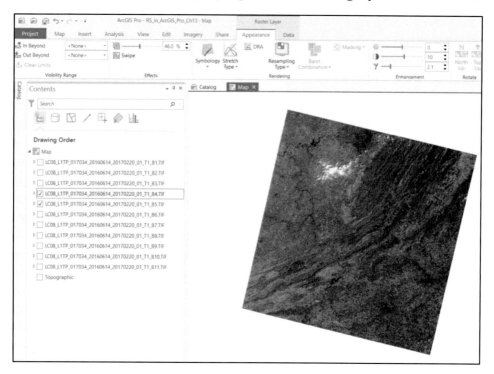

However, even after changing the grayscale to a color scheme, it is still difficult to distinguish differences with transparency:

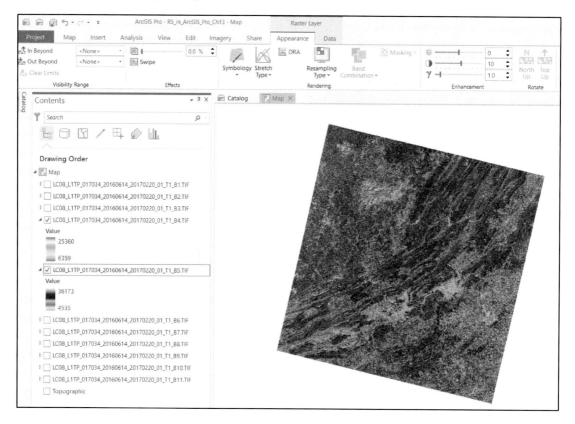

The swipe tool also provides an ability to view parts of two different images (or layers) at the same time. This tool works much better with images that share pixel boundaries. Highlight the top layer in the *Contents* window and then click on the Swipe button. The place the cursor on the image, holding the left mouse button down.

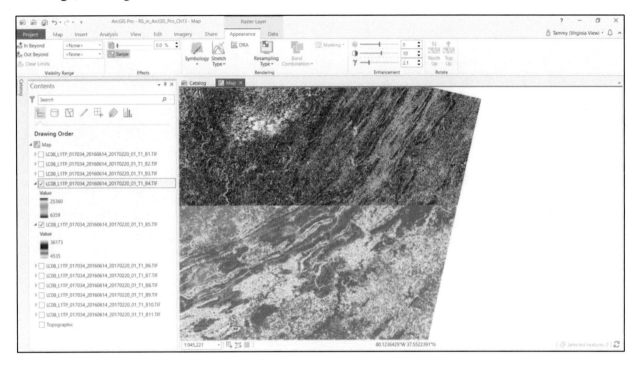

Swipe is an important tool that we will use in the last chapter: *Chapter 23 – Accuracy Assessments.*

We have introduced some readily available metadata and important tools for displaying the imagery. Now that the images are displayed, additional metadata is available.

Right-click on any layer name, go to *Properties* and *Source*. The Data Source dialog box provides the number of columns and rows for the image, that the image is 1 band, the cell size - X and Y - are 30. In Chapter 8: Metadata, we demonstrated how to find and interpret basic metadata elements. This is another way to view basic metadata for your image.

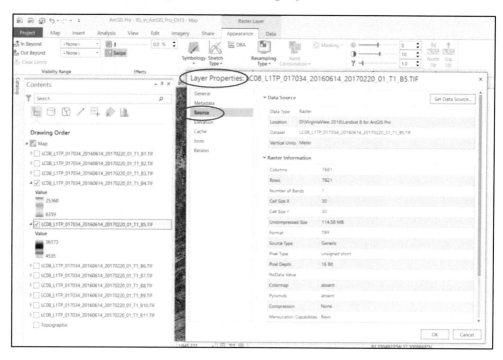

And scroll down to *Spatial Reference* to see more detail – the scene's Projection, unit of measurement – meter, and other details are provided.

It is important to note that metadata for Landsat 8 imagery, as viewed in the original text file (that was downloaded from the USGS), does not import into ArcGIS® Pro.

Now, right click on the same layer's name and go to *Symbology*. We already set the symbology but there is additional information about this specific image under symbology.

First is the *range of brightness values*.

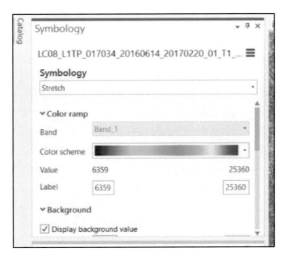

Scroll down and it shows that for the *Stretch* symbology, Stretch type is *Percent Clip* and the percentages used to calculate the stretch.

Expand the options associated with *Stretch type*, and, other options are displayed:

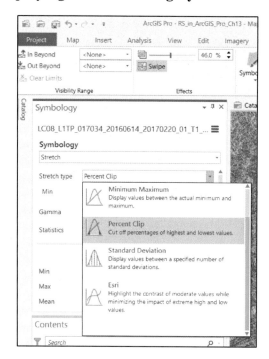

We are going review some of these when we analyze imagery in subsequent chapters. But, if knowing the differences is important, go to ArcGIS® Pro help (http://pro.arcgis.com/en/pro-app/help/data/imagery/raster-display-ribbon.htm).

Summary

In this chapter, we demonstrated how to add the downloaded Landsat bands into ArcGIS® Pro, display them, change their order in the *Contents* window, change symbology, and we reviewed areas of metadata. In the next chapter (Chapter 14: Creating a Composite Image for Landsat 8 Imagery), we will show how to combine multiple bands into one single image (composite image).

Landsat images are acquired in grayscale, so when added to ArcGIS® Pro, each image file (or band) is listed separately in the *Contents* window. Familiarity with a Landsat scene is important in order to complete different analyses, such as change detection, unsupervised classification, supervised classification, and to generate different indices (i.e., NDVI). Image processing and image analysis techniques are covered in subsequent chapters.

Creating a composite image means creating one image from several different bands. With a composite image, Landsat images can be displayed in color or red-green-blue (RGB format). Displaying multiple bands in color allows features within a scene to be distinguished from each other. This is helpful for differentiating between types of land cover, which could include urban areas, forests, agriculture, and water bodies, for example.

Remember, from discussions in prior chapters, data contained in each band is comprised of a different slice of the electromagnetic spectrum. Wavelengths can vary in bands between different Landsat sensors (i.e., Landsat 7 and Landsat 8) and from one satellite system to another (e.g., Landsat and Sentinel). The following table provides the different wavelengths covered by Landsat 8 sensors.

Reference

Barsi, J.A.; Lee, K.; Kvaran, G.; Markham, B.L.; Pedelty, J.A. The Spectral Response of the Landsat-8 Operational Land Imager. *Remote Sens.* **2014**, *6*, 10232-10251. doi:10.3390/rs61010232

Landsat 8 Operational Land Imager (OLI) and Thermal Infrared Sensor (TIRS)	Bands	Wavelength (micrometers)	Resolution (meters)
	Band 1 - Ultra Blue (coastal/aerosol)	0.435 - 0.451	30
	Band 2 - Blue	0.452 - 0.512	30
	Band 3 - Green	0.533 - 0.590	30
	Band 4 - Red	0.636 - 0.673	30
	Band 5 - Near Infrared (NIR)	0.851 - 0.879	30
	Band 6 - Shortwave Infrared (SWIR) 1	1.566 - 1.651	30
	Band 7 - Shortwave Infrared (SWIR) 2	2.107 - 2.294	30
	Band 8 - Panchromatic	0.503 - 0.676	15
	Band 9 - Cirrus	1.363 - 1.384	30
	Band 10 - Thermal Infrared (TIRS) 1	10.60 - 11.19	100 * (30)
	Band 11 - Thermal Infrared (TIRS) 2	11.50 - 12.51	100 * (30)

* TIRS bands are acquired at 100 meter resolution, but are resampled to 30 meter in delivered data product.

Table from: https://landsat.usgs.gov/what-are-band-designations-landsat-satellites

If working with a scene from a different sensor, please see http://pubs.usgs.gov/fs/2012/3072/fs2012-3072.pdf for more information on band coverage of the electromagnetic spectrum.

Please be sure to complete Chapters 12 and 13 before completing this chapter.

Creating One Composite Image for 11 Bands:

Open ArcGIS® Pro. *Create a New Blank Map Project*, and save it on the computer in the designated project file folder.

For this exercise, we are going to generate a composite of all 11 bands into one multispectral image. Remember, each band will be listed, separately, in the *Contents* window and layered in ArcGIS® Pro on top of each other, so only the image listed on top is actually seen in the map window. Add the bands for the image downloaded in Chapter 11, eliminate background values, make sure the project is connected to its folder, and unpin Catalog, so the project looks like the figure below. Note that all of these steps have been covered in previous chapters.

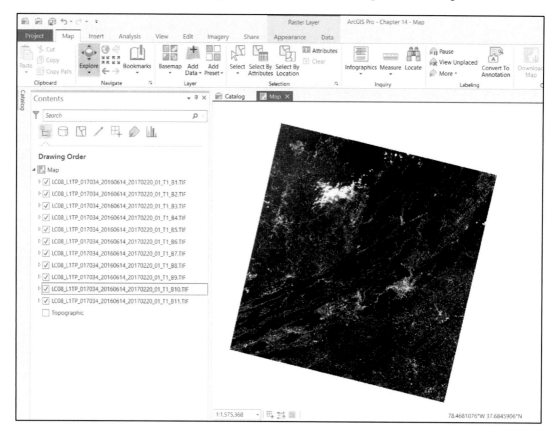

Next, check the workspace environments by going to the *Analysis* tab

and click on *Environments* (the icon that looks like a hammer and wrench).

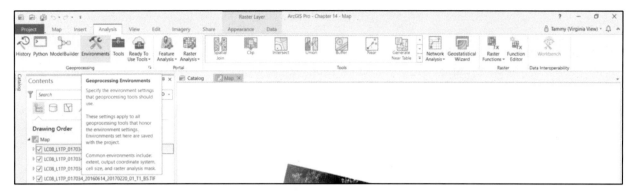

Make sure the *Current* and *Scratch Workspaces* (red box below) are set to the project's
geodatabase. If not, then select the browse option on the end of the dialogue box (below) to
navigate and connect.

Now we are ready to create a composite image containing Band1 through Band 11 into one
image.

Under the *Analysis* tab, select the *Tools* icon – the red toolbox (*Tools* provides a shortcut to
Geoprocessing capabilities).

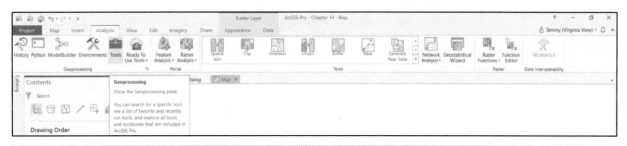

In the top of the Geoprocessing window is a search option (black box). Since we want to generate a composite image, type *Composite Bands* to search for the composite bands tool, and then hit enter on the keyboard.

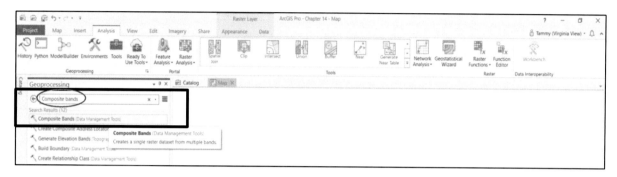

The *Composite Bands* tool opens.

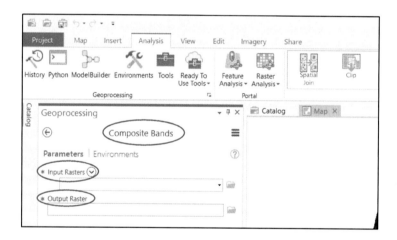

The *Input Rasters* consist of the individual bands and the *Output Raster* will be the name of the newly created composited image. Choose the *Input Rasters* by clicking on the down arrow. Choose Band number 1 from the list.

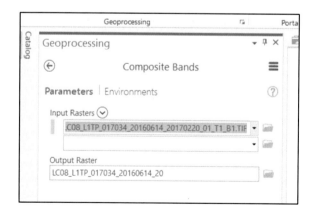

The *Input Raster* option populates in the box and adds a line to enter the next band. Click again on the down arrow and now choose Band 2. Continue with this process until all 11 bands are entered.

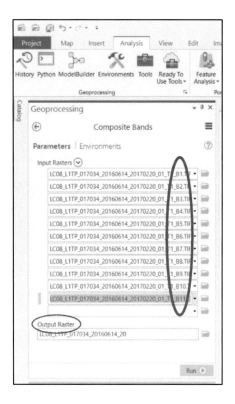

Please make sure that the bands are entered in numerical order and appear that way in the tool (red oval in above figure). This importance will become clear when the composite image has been generated.

Under *Output Raster*, name the new raster file. For ease in remembering what this new file will represent, we have named the newly created composite file *LC08_1thru11*. Be sure, when typing the name that the file is saving into the geodatabase (.gdb)! (Remember that the geodatabase was automatically created when the new blank project was initially created.)

Once everything is populated, click on *Run* at the bottom of the tool.

And wait for the tool to run. Be patient, each of these 11 bands is represents a large file individually. Now they will all be combined to form one (really large) composite multispectral image. Watch the processing status at the bottom of the tool's window. Once the process is finished, the processing status box will turn green. Close the Geoprocessing window.

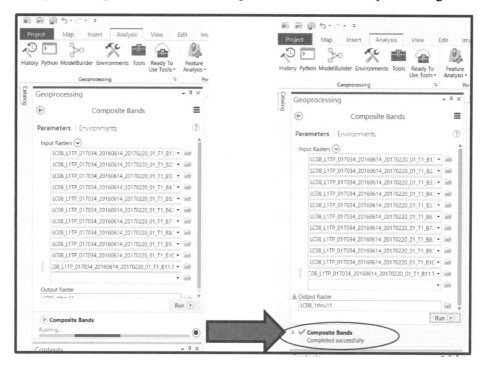

If instead of the green box with messsage – *Completed Successfully*, a red message appears stating that the ***processing failed***, try the tool again and make sure the output raster is being saved in the geodatabase.

Once the tool has completed, the *Contents* and map windows have a new file – a composite (multispectral) image that was created by combining the 11 separate bands together. The file listed in the *Contents* window displays the symbology as red, green, and blue. The image in the display window appears in color. A black box is around the new image, remember ArcGIS® is trying to make the image square so adds pixels with no data.

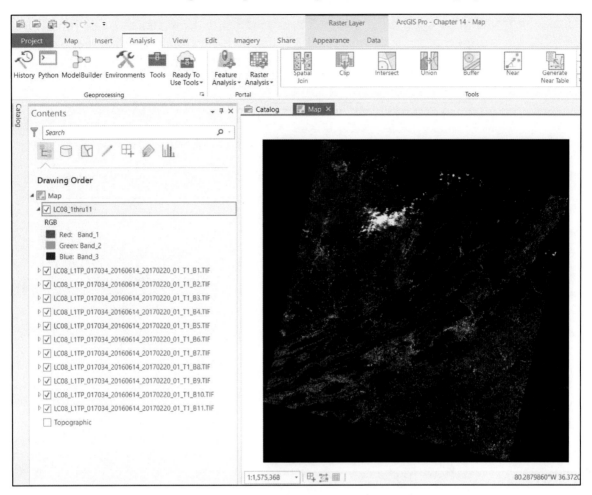

Turn off the individual bands and eliminate the background values on the new composite image.

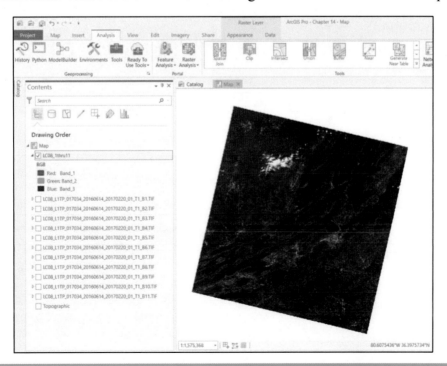

It is apparent from the *Contents* window that 3 bands are being displayed. – Band 1 is displayed in Red, Band 2 is displayed in Green and Band 3 is displayed in Blue. Are the other bands present? Check the *Properties/Source* tab for the image, it is now an 11 band image with information related to each band.

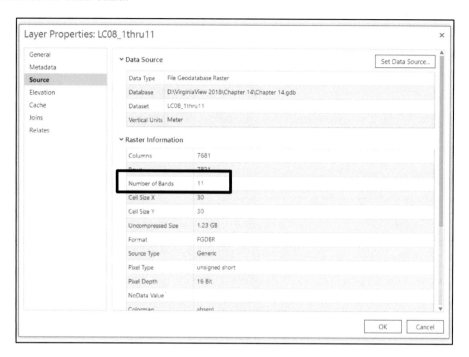

Selecting and expanding *Statistics* reconfirms that all bands are contained in this one composite image.

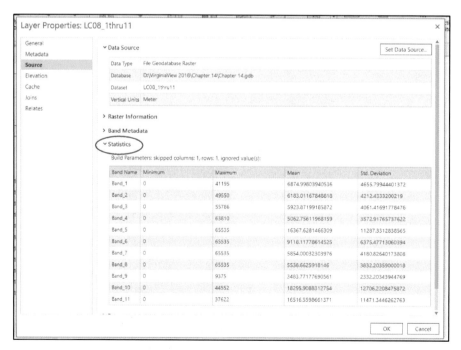

Check the symbology for this image. We can change the symbology, display different bands with either red, green or blue color combinations. This process will be covered in more detail in Chapter 16: Band Combinations using Landsat 8 Imagery.

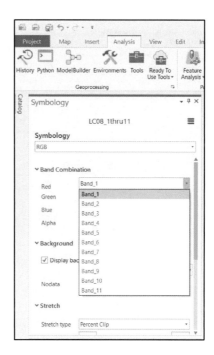

Notice that, although the image is in color, the color does not appear "natural," it actually looks a slightly blue (and the colors and contrast appears to be somewhat 'muted').

Recall from the table on the first page – Landsat 8, Band 2 is the blue visible range of the electromagnetic spectrum, Band 3 is the green visible and Band 4 is the red visible (red box below).

Reference

Barsi, J.A.; Lee, K.; Kvaran, G.; Markham, B.L.; Pedelty, J.A. The Spectral Response of the Landsat-8 Operational Land Imager. *Remote Sens.* **2014**, *6*, 10232-10251. doi:10.3390/rs61010232

Landsat 8	Bands	Wavelength (micrometers)	Resolution (meters)
Operational Land Imager (OLI) and Thermal Infrared Sensor (TIRS)	Band 1 - Ultra Blue (coastal/aerosol)	0.435 - 0.451	30
	Band 2 - Blue	0.452 - 0.512	30
	Band 3 - Green	0.533 - 0.590	30
	Band 4 - Red	0.636 - 0.673	30
	Band 5 - Near Infrared (NIR)	0.851 - 0.879	30
	Band 6 - Shortwave Infrared (SWIR) 1	1.566 - 1.651	30
	Band 7 - Shortwave Infrared (SWIR) 2	2.107 - 2.294	30
	Band 8 - Panchromatic	0.503 - 0.676	15
	Band 9 - Cirrus	1.363 - 1.384	30
	Band 10 - Thermal Infrared (TIRS) 1	10.60 - 11.19	100 * (30)
	Band 11 - Thermal Infrared (TIRS) 2	11.50 - 12.51	100 * (30)

* TIRS bands are acquired at 100 meter resolution, but are resampled to 30 meter in delivered data product.

Now look in the *Contents*, when the bands are composited together and ArcGIS® Pro displays the results as Band 1 = Red, Band 2 = Green, and Band 3 = Blue. So the natural colors are not being displayed.

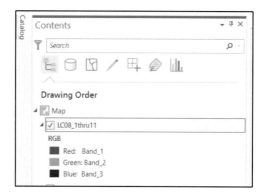

Let's change the symbology. Right-click on the new layer's name and go to *Symbology*. Click on the Arrow at the end of Red's (Band 1) box. Change Band_1 to Band_4.

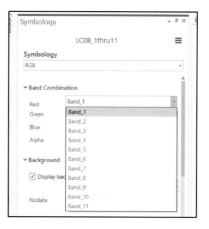

Under Green, change it to Band_3 and under *Blue*, change it to Band_2. Your final selection should be similar to the figure below.

Now, a "natural" color image is displayed. This means that the colors in the image now mimic those humans see in nature with the naked eye. Again, we will talk more about band combinations in Chapter 16: Band Combinations for Landsat 8 Imagery.

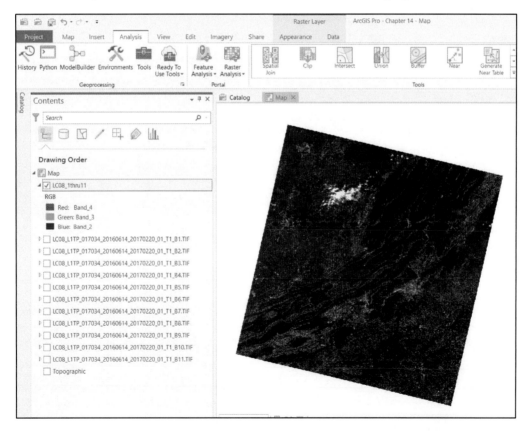

Is it necessary to use all 11 bands of a Landsat 8 scene when creating a composite image? No, a composite image can be accomplished using with any selection of bands. We recommend that, when creating a composite imagey, that you only include the specific bands that are required for the project. However, please be careful, when generating a composite image, ArcGIS® Pro will renumber the bands if all the bands are not used or one band in a sequence is eliminated. For example, if Bands 2 – 5 are the only bands that are used (blue visible through near infrared), once composited, the band numbers will be represented in ArcGIS® Pro as bands 1 – 4. In this case, carefully document and make note of the specific bands used.

But what if, during the Geoprocessing operation, you failed to make a note as to which bands were actually used? How do you verify which bands were used and if used, and in which order ?

ArcGIS® Pro documents your processing steps.Go to the *Analysis tab*, and click on *History.*

History opens in *Catalog*. In the window below. In the example below, two geoprocessing results are displayed. The geoprocessing step at the bottom has a red exclamation mark because the first time we ran the tool, we forgot to make sure that the file was saved in our geodatabase, so the tool failed.

The more recent geoprocesses appear on top. So, now click on the results - the one with the green check mark - and the tool results open and shows the bands used to generate the composite image and the order that they were used.

Why do we bother creating a composite image? The human eye can only see that portion of the electromagnetic spectrum within the visual spectrum. By creating a composite image , we can display, using the RGB color scheme, different bands that not only include data from the visible spectrum (that we typically see), but we can also substitute bands from outside the visible spectrum to expand the scope of the regions of the spectrum our image can display. This provides us with broadened perspectives to record images of features we cannot normally "see".

Integrating data (imagery) from outside of the visible spectrum is very powerful analysis tool. Thermal data, for example, can provide support for emergency management applications (identification of hot spots when fighting wildfires, etc.). Image analysis that incorporates the near infrared spectrum is often used to identify stress in agricultural crops, long before the stress is evident to the human eye. This provides agricultural operators with the ability not only to prevent crop loss and to maximize production while minimizing inputs (fertilizer, herbicide, pesticide, water, etc.).

We will be using the composited image created here (in this chapter) in Chapter 15: Sub-Setting a Landsat 8 Image.

Instead of an entire Landsat scene, the area of interest may be only one specific region within that scene, or only specific bands. The previous chapter provided instruction on how to generate a single composite image consisting of all eleven Landsat 8 bands. In that chapter, 11 bands were used. As previously discussed, a composite image can consist of any number of bands: 3bands, 4 bands, (etc.) or all 11 bands. This chapter provides instructions on how to limit the areal extent of the scene to a specific region (*sub-setting* an image, aka in GIS term, *clipping*).

For this chapter, use the new band composite image created in the previous chapter.

Sub-Setting (aka clipping) by Spatial Extent

Open ArcGIS® Pro. Open the project created in the previous chapter, or open a new blank project. For our purposes, we created a new project and added the composite image. *Note - be sure the project's folder is connected and workspaces are set.*

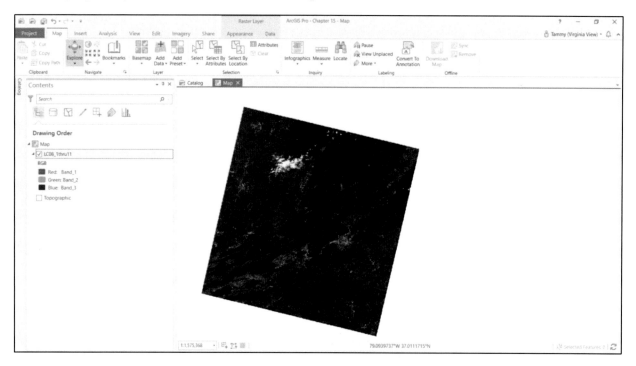

Limiting the spatial extent of this image can occur in multiple ways. First, we need to review the tool.

Highlight the composite image in the *Contents* and the *Raster Layer* tab enables, click on the *Data* tab.

On the far left is *Export Raster*, click on it and the *Export Raster* tool opens.

As seen, the composite image automatically populates in the top blank.

Next is the *Coordinate System* (note this is where the projection is changed, if required – but this option is beyond the scope of this book, so refer to the appropriate literature).

Click on the down arrow next to *Clipping Geometry* – several options are presented:

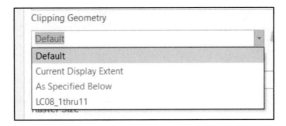

Default clipping setting is used when doing other types of changes, such as changing the coordinate system. That option will not be used in this chapter.

Current Display Extent – use this setting if the map is zoomed in to a specific region – this option will be used in the example below.

As Specific Below –use this setting if the specific coordinates for each corner of the desired region are known. We will actually note this further below.

The next item is the name of our *composite image* – for any other files listed in the project with a different extent than the composite image, this will snap to that extent. We will use this option below.

The next several figures provide an overview of the entire tool. Again, use this tool to export any raster file and change the parameters within that file. For our purposes, we are only sub-setting to areal extent (aka clipping the image).

To show all available settings within the tool, use the scroll bar on the right side of the tool.

Look at the *Raster Size* (red oval) in *Columns* and *Rows* – note the values in these boxes are the same as the entire scene (to compare, please go back to Chapter 13: Displaying Landsat 8 Imagery in ArcGIS® Pro).

Of additional note is the *NoData value* (black oval) – why not 0? Because 0 is already in use for brightness values.

The following figure reveals the last part of the tool options under the *General* tab. For this chapter, no changes to these settings will be made.

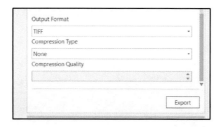

Now select the *Settings* tab. The following 3 figures provide examples of all available options. We are going to leave these as default – many of these settings are used for other types of processing.

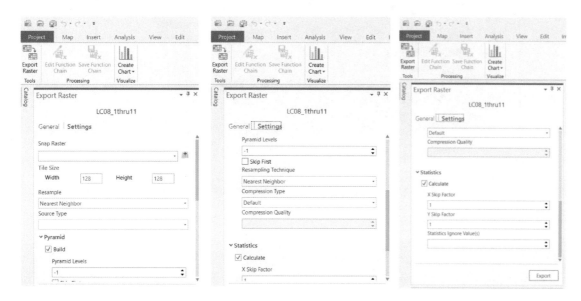

Note - our purpose here is not to evaluate the results from each type of setting, but provide the basics for accomplishing the task at hand. Refer to ArcGIS® Pro Help and current literature to determine if the project requires any other setting(s).

Clipping to the Extent of the Current Display

Now that we have reviewed the tool, let's set some parameters. First, we are going to clip to the extent that is displayed in the map viewer. Zoom in on the southeastern region of the image – it will include the city of Roanoke – (white circle), the Christiansburg/Blacksburg area (red circle) and Smith Mountain Lake (blue circle).

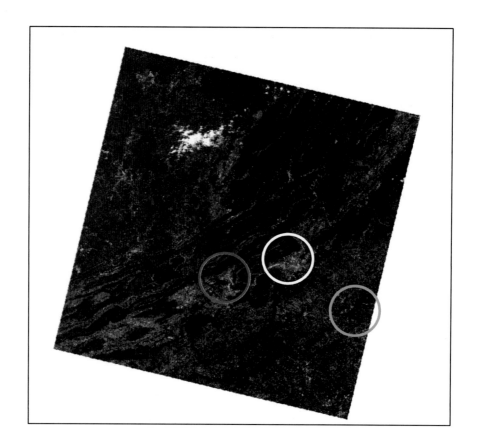

When zoomed in, it should look like this in the map window:

Within the *Export Raster* tool, under *General*, choose *Current Display Extent*

ArcGIS® Pro automatically changes it to *As Specified Below* and added the coordinates to limit the extent:

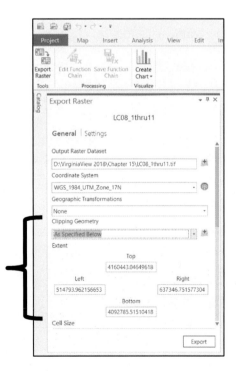

The number of *Rows* and *Columns has also changed.* Remember, we are clipping the scene to a smaller areal extent.

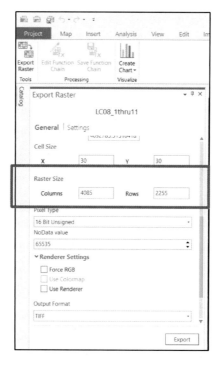

Leave the all other parameters as *Default* and then click on *Export*. In the bottom of the processing window, watch the progress of the processing (red box). When it finishes, a green message displays in the top of the window (green box).

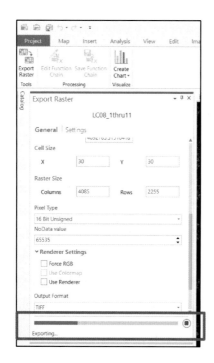

In the map window, the image has changed colors (we will discuss the color change in a bit):

Close the *Export Raster* window. Turn off the original composite image. A second layer is present in *Contents*. The name appears the same, except that it has a .tif.

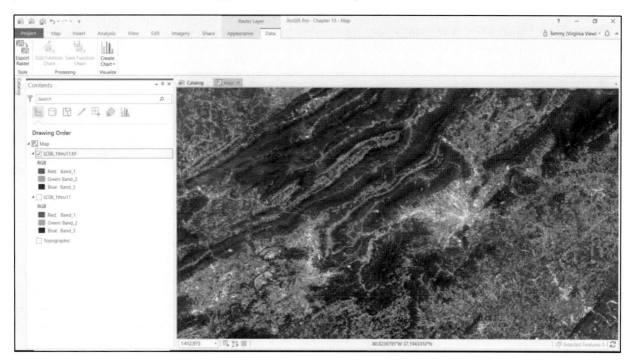

Turn the original composite image back on. Put the mouse cursor in the map window over the image and roll the mouse wheel backwards to zoom out. The image is clipped smaller than the original composite:

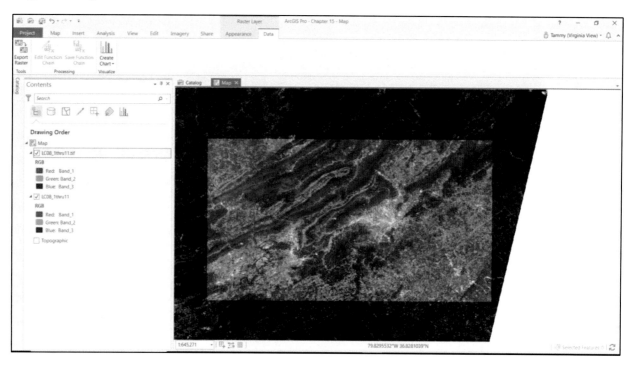

Notice that the image appears to have changed colors when comparing to the original image. Actually, the symbology is the same; the range of brightness values have changed, so the image appears a bit differently.

The figure below lists the brightness values of the newly clipped image:

The figure below lists the brightness values of the original composite image:

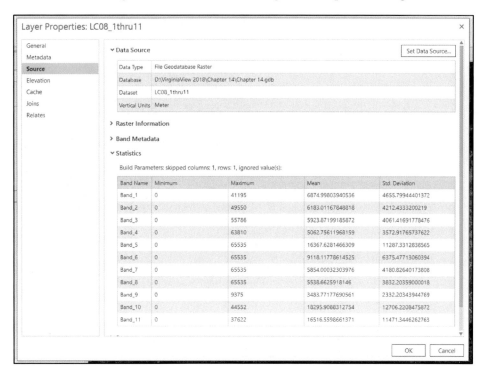

While it appears that the brightness values are the same, in the new clipped image, the range of values is much smaller.

We will continue to show 2 additional methods of clipping, but this specific clipped image will be used in many of the subsequent chapters.

Clipping Using a Polygon File

Another clipping option is to clip to an existing polygon file.

To do this, go ahead and add a polygon vector file that represents the spatial extent of the area desired. In this example, we have added two polygon files to demonstrate the process – Montgomery County, Virginia and a square around Roanoke, Virginia. *(If boundary shapefiles for the United States are needed, go to the US Census Bureau at* *https://www.census.gov/geo/maps-data/data/tiger-cart-boundary.html for Tigerline® files)*

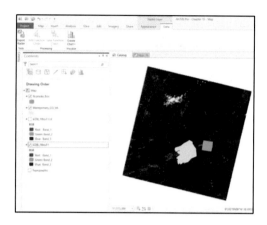

We are using the original composite image (not the clipped image), so make sure that the original composite image is highlighted in the *Contents*. As seen in the figure below, additional files are listed (beyond the original composite image), including the two new polygon shapefiles. Open the *Export Raster* tool. Choose the desired polygon file - we choose the polygon file <Roanoke Box> as the *Clipping Geometry* option and, again leave all other settings as the default. Remember – the *Clipping Geometry* will change to *As Specified Below*. Then click *Export*.

Once the tool as run, the message – *Exported successfully* – displays

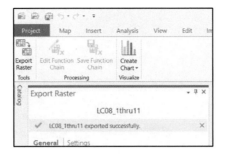

Results – note all the other layers are turned off and the image zoomed to the most recent clipped image (the one on the top in *Contents*). The composite image is clipped to the polygon file – a box around Roanoke Virginia:

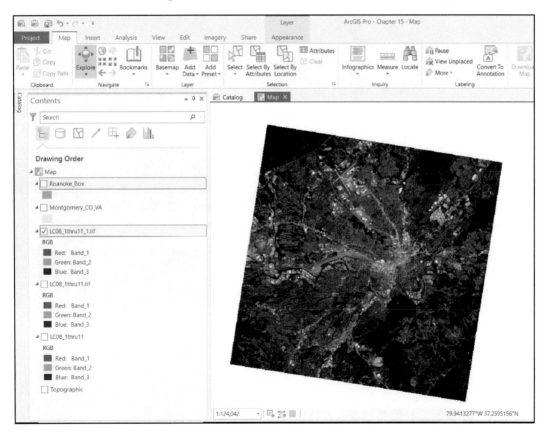

Now let's do it more one time, using the boundary file for Montgomery County – again, be sure that the original composite image is highlighted before setting the *Clipping Geometry* and running the tool.

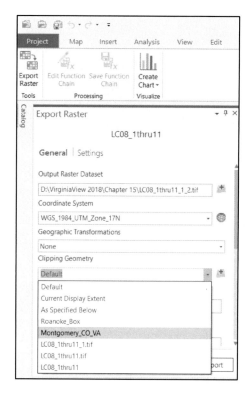

Results. Why did we do this a second time? To demonstrate that clipped parameters can be a polygon of any extent (not just straight lines). Please note that each time the tool ran, ArcGIS® Pro automatically named the file – but each file has a new number at the end (red boxes).

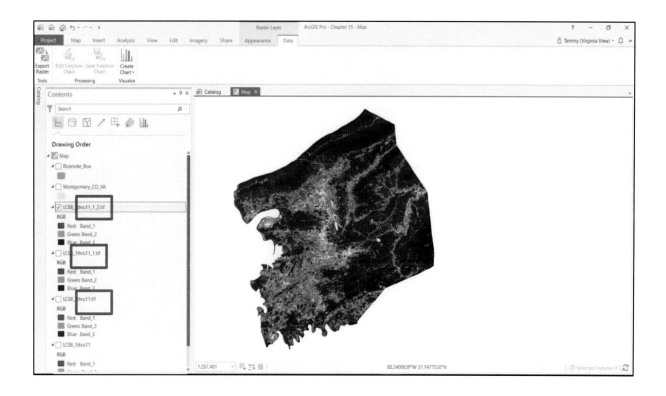

Compositing and Clipping in One Step

We are going to demonstrate one more process – compositing and clipping can be done all at the same time. Don't get upset, the results are different as we will demonstrate. In this method, we are going to use *Processing Extent*, found under *Environments*.

Remember - go to *Analysis* tab, *Environments* (here is where the workspace was set), go to *Processing Extent.* Click the down arrow and choose the file with the desired extent – yes, a raster file or a vector file is usable. We choose Montgomery County, Virginia.

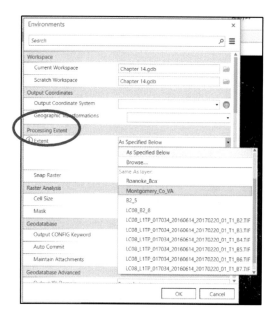

Once we chose Montgomery, County, Virginia, and ArcGIS® Pro populated the coordinates for that extent.

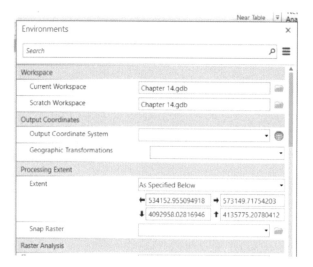

Now, open the *Composite Bands* tool, and redo the composite (if you forgot how to accomplish this, go back to the prior chapter). In the screenshot below, we are using Bands 2 – 5 (only 4 bands). Once populated and the new file has a name, click *Run*.

Results (please remember what we said about the band numbers in the prior chapter. When only using a limited number of bands from the scene, ArcGIS® Pro renumbers the bands). In the screenshot below, we turned off all the layers except the polygon for Montgomery County, Virginia and the new clipped image.

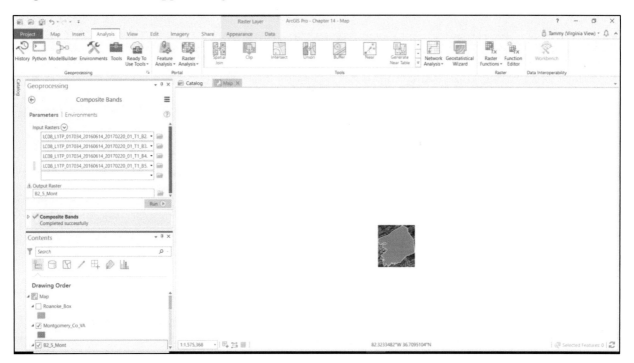

Right click on the new layer and *Zoom to Layer*. Turn off the Montgomery County, Virginia polygon.

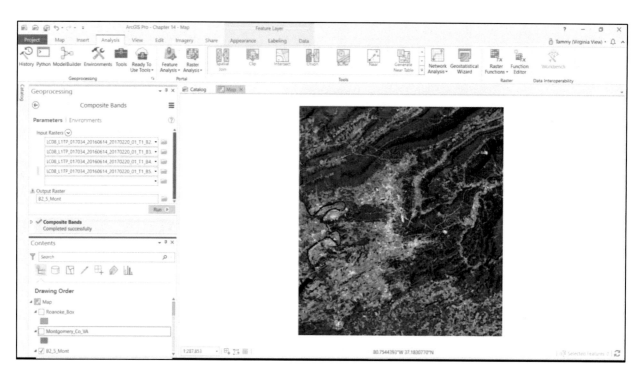

See the difference? The *Processing Extent* setting in *Environments* created a new composite image with straight lines, while the *Export Raster* tool creates a new image with the exact boundaries of the polygon. Which approach is better? There is no right or wrong answer as this is contingent on the project's parameters. One approach provides a subset of a general region. The other approach provides a subset of a more specific user-defined extent (which could include a watershed boundary, a political boundary, etc.).

Please proceed to the next chapter (Chapter 16: Band Combinations for Landsat 8 Imagery). The 11-band composite image clipped to the *Extent of the Display* will be used in the next few chapters.

In this chapter, we discuss band combinations and how to use them within ArcGIS® Pro. We begin with a brief review of Landsat 8 spectral channels and a discussion on band combinations, spectral values for features on the surface of the Earth, and how different features can be identified with specific bands.

Introduction

Landsat 8 images are acquired in grayscale and each band covers a different region of the electromagnetic spectrum. By combining 3 or more bands, images can be displayed in red, green and blue (RGB format). Remember, from prior chapters discussing Landsat 8 imagery, each spectral channel (designated as a *band* for satellite imagery) is defined by its own distinctive region of the electromagnetic spectrum. Each band is specifically tailored to help distinguish separate features on the Earth's surface *(See table below. Additional notes at the end of this chapter provide details on usefulness of individual bands and combination thereof for identifying specific surface feature).*

Furthermore, different features on the surface of the Earth respond to various wavelengths of the electromagnetic spectrum, as features absorb, reflect and re-emit the radiation in diverse ways. Using different band combinations to display the scene in color allows these dissimilar features to be more easily detected and identified. This process does take some experience. Users must become familiar with the scene, in order to identify, for example, urban areas, forests, agriculture, and water bodies. Familiarity with any satellite platform (Landsat, Sentinel, etc.) is vital for different analyses, such as unsupervised classifications, supervised classifications, and different indices (ex: NDVI). Such analyses are covered in subsequent chapters.

Using data outside the visible spectrum

Examine the tables at the end of this chapter. These tables provide several examples of how data outside the visible spectrum can be used to more effectively identify features on the Earth's surface. For example, the near infrared (NIR) wavelengths are very useful for water bodies, as clear, calm water absorbs NIR wavelengths and thus water bodies appear very dark, almost black on a color infrared image. Additionally, healthy vigorous vegetation is also more readily identified using the NIR bands, much more so than by using the green band. Refer to the figure below for general information regarding the potential applications of various wavelengths of Landsat 8.

Reference

Barsi, J.A.; Lee, K.; Kvaran, G.; Markham, B.L.; Pedelty, J.A. The Spectral Response of the Landsat-8 Operational Land Imager. *Remote Sens.* **2014**, *6*, 10232-10251. doi:10.3390/rs61010232

Band	Wavelength	Useful for mapping
Band 1 – Coastal Aerosol	0.435 - 0.451	Coastal and aerosol studies
Band 2 – Blue	0.452 - 0.512	Bathymetric mapping, distinguishing soil from vegetation, and deciduous from coniferous vegetation
Band 3 - Green	0.533 - 0.590	Emphasizes peak vegetation, which is useful for assessing plant vigor
Band 4 - Red	0.636 - 0.673	Discriminates vegetation slopes
Band 5 - Near Infrared (NIR)	0.851 - 0.879	Emphasizes biomass content and shorelines
Band 6 - Short-wave Infrared (SWIR) 1	1.566 - 1.651	Discriminates moisture content of soil and vegetation; penetrates thin clouds
Band 7 - Short-wave Infrared (SWIR) 2	2.107 - 2.294	Improved moisture content of soil and vegetation and thin cloud penetration
Band 8 - Panchromatic	0.503 - 0.676	15 meter resolution, sharper image definition
Band 9 – Cirrus	1.363 - 1.384	Improved detection of cirrus cloud contamination
Band 10 – TIRS 1	10.60 – 11.19	100 meter resolution, thermal mapping and estimated soil moisture
Band 11 – TIRS 2	11.50 - 12.51	100 meter resolution, Improved thermal mapping and estimated soil moisture

Landsat 8 Bands and Associated Mapping Applications. Table from: https://landsat.usgs.gov/what-are-best-spectral-bands-use-my-study

An in-depth discussion of the spectral properties of individual features on the surface of the Earth is beyond the scope in this book. Additional information about this topic can be acquired from various online resources, including:

- https://egsc.usgs.gov/isb//pubs/factsheets/fs12901.pdf
- https://earthobservatory.nasa.gov/Features/FalseColor/page6.php
- http://www.mngeo.state.mn.us/chouse/airphoto/cir.html
- https://www.altavian.com/knowledge-base/cir-imagery/
- https://publiclab.org/wiki/near-infrared-imaging

Recall from Chapter 10 that, when downloading scenes collected from a specific satellite platform, it is important to note that each band conveys information. Unfortunately, the spectral properties of the band numbers are often not consistent between different satellite platforms (even if the band numbers are the same). For example, the spectral properties of a Band 5 image collected by Landsat 4 will not match the spectral properties of a Band 5 image collected by Landsat 8. We have attempted to consolidate much of the information associated with the bands of Landsat family (Landsat 1-8) in the "Additional Notes" section at the end of this chapter. For more information, please consult: http://pubs.usgs.gov/fs/2012/3072/fs2012-3072.pdf

Creating Different Band Combinations

This section will provide step by step instructions to change and explore band combinations of Landsat imagery using ArcGIS® Pro.

Open ArcGIS® Pro. For this section, we will use the composite image that was created in Chapter 15: *Sub-setting a Composite Landsat 8 Image*. Don't forget to set workspaces and link the project's folder. The map project should look similar to the figure below.

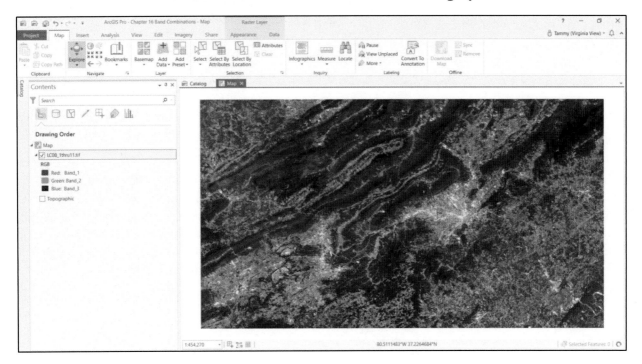

There are several ways to change the combination of bands for a color composite image. We will start with two default options.

Short Cut Button for Band Combinations

Click on the *Raster Layer* tab and then *Appearance*. Under this tab is a button called *Band Combinations*.

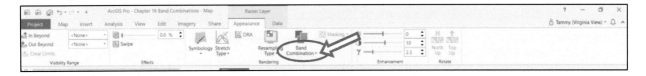

Click on the down arrow at the end of the word *Combination* and three options are revealed – *Natural Color, Color Infrared*, and *Custom*. Each of these options will be discussed, but more so as a cautionary note when using this shortcut button. This will become clear as we proceed.

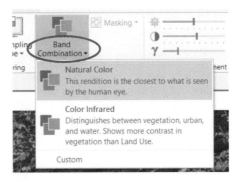

Hover the mouse over *Natural Color.*

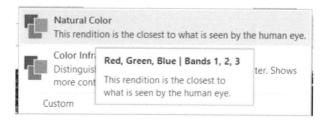

Natural color uses the wavelengths of the electromagnetic spectrum in the visible range – red, green and blue (what ArcGIS® Pro calls Bands 1, 2, 3) to display the image. Reference the table provided at the beginning of this chapter. The table above for Landsat 8, depicts Band 2 as Blue, not Red and Band 3 as Green, not Blue and Band 4 as Red. ArcGIS® Pro defaults to Red, Green, Blue. Blue is a shorter wavelength than Red so the Blue band actually comes 1st in the visible range of the electromagnetic spectrum and labeling for satellite bands.

Hover the mouse over the *Color Infrared* option:

Color infrared uses wavelengths from the green and red visible along with the wavelengths from the very next region of the electromagnetic spectrum – near infrared. But again, the band designations in ArcGIS® Pro do not correspond to the band sequence of Landsat 8, as Band 5 should be associated with the near infrared band.

The third option under band combinations is *Custom.* Using this option, users can set a specific band combination to use on a regular basis. When regularly using Landsat 8 Natural Color, set the *Custom* parameters to the following: Red to Band_4, Green to Band_3 and Blue to Band_2. Name your custom display *Landsat 8 Natural Color.* (Note – please be careful when setting these values. For our composite, we used all 11 bands and thus the band number within ArcGIS® Pro remains the same as the Landsat 8 original designations).

Click on *Add,* and we have a natural color, 432 Band Combination Landsat 8 image. The image in the display window (see figure below) does now look more like features seen on the Earth. This is how 'natural' color (or true color) should appear.

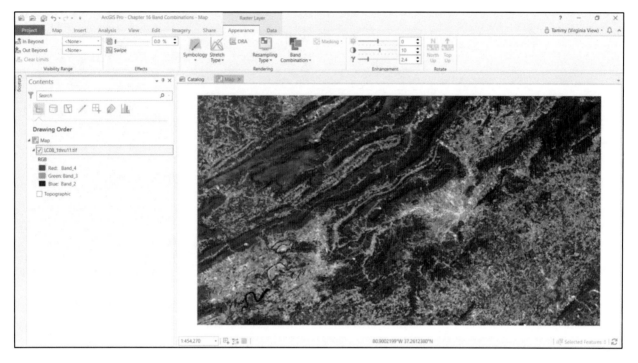

Use the *Custom* setting one more time, but this time, use the band combinations for Landsat 8 Color Infrared (hint: reference the chart provided at the end of this chapter).

After creating a Color Infrared image, your display window should appear similar to the figure below. Does the image look like the one below? The Landsat 8 bands for Color Infrared are 5-4-3 (Band 5 = red, Band 4 = green, and Band 3 = blue).

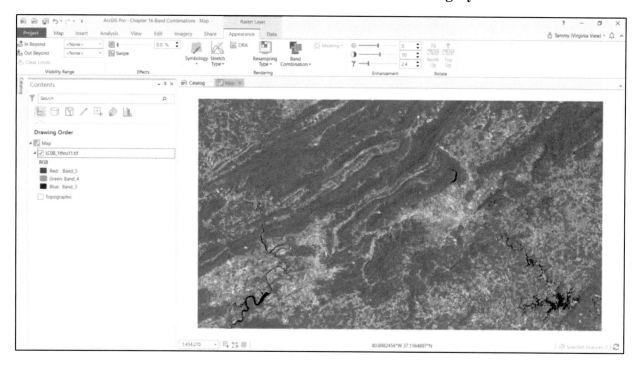

Landsat 8's Band 5 is the near infrared. Normally, we cannot 'see data from this segment of the electromagnetic spectrum, but we have arranged Band 5 so that the ArcGIS® Pro display window will display the near infrared band as the color red. Using this band combination, vegetation appears bright red (healthy/more vigorous vegetation is highly reflective in the near infrared band). The healthiest vegetation (or vegetation that is mature, or at its peak) within this scene will show as red. That does not mean that the landcover associated with pink hues (less red saturation) are unhealthy vegetation. It is possible, for example, that this vegetation could be less dense, less mature, etc. This exemplifies the importance of *in-situ* verification.

There is a tremendous difference between the two images (Natural/True color image and NIR image). We will discuss the differences in more detail a bit later. But first, we will explore another option for changing and visualizing different band combinations of a composite image.

Band Combinations using Symbology

Go to *Symbology* for the image. You can access the *Symbology* icon either under *Appearance* or under *Properties* for the layer (either option works).

Under *Symbology*, we can create any band combination that we want. We can display a **432** image (Landsat 8 Natural Color); a **543** image (Landsat 8 Color Infrared), or **757**, **657**, etc. Again, it is vital to remember which bands were used when creating the composite image. If all of the 11 Landsat bands (starting with 1, and added in order) were not used, the band combinations using band numbers will be different in ArcGIS® Pro than what the actual Landsat designations are. It is extremely important that this information is retained when doing analyses. And remember, we are assigning different wavelengths of the electromagnetic spectrum to colors that we can see with the naked eye. Humans are unable to see the NIR and other 'nonvisible' wavelengths. But with software's help, we can display them with color, and are therefore able to visualize them.

Once *Symbology* is open, just change band numbers to the appropriate colors. Right now, for our image, the combination is 5-4-3.

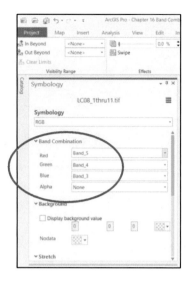

Using the drop down arrow at the end of each color's field, change the following:

Red to Band_4; *Green to Band_3*; *Blue to Band_2* – this is the natural color combination. Your image display should look similar to the figure below.

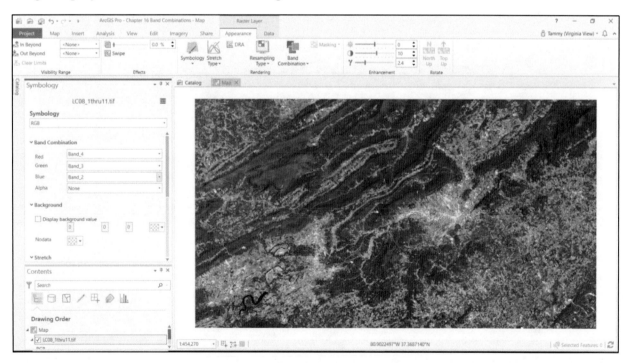

Now change it to Color Infrared. Your displayed image should look similar to the figure below.

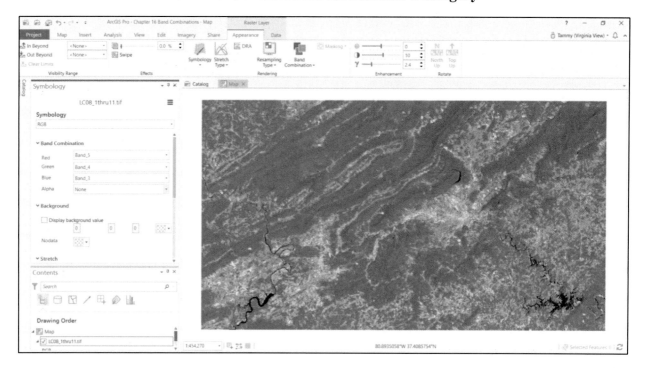

Let's do a closer comparison of these two combinations (we will visualize another band combination later). The next two screenshots are the Natural Color compared to the Color Infrared. Can you identify some specific differences?

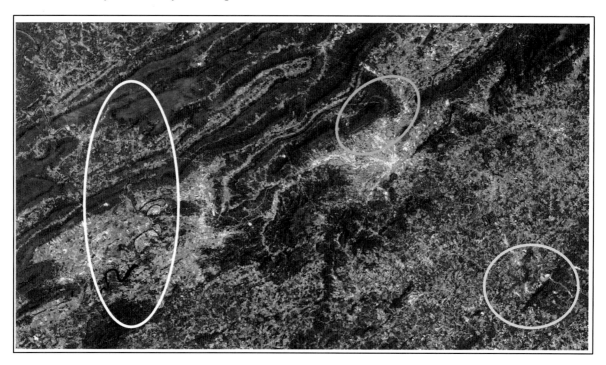

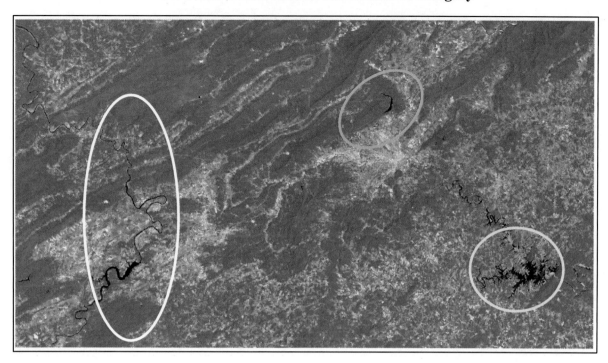

Within the various circles in the two images above are water bodies. Inside the white oval is the New River. The New River is fairly evident in the Natural Color image (the southern wider portion). In the Color Infrared, the entire course of the river is quite obvious. The lime green circle in the north is Carvin's Cove, a reservoir for the City of Roanoke. Carvin's Cove is barely visible on the Natural Color image, but is very prominent on the Color Infrared image. Finally, Smith Mountain Lake, located in the southeast section of the image, is located within the yellow circle. Now that we have pointed it out, you can see the lake in the Natural Color image, but the lake is clearly evident in the Color Infrared image. Additionally, note that the lake is not all dark. Smith Mountain Lake is a reservoir and north of the dam, the river which flows into the lake is heavily laden with sediment (which is displayed as a bright light blue).

How do these two image combinations display vegetation? Green in the first image (the natural or true color image) is associated with vegetation. Remember that this is a summer image in Virginia (June 14, 2016) and within this region are extensive forests, and include both a National Forest and a State Forest. Red in the second image shows vegetative cover – much more prominently. Virginia is a heavily-vegetated state with both forests and agriculture. Zoom in.

Although not apparent in the natural color – the agriculture fields appear as lighter shades of green (true color image) and as various shades of pink (Color Infrared image). Refer to the next set of images.

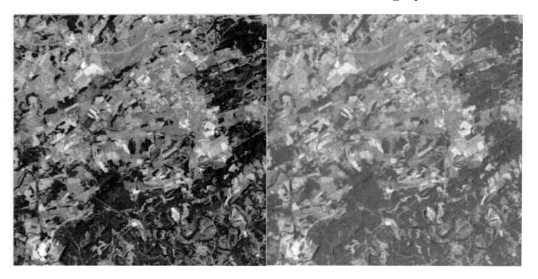

Let's try another area of the scene-- the city of Roanoke. Roanoke is the largest urban area in southwest Virginia and within this Landsat scene. What do you find in urban areas *(hint – long linear features like roads, things with definite angles like buildings, perhaps an airport).* Can you find the city?

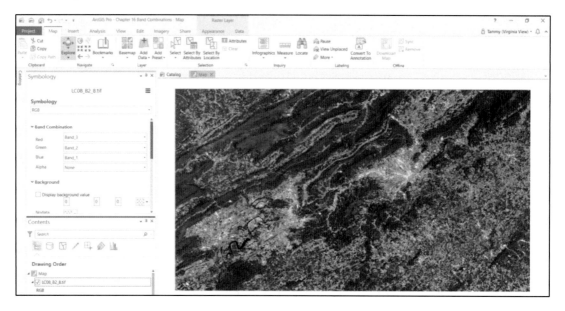

Zoom into the City of Roanoke. Can you ascertain any specific features within the city – roads? The Airport? Some golf courses?

Remain zoomed into Roanoke and now explore the city using a Color Infrared display. Roanoke looks a lot different doesn't it? The Roanoke River runs through Roanoke southeast to Smith Mountain Lake. The river is barely visible in the Natural Color (can you see it?). In the Color Infrared image, the river is visible in the southeast of Roanoke but within Roanoke, the river almost disappears.

Can you find one of the golf courses? *(Hint – infrared is showing bright red for healthy vegetation – what do you find in a golf course year round?)* What other features are present on a golf course that might be visible with Landsat imagery. Can you identify the fairways and putting greens along the golf courses? What about sand traps? Would sand traps be displayed as bright red on a Color NIR image?

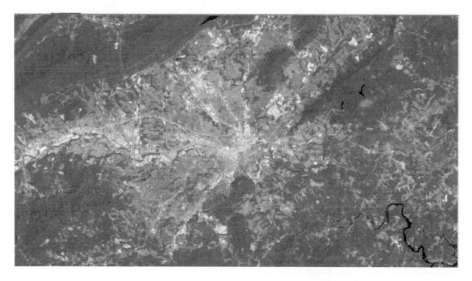

The figures below show a specific area of Roanoke using different band combinations: Natural Color (left), Color Infrared (middle) and a new Band Combination (more information about this image later!). You can see that there are very distinctive differences between these 3 images. They all highlight different features on the Earth.

The image (3rd on the right, and below) uses a band combination of 5 - 6 – 8. All of the bands associated with this image are outside of the visible spectrum. But, the river channel is now a distinctive line meandering on the south side and through the city.

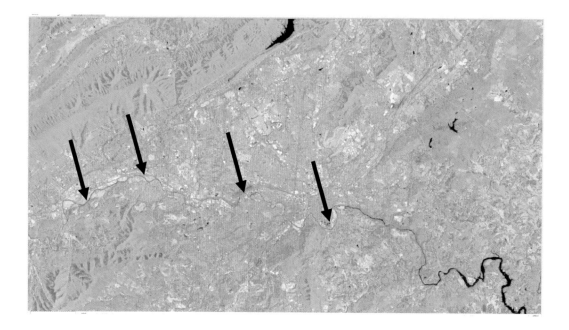

Why do the different bands placed within those specific channels make a difference? *(See Landsat Table above and additional notes at the end of this chapter.)*

What else can you now identify with this band combination that you could not discern from the natural color combination? The same band can be used multiple times. Here is a 7-5-7 band combination.

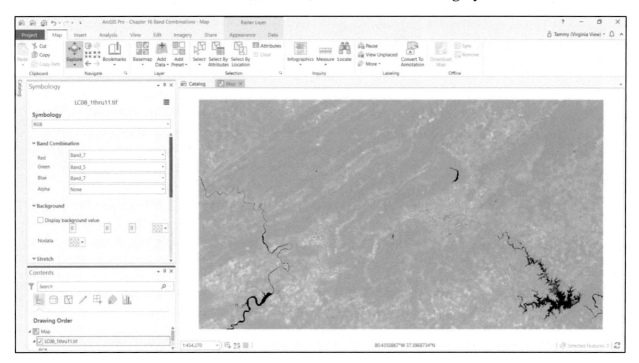

Note that the same band can be displayed more than once (as 2 different colors). This again changes the display in the map document window. Does this band combination facilitate seeing anything more distinctly in the forested mountains? *(Answer- no, Band 4 (near infrared) is the most effective band for identifying healthy vegetation and Band 4 is not used in this combination.)* But the water bodies are even more prominent and in this image-- we can even see some smaller water bodies and another river in the northeast, only slightly seen in the 5-4-3 Color Infrared combination (shown in various locations within the black ovals).

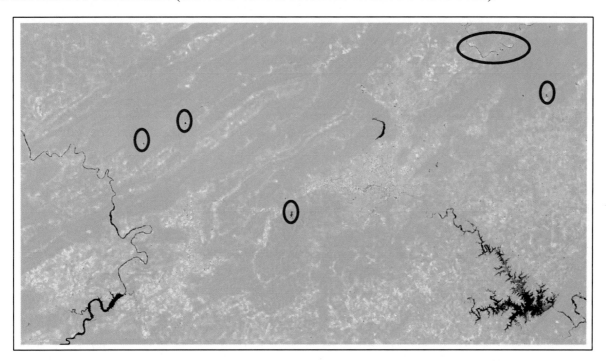

Go ahead and explore different band combinations. Follow the tables and charts at the end of this chapter. Try different combinations for the whole scene, and then for different localized regions of the scene (by zooming-in).

Note – many aerial images (from airplanes, drones, and other platforms) are acquired in 4 bands – the three visible bands (RGB) and also the near-infrared. The USDA NAIP (National Agriculture Imagery Program) imagery is acquired with 4 bands because the purpose is to evaluate agricultural productivity and these images are usually acquired during the growing season (see https://www.fsa.usda.gov/programs-and-services/aerial-photography/imagery-programs/naip-imagery/ for further information). This 4-band imagery can be loaded into ArcGIS® Pro and displayed using the different band combinations in similar fashion or loaded with a GIS Server connection (see Chapter 4: Connecting to a Folder or an Online GIS Server). These images are typically distributed as a single, 4-band, composite image (not as separate image bands as is the case with Landsat imagery).

You are now ready to proceed to the next set of chapters, which discuss image enhancement techniques. We will be using the sub-setted 11-band composite image in those chapters. The following pages of this chapter discuss single band sensitivities and specific band combinations.

ADDITIONAL NOTES

Single Band Sensitivities

LANDSAT Thematic Mapper (TM &ETM+)

0.45-0.52 μm BLUE (BAND 1)
- Shorter wavelengths most sensitive to atmospheric haze, so images in this region may lack tonal contrast
- Shorter wavelengths have greatest water penetration (longer wavelengths more absorbed); optimal for detection of submerged aquatic vegetation (SAV), pollution plumes, water turbidity and sediment
- Detecting smoke plumes (shorter wavelengths more easily scattered by smaller particles
- Good for distinguishing clouds from snow and rock, and soil surfaces from vegetated surfaces

0.52-0.6 μm GREEN (BAND 2)
- Sensitive to water turbidity differences, sediment and pollution plumes
- Covers green reflectance peak from leaf surfaces, can be useful for discriminating broad vegetation classes
- Also useful for detection of SAV
- Also useful for penetration of water for detection of SAV, pollution plumes, turbidity and sediment

0.63-0.69 μm RED (BAND 3)
- Sensitive in a strong chlorophyll absorption region, i.e. good for discriminating soil and vegetation
- Senses strong reflectance regions for most soils
- Effective for delineating soil cover

0.76-0.9 μm NEAR IR (BAND 4)
- Distinguishes vegetation varieties and vegetation vigor
- Water is a strong absorber of NIR, so this band is good for delineation of water bodies and distinguishing between dry and moist soils

1.55-1.75 μm MID OR SWIR (BAND 5)
- Sensitive to changes in leaf-tissue water content (turgidity)
- Sensitive to moisture variation in vegetation and soils; reflectance decreases as water content increases
- Useful for determining plant vigor and for distinguishing succulents vs. woody vegetation
- Especially sensitive to presence/absence of ferric iron or hemitite in rocks (reflectance increases as ferric iron increases)
- Discriminates between snow and ice (light toned) and clouds (dark toned)

2.08-2.35 μm MID OR SWIR (BAND 7)

- Coincides with absorption band caused by hydrous minerals (clay mica, some oxides, and sulfates) making them appear darker; e.g. clay alteration zones associated with mineral deposits such as copper
- Lithologic mapping
- Like band 5, sensitive to moisture variation in vegetation and soils

10.4-12.5 μm LWIR, THERMAL (BAND 6)

- Sensor designed to measure radiant surface temps -100 degrees C to +150 degrees C; day or nighttime use
- Heat mapping applications: soil moisture, rock types, thermal water plumes, household heat conservation, urban heat generation, active military targeting, wildlife inventory, geothermal detection

Electromagnetic Spectrum and Band Coverage - Landsat 4, 5, 7 and 8

Landsat 8 uses more bands relative to those of sensors used by the earlier Landsat satellites. In addition, Landsat 8's divisions of the electromagnetic spectrum differ from those of TM and ETM+ sensors aboard Landsat 4, 5 and 7 – see the following table for comparisons. As such, when working with Landsat 8 imagery, be careful to use the appropriate bands when selecting band combinations.

Band Number	Landsat 8: Operational Land Imagers (OLI) & Thermal Infrared Sensor (TIRS)	Landsat 4 & 5: Thematic Mapper (TM) Landsat 7: Thematic Mapper Plus (ETM+)
1	0.43 - 0.45 μm – coastal aerosol	
2	0.45 - 0.51 μm - blue	0.45- 0.52 μm – blue-green
3	0.53 - 0.59 μm - green	0.52 – 0.61 μm - green
4	0.64 - 0.67 μm - red	0.63 – 0.69 μm - red
5	0.85 - 0.88 μm - NIR	0.76 – 0.90 μm - NIR
6	1.57 - 1.65 μm - SWIR 1	1.55 – 1.75 μm - SWIR
7	2.11 - 2.29 μm - SWIR 2	10.40 – 12.50 μm – thermal
8	0.50 - 0.68 μm - Panchromatic	2.08 – 2.35 μm - SWIR
9	1.36 - 1.38 μm - Cirrus	0.52 – 0.90 μm Panchromatic (ETM+ only)
10	10.60 - 11.19 μm - TIRS 1	NONE
11	11.50 - 12.51 μm – TIRS 2	

SWIR = Short-Wave Infrared
Cirrus = Defined to detect and screen out contamination of cirrus clouds in other bands.
     (Not intended for analysis as separate channel.)
Coastal aerosol = Defined to analyze, and to estimate depths of, shallow coastal waters.

Landsat Band Combination Sensitivities

OLI (Landsat 8)

4-3-2
Simulates a natural color image.

5-6-4
Used for the analysis of soil moisture and vegetation conditions. It is also useful for location of inland water bodies and land-water boundaries.

5-4-3
Known as false-color Infrared, or CIR (color infrared); this is the most conventional band combination used in remote sensing for vegetation, crops, land-use and wetlands analysis.

7-5-3
Analysis of soil and vegetation moisture content and location of inland water. Vegetation appears green.

6-5-4
Separation of urban and rural land uses; identification of land/water boundaries.

5-6-7
Detection of clouds, snow, and ice (in high latitudes especially).

TM (Landsat 4 & 5) and ETM+ (Landsat 7)

3-2-1
This combination simulates a natural color image. It is sometimes used for coastal studies and for detection of smoke plumes.

4-5-3
Used for the analysis of soil moisture and vegetation conditions. It is also useful for location of inland water bodies and land-water boundaries.

4-3-2
Known as false-color Infrared; this is the most conventional band combination used in remote sensing for vegetation, crops, land-use and wetlands analysis.

7-4-2
Analysis of soil and vegetation moisture content and location of inland water. Vegetation appears green.

5-4-3
Separation of urban and rural land uses; identification of land/water boundaries.

4-5-7
Detection of clouds, snow, and ice (in high latitudes especially).

The next three chapters introduce image enhancement using ArcGIS® Pro. This chapter demonstrates radiometric enhancement.

Image Enhancement, An Introduction

Image enhancement denotes processing of remotely sensed imagery to adjust brightness values (displayed as digital numbers [DN]), thereby improving the image's visual qualities for a specific purpose. The brightness values of individual pixels are changed to improve qualities such as color balance, brightness, contrast between pixels, or other characteristics.

An image's visual quality is connected to the range of pixel brightness values, known as *contrast*. An image with high contrast has a narrow range of brightness values - largely only blacks and whites. An image with low contrast has a wide range of brightness values, and is often associated with black and white images and include gray pixels. Usually, extremely low contrast is undesirable, as features will appear, not as blacks and whites, but as intermediate greys. Often, these values may better record the important features of an image (than just black and whites), but the gray tone may also suppress key features within the image. On the other hand, extreme reduction of contrast may conceal distinctive features within a scene.

Image enhancement permits the application of a level of contrast appropriate for a specific purpose. Of special significance is recognition that the intent of image enhancement is to improve an image's appearance for that specific purpose. Because analyses have different objectives, and images have differing qualities, preferred enhancement techniques vary from one application to the next. Image enhancement is a manipulation of an image's appearance, so, fundamentally, image enhancement is cosmetic and should not be used as an input for analytical purposes.

Most remotely sensed images require some form of image enhancement because images use only a small range of the brightness available on a computer's display. As such, many features on the image are not visible to the analyst. As a result, in its unenhanced form, the image's suitability may be lacking for a specific purpose. Image enhancement expands the range of brightness used to display the image, thus revealing features not visible in the unenhanced version.

Enhancing images dynamically in a map project viewer is much faster than writing a permanent image file for every enhancement operation. Dynamic enhancement in a map viewer does not change the actual values of the pixels in the original image.

Histogram Enhancement Techniques

An image's frequency histogram provides the best context for beginning an image enhancement discussion. A frequency histogram displays image brightness along the horizontal axis, and numbers of pixels at each brightness level along the vertical axis. The shape of a specific histogram is related to the features represented within a scene, and conditions under which the image was acquired. We provide examples of histogram enhancement techniques in this chapter. Some of these techniques are summarized below.

- A **Linear Contrast Stretch** expands the range of brightness values by extending the values to occupy the full range of brightness available within the image by creating new intermediate values.

- **Histogram Equalization** expands the range of brightness by sliding the brightness along the brightness scale so that they occupy the full range of brightness available in the display. The histogram of the enhanced image shows gaps between the brightness values because they have been separated to create a wider range of brightness in the image.

Digital Image Enhancement Techniques

A great variety of digital image enhancement techniques are available. Choosing a particular technique(s) depends on the application, data available, experience and preferences of the analyst or the analyst's customer. In this and the next two chapters, we demonstrate the three most important and widely used groups of enhancement techniques:

- **Radiometric Enhancement** - Enhancing images based on the values of individual pixels (this chapter)

- **Spatial Enhancement** - Enhancing images based on the values of individual and neighboring pixels (see Chapter 18: Spatial Enhancement of Landsat 8 Imagery)

- **Spectral Enhancement** - Enhancing images by transforming the values of each pixel on a multiband basis (Band Ratios, Vegetation Indices - see Chapter 19: Spectral Enhancement of Landsat 8 Imagery).

Radiometric Enhancement using ArcGIS® Pro

We will be using the first clipped 11-Band Composite Image created in Chapter 15: Sub-setting a Landsat 8 Image (the image that was clipped to the extent of the display). Note – while we will be using the 11-band composite image in this chapter, enhancement techniques discussed in this chapter can also be accomplished on a single-band image.

To being, create a new map project, be sure to name it, connect to the project's folder, and set the workspaces. Then, add the 11-band composite and sub-set image. Display the image with band combination 5-4-3 (color infrared). Click on the Raster Layer > Appearance tab. This chapter discusses some of the tools that are listed under the Appearance tab (some tools are also discussed in the next two chapters). The display should look similar to the image below.

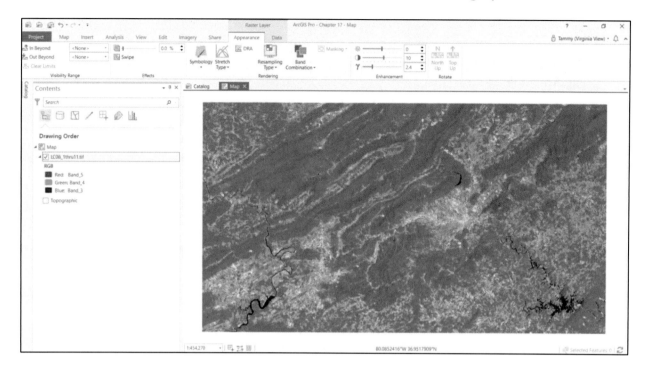

We start with the *Enhancement* icons shown in the next figure - *Brightness, Contrast, and Gamma* – found on the left side of the *Appearance* toolbar.

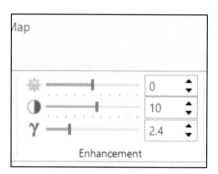

The name of the enhancement tool, can be acquired by hovering the mouse over one of the icons (tool tip). Place your mouse and hover over the Sun icon. The following tool tip should appear.

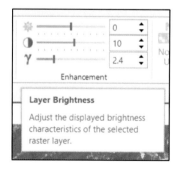

These three enhancement tools are used by either sliding the bar, or by placing a numeric value in the box at the end of the sliding bar. Do not make any changes yet. Once the values are changed, the image can always be reset to the default values. To reset the image to the original setting, just click on the icon itself:

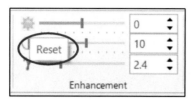

Now, we will change the values, one at a time. Observe the changes in the display (again these techniques only change the display, not the pixel values in the original image). Each enhancement technique changes the image display in different ways.

Adjusting Image Brightness

Brightness will make the image appear lighter or darker. The default value is 0 and the value can be negative or positive. Change the value as illustrated in the following two figures.

Negative values will darken the image. In the figure below, this value was set to -34 (negative 34).

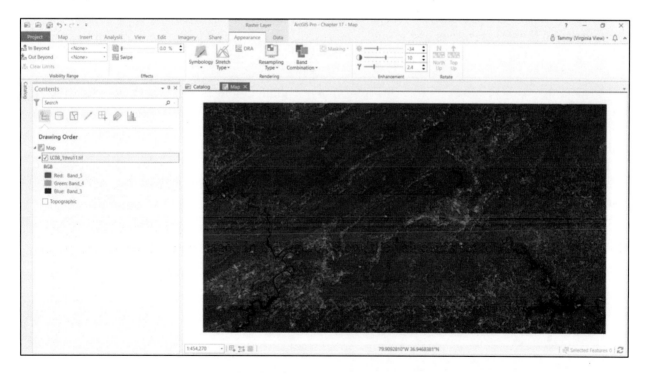

Positive values brighten the image. In the figure below, the value was set to +14.

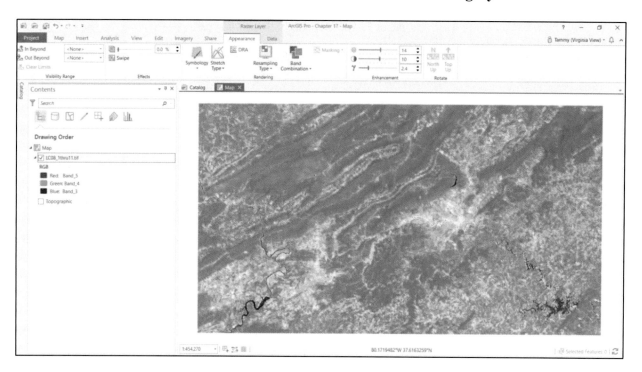

As demonstrated in the above two examples, brightening or darkening the image changes the individual features in different ways. Which enhancement technique is most appropriate is contingent on the requirements of the specific project. Go ahead and change the brightness values to several different settings to see how the image changes.

When you are ready to move on to a different image enhancement technique, be sure to click on the *Sun icon* to reset the image to default values before proceeding to *Contrast*.

Adjusting Image Contrast

Contrast changes the range of differences between the darkest and lightest objects. The *Contrast* value is not set to 0. For this specific image, it is set to 10, and the sliding bar is not centered. ArcGIS® Pro automatically sets this value, based on pixel values of the specific image. When using a different image, the software might display a different value.

Contrast, however, does have a range including negative numbers. Let's try two settings.

In the figure below, the contrast value was set to -34.

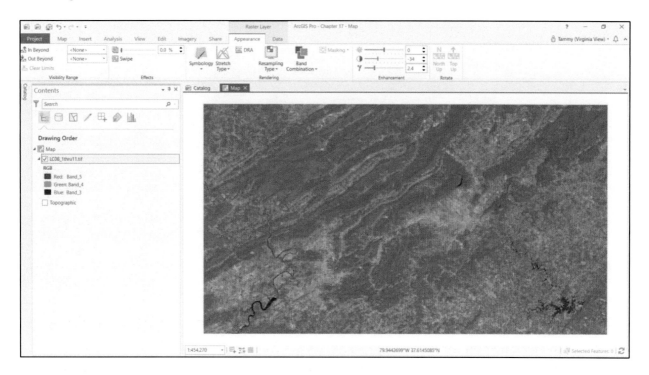

Notice that the image is not darker, it actually is not as sharp. The contrast is more muted. *Remember, this operation is changing the range of brightness values dynamically in the map document viewer. This technique does not actually change the original pixel values.*

Now, increase the contrast value to +35 and a much sharper image displays (figure below). – This setting has actually sharpened the difference between land and water bodies (the darker colored features).

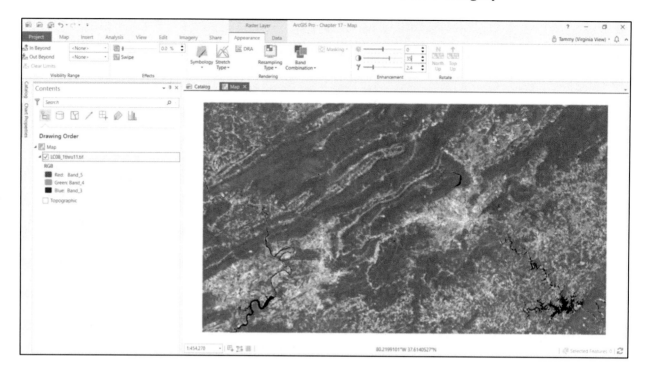

Go ahead and try other settings. When finished, do not forget to click on the icon to reset the values to default. For contrast, clicking on the *Contrast* icon, it will reset to 0, so be sure the contrast value is set to 10, which is what ArcGIS® Pro initially determined was the best contrast setting for this image.

Gamma Enhancement

Gamma controls relationships between the brightness of original scene and that on the display. (For example, at a gamma of 1.0, the two images will use the same scale of brightness, whereas at gammas of 0.5 or 1.5, the display shows, respectively, either compressed, or expanded, scales of brightness relative to the original.) For our image, ArcGIS® Pro determined that 2.4 was the best setting. *Gamma* values range from 0 to 10.0.

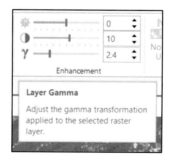

In the figure below, the *Gamma* value was set to 0.

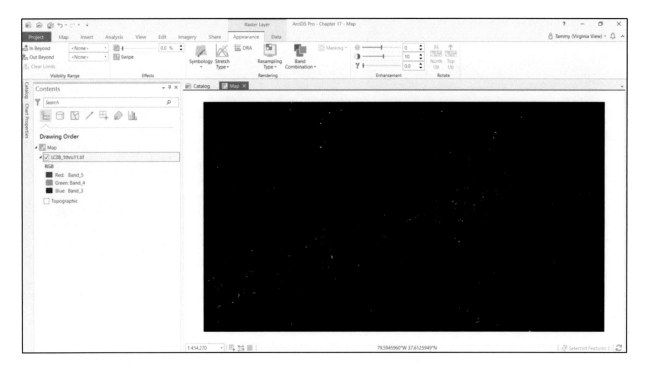

In the figure below, the *Gamma* value was set to 10.

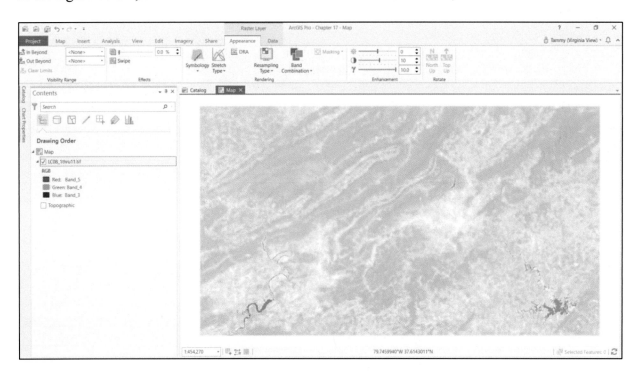

In the figure below, the *Gamma* value was set to 1.7.

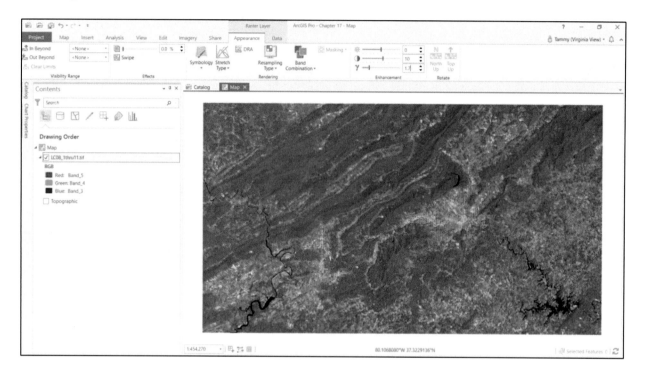

What is the purpose of the first 2 settings demonstrated? For this image, possibility nothing. But again, image enhancement settings used depend on the application demands and the purpose of the project.

Now reset the Gamma value to 2.4 – the default setting used by ArcGIS® Pro.

Now, let's look at another icon:

Dynamic Range Adjustment (DRA)

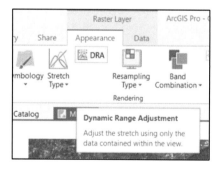

Dynamic range adjustment adjusts an image dynamically in the viewer when zooming in and out (again-- it does not change the original image). The stretch type does not change, only the range of values changes (based on the image displayed in the viewer). This technique is used to help enhance a specific region seen within the viewer.

The figure below illustrates an example without DRA enabled.

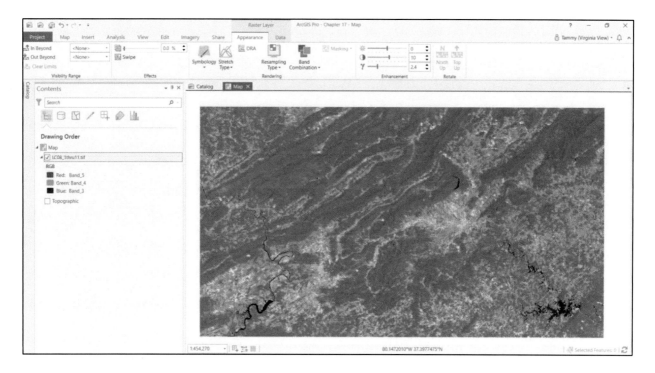

The figure (below), shows the same image, zoomed in to view Carvin's Cove (the crescent-shaped lake), without DRA enabled.

The figure below provides an example of a DRA-enabled view, of an entire scene. Visually, this figure is no different than a full image without DRA enabled. The difference in the image display occurs when zooming in:

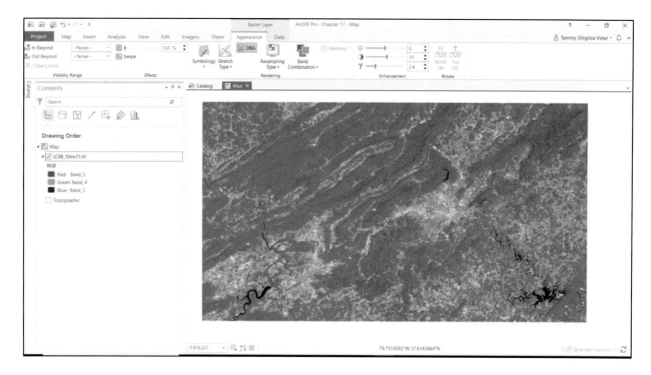

Zoom into Carvin's Cove (see figure below) with DRA enabled. The image is much sharper, especially the boundaries of the water body.

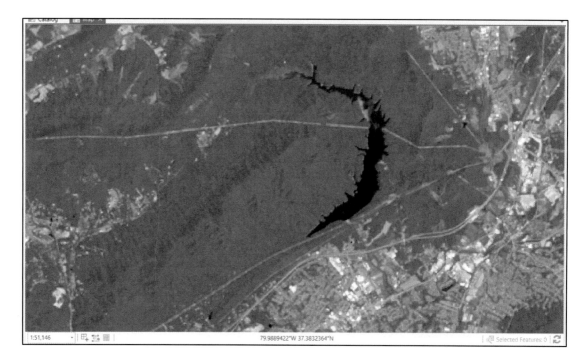

These tools are useful when conducting image classification (covered in subsequent chapters) to help discern different features within the image.

Please be sure that your image enhancement tools (*Gamma, Contrast, Brightness*) are set back to their original values before proceeding with the next section.

Histograms

As stated in the introduction, histograms plot the frequencies of brightness values (the digital numbers [DNs], plotted along the x-axis) against the number of pixels associated with each value (y-axis). The shape of a histogram is determined by the features represented in the image, and their brightness values.

Changing the *Stretch Type*, changes the histogram and how the image appears in the map viewer. Go to the *Raster Layer > Appearance* tab. Select *Stretch Type* (the icon with the histogram on it).

A list of *Stretch Types* is provided. We will review each enhancement tool briefly and then discuss each tool in more detail.

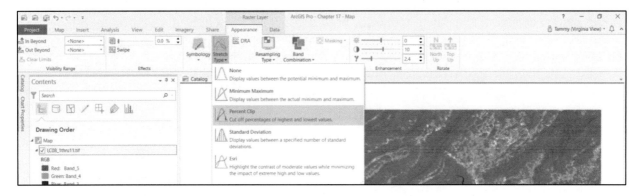

- *Percent Clip* is highlighted because it is the default. Percent Clip eliminates the minimum and maximum values ends of a histogram based on a percent. These values can be changed.
- *None* displays all potential values, for a 16-bit image this is between 0 and 65,536.
- *Minimum-Maximum* displays values between the actual minimum and maximum values or values that you can independently set.
- *Standard Deviations* displays values between a chosen number of standard deviations.
- ESRI is a software defined Histogram.

Let's start by looking at the *Percent Clip* options. Go to *Symbology* and scroll down until *Stretch type* is visible:

Here it shows the minimum and maximum ends of the *Histogram* were clipped by 0.250. These values can be changed. Change it to 5.0 for both ends. There is a substantial change in in the map viewer, especially around the urban areas. The *Statistics* have not changed from the original setting because it is based on the dataset values (remember this is dynamic enhancement).

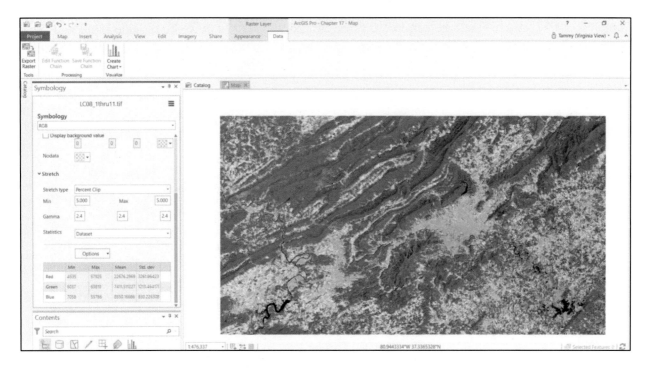

To change that, click on the down arrow at the end of the line containing the word dataset:

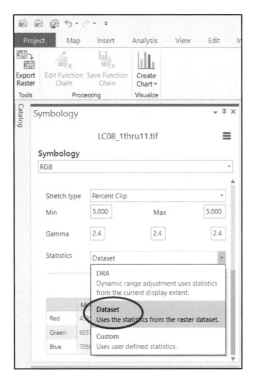

Here the basis of *Statistics* can be changed. *DRA* will base statistics from the display in the map viewer.

Using the *Custom* option under *Statistics,* the Histogram can be equalized across all bands with DNs over the entire range of values. To change this, click inside the box of the values needing changed. Remember, that a 16-bit image has values from 0 to 65,536. In this image, the NIR band (Band 5) only has values from 4545 through 57925. Should these be changed to 0 and 65,536? That discussion is beyond the scope of this chapter because the range of values needed for any one specific band is contingent on the project for which the image is being analyzed.

Notice under *Stretch* type, *Gamma* is also present. All of the settings for different forms of radiometric enhancement can be changed. These options do not need to be changed independently of each other. So, after adjusting settings under *Percent Clip*, *Brightness*, *Contrast* and *Gamma* can also be adjusted.

Change the *Stretch* type to see how this modification changes the image. Change to *Minimum Maximum*. How has the image and *Symbology* window changed? *(The Minimum and Maximum Percent* boxes are gone)*. This option provides the ability to perform a contrast stretch separately for each band by choosing *Custom* under *Statistics* and adjust the minimum and maximum values by entering a specific value into each box for each band.

Explore the various methods of histogram stretch with different band combinations. Which method is best will depend on the purpose of the project and likely a decision the analyst makes at the time of the project. The goal of this chapter, and subsequent chapters, is to provide a summary of the methods and techniques available in ArcGIS® Pro and not to advise on which techniques to use.

Density Slicing

A final radiometric enhancement method is *density slicing*. However, density slicing is not an available option on a composite image. *Density slicing* can only be performed on each individual band image in ArcGIS® Pro. Density slicing differs from contrast stretch in that it assigns colors to specific brightness values. The colors do not add additional information, but simply permit the analyst to make sharper distinctions between brightness classes in the image. This technique is beyond the scope of this chapter.

Viewing and Exporting a Histogram

To view the actual histogram associated with a specific band, highlight the raster layer (the composite image) in *Contents*. Click on the *Raster Layer* tab and then *Data*. Select *Create Chart – Histogram* (currently *Histogram* is the only option under *Create Chart*).

Another window opens under the map viewer:

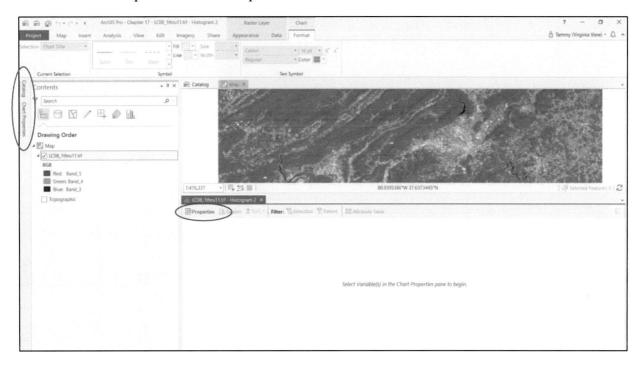

Select the *Properties* tab at the top of this new window and another window opens to the left – *Chart Properties*.

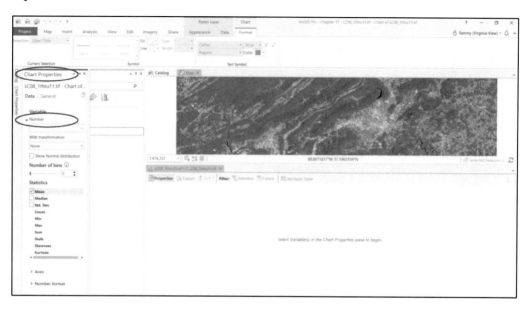

Under *Chart Properties*, click on the drop down arrow on the *Number* line and select the band – note the only bands available are those bands being displayed – remember we displayed bands 5-4-3.

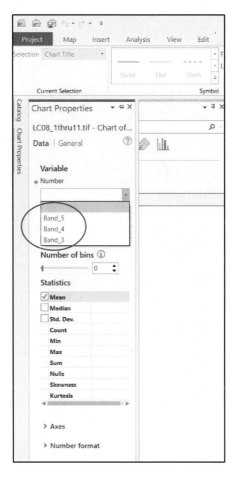

As soon as a Band number is selected – we chose *Band_5*, the histogram appears in the *Chart* window. The red line on the *Histogram* is the mean line – because *Mean* is the only Statistic checked in the *Chart Properties* window.

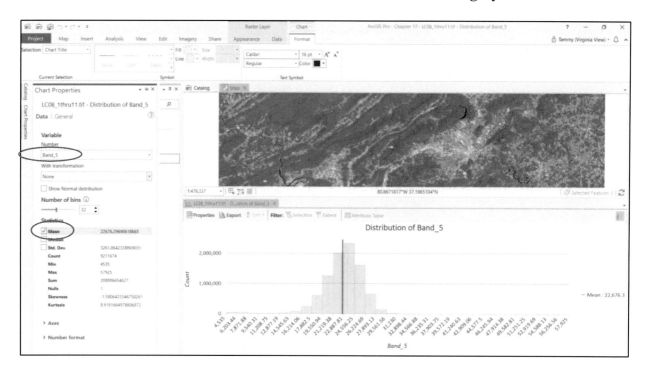

Choose the other two statistics – *Median* and *Standard Deviation*.

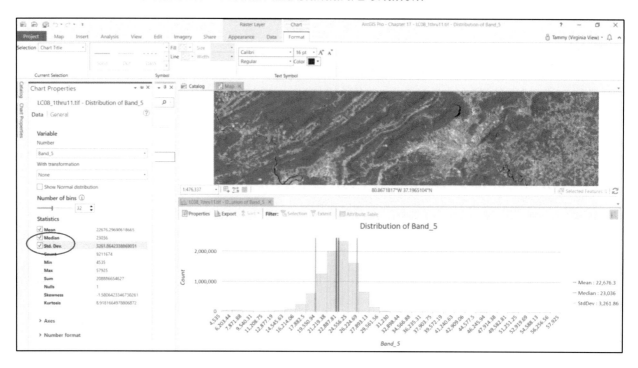

Expand the arrows next to *Axes* and *Number Format* – these two areas can be changed but these just change the formatting of the *Histogram*.

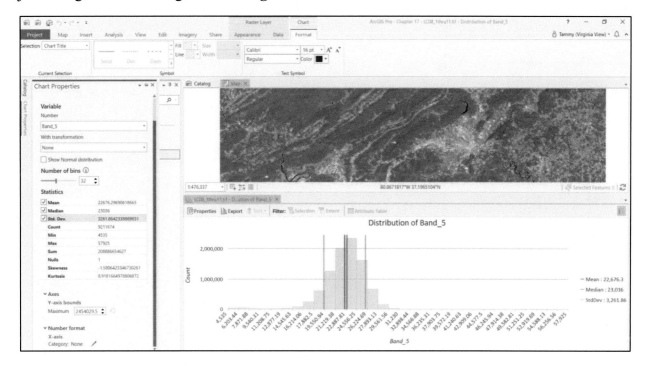

Selecting the *General* tab at the top of the *Chart Properties* windows provides additional options to display the *Histogram*:

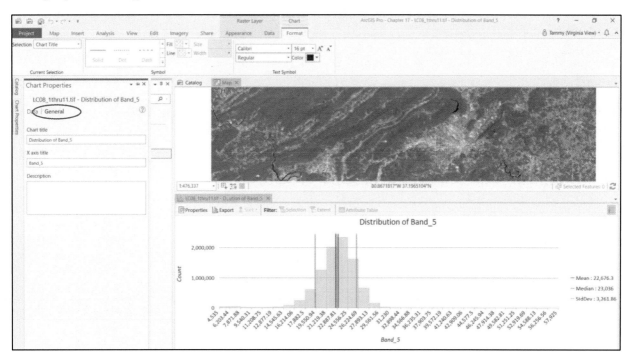

Now change the Band number to Band_3:

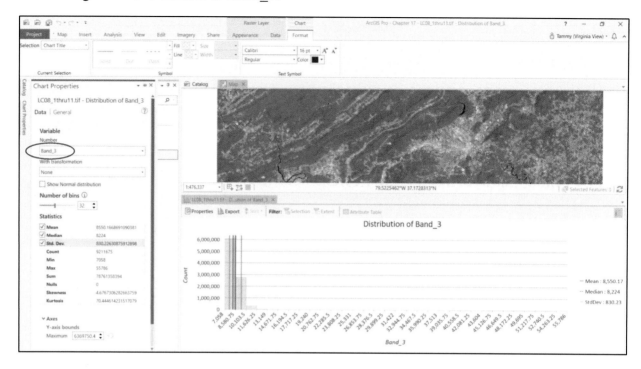

The Histogram now looks very different. Recall the discussion about *Band Combinations* from Chapter 16? Chapter 16 also provided an overview of the spectral properties of features on the Earth's surface. Remember that each feature on the Earth's surface reflects, absorbs and re-emits different types and values of electromagnetic radiation in different ways. These features often have unique spectral signatures. The variation in histograms between the different Landsat Bands demonstrates these spectral variations.

If a histogram is needed for a figure in a non-GIS format, click on *Export* in the *Chart* window.

This ends the chapter on Radiometric Image Enhancement. We will discuss further Image Enhancement techniques in the next two chapters – Spatial Enhancement (Chapter 18) and Spectral Enhancement (Chapter 19). Spatial Enhancement enhances images based on the values of individual and neighboring pixels. Spectral Enhancement transforms the values of each pixel on a multiband basis, e.g., Band Ratios, Vegetation Indices, etc.

Image Enhancement: An Introduction

As a reminder from *Chapter 17: Radiometric Enhancement of Landsat 8 Imagery* -- image enhancement denotes the processing of remotely sensed imagery to adjust brightness values (displayed as digital numbers [DN]). This improves the image's visual qualities for a specific purpose. Brightness values of individual pixels are changed to improved color balance, brightness, contrast between pixels, or other elements associated with image display.

While radiometric (Chapter 17) and spectral enhancement (Chapter 19) operate on each pixel individually, spatial enhancement deals largely with spatial frequency and modifies the pixel's brightness values based on the values of neighboring pixels.

This chapter focuses on spatial enhancement and demonstrates two different processes for spatial enhancement. The first process is a *dynamic process* – it changes the image within the viewer itself, but does not change the original file. The second process uses tools in the ArcGIS® Pro toolbox and creates a new permanent image file. The brightness values of this new file are modified by the specific enhancement method.

This chapter provides a very basic discussion of image enhancement techniques. There is an array of information associated with image enhancement available online that can provide a more thorough discussion of these techniques, including:

- Faust (date unknown) Georgia Institute of Technology: http://knightlab.org/rscc/legacy/RSCC_Spatial_Enhancement.pdf
- Natural Resources Canada. Image Enhancement: https://www.nrcan.gc.ca/earth-sciences/geomatics/satellite-imagery-air-photos/satellite-imagery-products/educational-resources/9389

Dynamic Spatial Enhancement

Open a new map project, save it, and add the image we created in the chapter on *sub-setting a Landsat 8 image*, the image clipped to the spatial extent of the window – the image display shows Roanoke, Blacksburg, and Smith Mountain Lake. Go ahead and set the band combinations as color infrared image. Be sure that the workspaces are set to the appropriate project file folder.

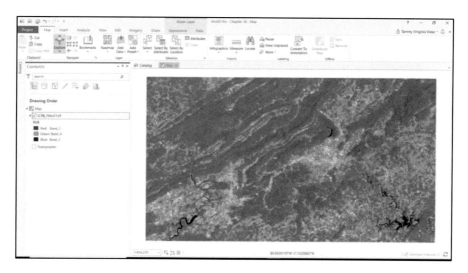

Go to the *Raster Layer* menu and select the *Appearance* tab.

Select *Resampling Type* and click on the down arrow. A number of different options are displayed. Again, with spatial enhancement, individual pixel values are changed using various tools based on neighboring pixel values. How do these values change? The changes are contingent on the method you select. When using any of these techniques, keep in mind that the change in the image display may not be apparent when zoomed out. For an example of resampling, zoom into the City of Roanoke, specifically to the airport area. Next, let's apply some of the resampling tools, including *nearest neighbor*, *bilinear*, and *cubic*.

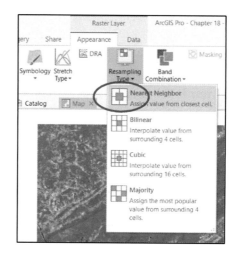

Nearest neighbor – the pixel is assigned the value of the cell closest to it. Looking at the dropdown list, Nearest Neighbor is highlighted because Nearest Neighbor is the one already used within the image. Check the layer's properties – go to *Properties > Source > Raster Information*. This shows that the method used for display is *resampling Nearest Neighbor*.

Go back to the *Raster Layer* menu and select *Appearance* and click on *Bilinear*. This technique creates a smooth-looking result, because it averages the brightness values of pixels from the 4 neighboring cells. Again, this is a dynamic method – it just changes the display in the viewer.

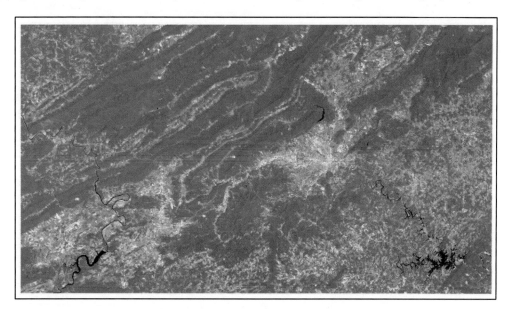

Can you see a difference? Zoom into the Airport area in the City of Roanoke:

Before bilinear   After bilinear

Notice in the *Before* image (native image), the outlines of the individual cells are visible, as a jagged edge (from the corners of the pixels) but in the *After* image (after bilinear enhancement), the runways (and nearby highway) now appear to be a straight line (because the bilinear algorithm has blended the pixel corners into a straight edge).

Remember, these processes are dynamic. These enhancement techniques only change the image display in the viewer, not the underlying properties of the image (this technique does not actually change the pixel values). Checking the *Properties > Source > Raster Information* dialog box, it still shows nearest neighbor:

Now, go back to *Raster Layer > Appearance* and select *Cubic* – which (according to the information displayed above, when the mouse cursor was hovered on the information) uses the surrounding 16 cells.

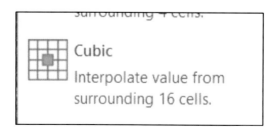

It creates a sharper-looking airport area.

Select *Majority*. This is not a good resampling method for the airport area, because this option chooses the most frequent value from the surrounding 4 cells and "smooths the image". So, if definitive boundaries are needed for the analysis, this is *not* the one to use (see figure below).

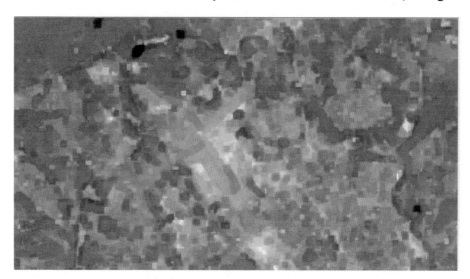

If more specific definitions are required for the methods, see *ArcGIS help:*

http://pro.arcgis.com/en/pro-app/help/data/imagery/resample-function.htm.

The method chosen to enhance the image will depend on the purpose of the project.

Reset the image to the default – *Nearest Neighbor*. We are now going to demonstrate how to use the resampling using tools in the Toolbox.

Spatial Enhancement Using Spatial Analyst Tools

Convolution Filtering

The *Convolution filtering* is a process that averages small sets of neighboring pixels across an image. This filtering changes the spatial frequency characteristics of an image. A *convolution kernel* is a matrix of numbers that assigns a weight to each cell within the matrix (choosing the kernel defines the neighborhood size.). As the kernel moves across the image, the values in each neighborhood are multiplied by the weights, then averaged. The resulting value is then assigned to the center pixel, and the kernel moves on to the next neighborhood. As a reminder - the filtering options in this section creates a permanent file after the tool runs, which means a new file is created with new properties.

Click on the *Analysis* tab and click on *Tools* to open the *Geoprocessing* window:

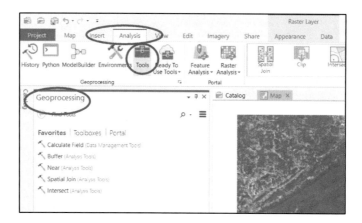

Under *Search*, use the word *Filter* (within the parenthesis for the first two filters are the words *Spatial Analyst Tools* – spatial analyst tools are used to perform geoprocessing on raster files.)

Select the first one option– *Filter*:

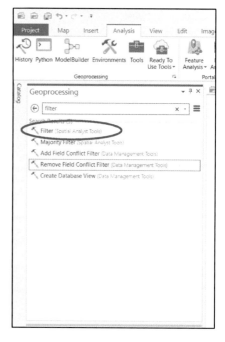

The tool opens. We are going to discuss options under *Filter type*.

Now, click on the down arrow at the end of the *Filter Type* line -- two options are present:

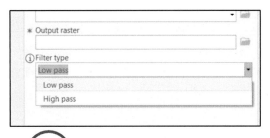

Click on the information icon: (i). Help is displayed.

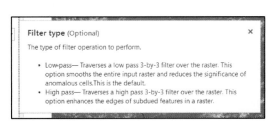

A low pass filter smooths edges and ***High pass*** filter enhances edges. Experiment and explore both methods and then we will compare them.

Input raster is the composite image (click on the down arrow at the end of the row, the image is listed, click on the image name and the field populates. Name the *Output Raster*. In this example, we named the output raster Filter_low (use a name that allows easy determination as to which process was used to create the new image). Click on *Run* in the lower right.

Then do the same for *High Pass*. The only inputs that need to be changed is the name of the new file and the *Filter type* (note -- additional parameters can be changed by clicking on the *Environments* tab [next to the word *Parameters*], but that is beyond the scope of this book). We will examine the images side by side after both have finished processing.

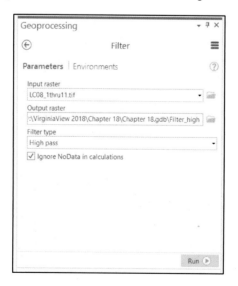

After running the tool, twice, two new files are listed in the *Contents* window and two new images posted to the viewer.

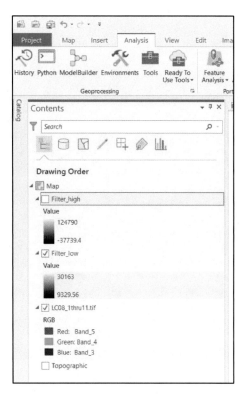

In the viewer window. Low pass results are smoothing of the image. Within the low pass image, what is clearly visible?

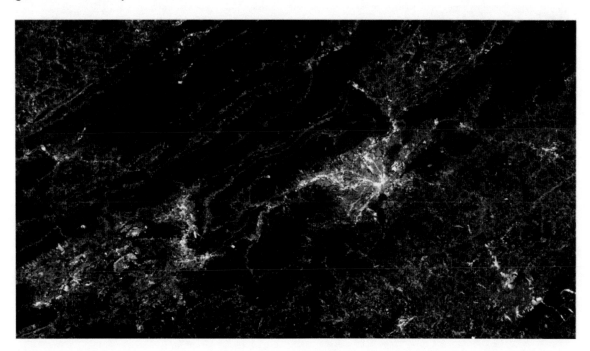

On the High pass image, only certain features are enhanced the image (yellow circles). Let's zoom in to these areas.

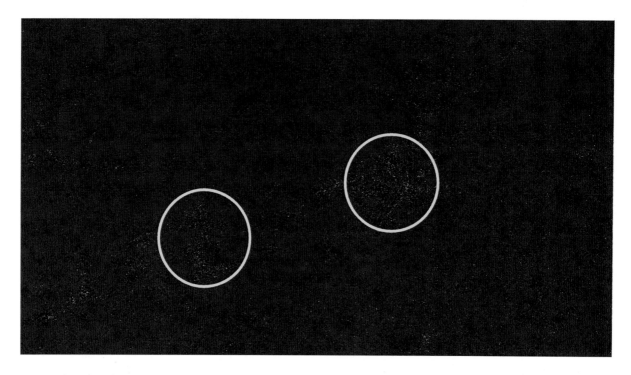

Remember, high pass enhances edges. What edges are now visible?

In the City of Roanoke – roads, the airport runways, some buildings are visible.

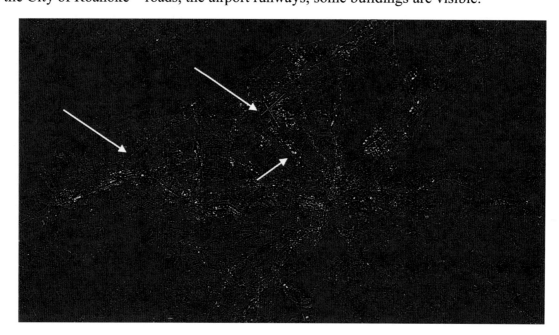

From a broader view of the New River Valley, we can discern populated areas (town of Blacksburg in upper right, town of Christiansburg in middle, city of Radford in the west and the New River on the left side).

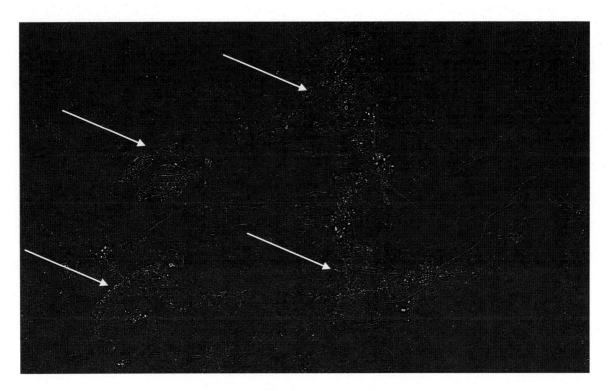

This specific tool – *Filter*, only has these two options for spatial enhancement. Again, which filter is appropriate for the project depends on the purpose of the project.

Now, we will use a second tool - *Focal Statistics*.

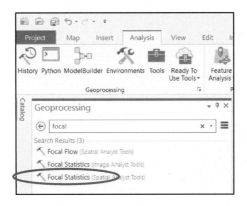

With the *Focal Statistics* tool, two items are the same the *Input raster* and naming the *Output raster* file. But with this tool, more decisions are made:

The first two decisions regard the neighborhood – those cells that are going to affect the new value of each cell in the new image.

1st decision -- the shape of the neighborhood. The shape does not have to be a rectangle!

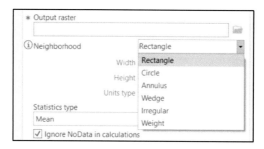

We will run examples of these, let's discuss other decisions first.

The 2nd decision is how big to make the neighborhood. The neighborhood means – how many pixels around a specific pixel is used to recalculate that pixel's new value. The figure below shows that the number of pixels used to generate the filter is 3x3. This is the default setting.

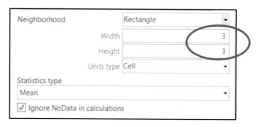

The 3rd and final decision is which statistic to use. When clicking on the *Statistic type* line:

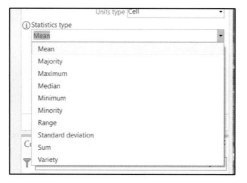

The information icon explains what each statistic in the list means. So, average (mean) can be used or another statistic type. Again, the specific choice is based on the project's purpose.

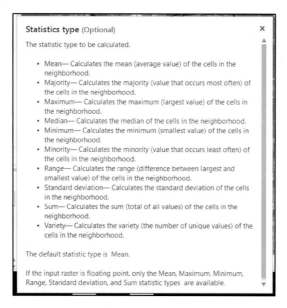

Now let's run a few filters. Once we have run the tool a few times, we will compare the different images. Start with the default – *Rectangle, 3x3, Mean*. Note again, that we have named the *Output raster* such that we know which method was used.

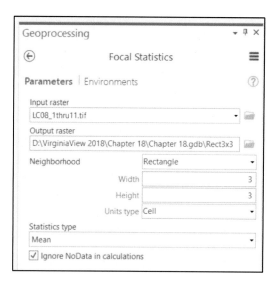

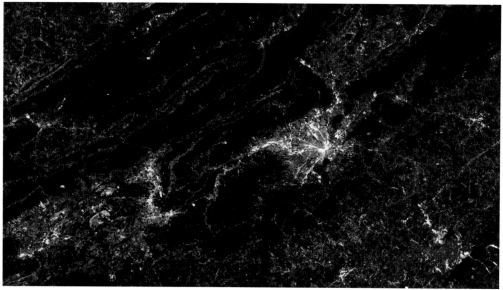

Next try – *Rectangle, 5x5, Mean*:

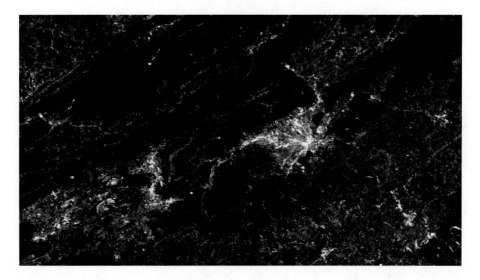

After that, try *Rectangle, 9x9, Median*: Please note that the larger the neighborhood, the longer the tool takes to process.

And, the results show more smoothing – remember, a 9x9 neighborhood to calculate the new value means each value is more like other values.

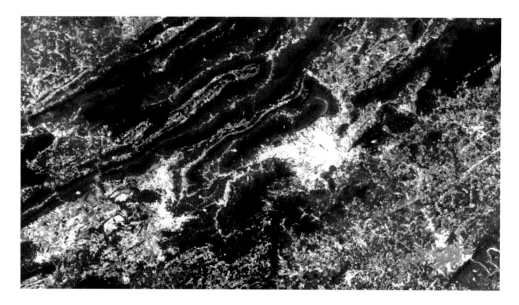

Now try Circle. Settings: *Circle, 6, Median*

We are not generating a subset as a circle from our clipped image. The filtering neighborhood is circular -- a set radius out from the middle pixel (the pixel for which the new value is calculated). As a reminder, the neighborhood moves across the image, changing the values of each pixel based on the neighborhood parameters.

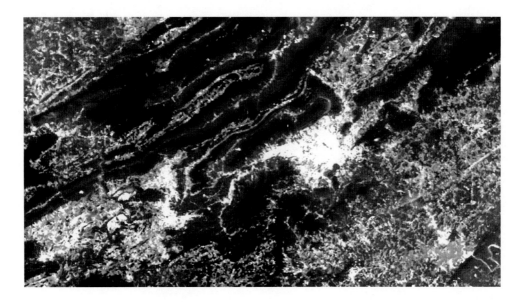

We will not do any additional examples now, so, continue to explore these options on your own.

A note on using two other methods - *Weight* and *Irregular*, which provides the *convolution kernel* options (see figure below, *convolution* was discussed above under dynamic processing). A .txt file, with the weights assigned, is required to use this function. But, using this tool for convolution provides options beyond the dynamic enhancement and allows generation of a new image.

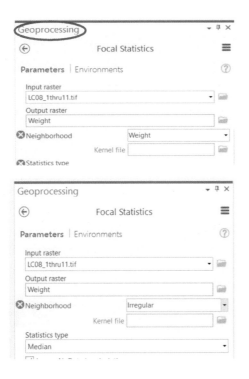

- Irregular Kernel file
  A custom neighborhood with specifications set by a user-defined file.
- Weight Kernel file

Now that the tool has run using several different parameters – do you see any differences between the images?   Why is the image sharper for the 5x5 rectangular neighborhood than the others? If a 3x3 neighborhood was used, would the image be sharper than the 5x5? Why would the rectangular produce sharper images compared to using a circular neighborhood?

Look at the new files in *Contents*. The range of Digital Numbers (DNs) is different for each result. Why? Recall, the values are being changed and the greater the number of pixels used as the neighborhood, the smaller the range of values.

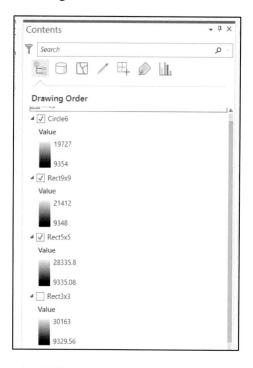

To do a visual examination on the differences in the viewer video, use the *Swipe* tool (under *Raster Layer> Appearance*).

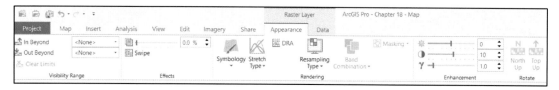

In the following image, *Circle 6* is unchecked so the image on display (on top) is *Rect9x9*. For *Swipe*, highlight the image *Rect9x9*. Then click on *Swipe* and click anywhere on the image in the viewer. When the double arrow turns on, hold the mouse button down and the top image swipes, so the next image (turned on in *Contents*) is seen (for the image below this is *Rect5x5*).

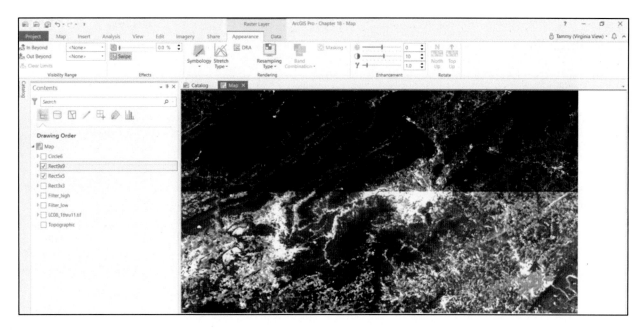

As seen on the image above, the 5x5 neighborhood is much more defined than the 9x9 neighborhood.

Go ahead and continue to try different methods, comparing the actual new images using *Swipe* and comparing the *Digital Numbers* in the *Contents*.

A composite image was used to complete the spatial enhancement, but single bands can also be used. Again, these can be explored on your own. Ultimately, the choice of methods is a decision dependent upon which is best for the specific project.

For a complete list of tools available under *Spatial Analyst:* see http://pro.arcgis.com/en/pro-app/tool-reference/spatial-analyst/complete-listing-of-spatial-analyst-tools.htm

Let's now proceed to the final image enhancement chapter – Chapter 19 *Spectral Enhancement of Landsat 8 Imagery.*

Introduction

As noted in the previous two chapters, image enhancement denotes processing of remotely sensed imagery to adjust brightness values (displayed as digital numbers [DNs]). This modification can improve the image's visual qualities for a specific purpose. Brightness values of individual pixels improve qualities such as color balance, brightness, contrast between pixels, or other qualities.

The prior two chapters covered radiometric enhancement (Chapter 17) and spatial enhancement (Chapter 18). Both processes can occur on a composite image or single band images.

Spectral enhancement is the process of refining new spectral data from available bands. This process relies on the spectral signatures of individual features on the Earth's surface. Spectral signatures are the distinctive qualities that denote the range of different features' reflected radiation wavelengths collected by satellite sensors. For example, spectral signatures can distinguish man-made objects from different types of vegetation. (For more information spectral signatures – see Campbell and Wynne (6th ed. forthcoming) or Keranen and Kolvoord, 2013).

New data are created on a pixel-by-pixel basis. Spectral enhancement applies an operation (e.g., subtraction, division) to corresponding pixels between two or more bands and creates a new image which may enhance features on the original image. This technique can be used to:

- Extract new bands of data that are more easily interpreted by the eye;
- Diminish redundancy in a multi-spectral dataset by merging bands of data that convey similar information (principal component analysis);
- Display a wider variety of data in the visible spectrum (R, G, B).

The most commonly used spectral enhancement techniques are:

- ***Spectral Ratios and Indices*** - Performs band ratios that are commonly used in vegetation and geologic studies;
- ***Principal Components Analysis (PCA)*** - Compresses redundant data values into fewer bands which are often more concise, more powerful. PCA provides representations of the original source data. It is often used to support image extraction, classification, and change detection analysis (PCA instructions are not provided in this book);
- ***Tasseled Cap*** – Transforms and rotates the data structure axes to optimize data display for vegetation studies (Tasseled Cap transformation instructions are not provided in this book).

Examples of band ratios and vegetation indices are provided in this text. Other techniques (including PCA and Tassled Cap) are beyond the scope of this book. The differences between image enhancement techniques are summarized accordingly:

- **Radiometric Enhancement** - Enhances images based on the values of individual pixels.
- **Spatial Enhancement** - Enhances images based on the values of individual and neighboring pixels.

- **Spectral Enhancement** - Enhances images by transforming the values of each pixel on a multi-band basis (within ArcGIS® Pro, this technique can used with single band or multi-band images).

Band Ratios process two or more different bands to enhance specific spectral properties. Processing includes addition, subtraction, division, etc. We will demonstrate two of these band ratios[1]:

- **5/4 Ratio - (NIR/Red)** - enhances the presence of vegetation. The brighter the tones, the denser the vegetation.
- **4 /7 Ratio - (Red/MIR)** – To see differences in water turbidity.

Indices are based more complicated mathematical equations (usually compound equations). To obtain additional information associated with common indices for Landsat Sensors, refer to:

https://landsat.usgs.gov/sites/default/files/documents/si_product_guide.pdf.

We will demonstrate one of these indices – *Normalized Difference Vegetation Index (NDVI)*. Once this process is demonstrated, users of this book will be able to repeat these processes for other indices. A discussion of NDVI is provided in more detail below.

There are at least 25 ratios in common use, and new ratios are developed to support emerging applications. An extremely important thing to remember is that a ratio is based on a region of the electromagnetic spectrum (EMS), not the band number. As discussed previously, the region of the EMS covered by a specific band often varies from sensor to sensor. For example, Landsat 5 - Band 1 covers a different slice of the EMS than Landsat 8 - Band 1 and Sentinel 2 - Band 1. Metadata for a specific sensor provides information on which band corresponds to which segment of the electromagnetic spectrum. The chart below provides information as a side-by-side comparison of Landsat TM, ETM+ and OLI, and Sentinel.

---

[1] For more information on Band Ratios, see https://erdas.wordpress.com/2007/12/30/4-band-ratios/

Band Number	Thematic Mapper (TM) - Landsat 4 & 5 Thematic Mapper Plus (ETM+) - Landsat 7	Operational Land Imagers (OLI) & Thermal Infrared Sensor (TIRS) – Landsat 8	Sentinel 2
1	0.45- 0.52 μm – blue-green	0.43 - 0.45 μm – coastal aerosol	0.443
2	0.52 – 0.61 μm - green	0.45 - 0.51 μm - blue	0.490 blue
3	0.63 – 0.69 μm - red	0.53 - 0.59 μm - green	0.560 green
4	0.76 – 0.90 μm - NIR	0.64 - 0.67 μm - red	0.665 red
5	1.55 – 1.75 μm - SWIR	0.85 - 0.88 μm - NIR	0.705
6	10.40 – 12.50 μm – thermal	1.57 - 1.65 μm - SWIR 1	0.740
7	2.08 – 2.35 μm - SWIR	2.11 - 2.29 μm - SWIR 2	0.783
8	0.52 – 0.90 μm Panchromatic (ETM+ only)	0.50 - 0.68 μm - Panchromatic	8 - 0.842 NIR
			8a – 0.865 NIR
9		1.36 - 1.38 μm - Cirrus	0.943
10	NONE	10.60 - 11.19 μm - TIRS 1	1.375
11		11.50 - 12.51 μm – TIRS 2	1.610
12	NONE	NONE	2.910

Creating Band Indices

We will explore some band indices. Open a new blank map project in ArcGIS® Pro and add the composite image used in the last two chapters. Be sure that the project workspaces are set. For ratios based upon use of two bands, there are two methods for creating simple indices.

- The first method uses the *Imagery* tab > *Raster Functions*.
- The second method is accessed from the *Geoprocessing/Spatial Analyst/Math* tools (these tools include divide, plus, square, square root, etc.)

Differences exist between the two methods. One method creates a permanent file, while the other method creates a file that can only be used in the current map project. One method uses a multi-spectral image, and the other method uses individual bands. We will discuss both methods.

Using Raster Functions for Band Ratios

Under the *Imagery* tab, find *Raster Functions*.

Click on the down arrow to find two choices – *Raster Functions* and *History*:

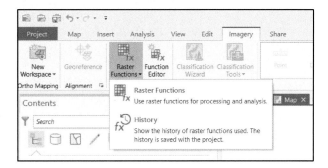

Select *Raster Functions* and a pick-list of functions is provided (many are also available under *Geoprocessing*). Each category expands to show the available tools. Click on *Math* to expand:

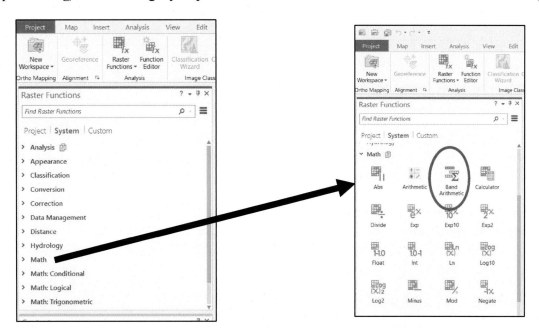

As seen in the figure above, individual *Math* tools are named *Divide*, *Minus*, etc. but there is also a tool called *Band Arithmetic* (red oval above). The individual tools - divide, minus, etc. - are used with single band images. *Band Arithmetic* is used for multiband images.

Click on *Band Arithmetic*. The default *Method* is *NDVI* (which we will discuss later).

Click on the down arrow at the end of the *Method*'s line, a list of available ratios is presented. For simple band ratios, select *User Defined*.

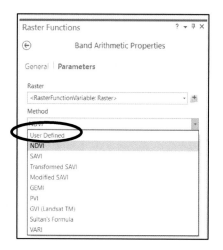

Now we will create a **5 /4 Ratio - (NIR/Red)** to enhance the presence of vegetation.

Referring to the next figure, under the *Parameters* tab, select the composite image as the *Raster*. Under *Band Indexes*, enter the equation (B5/B4) (red oval) – be sure to include the parentheses. Click on *General* (green oval) and name the file (black box) – here we spelled out the word divide because special characters cannot be used when naming files. Additional details can be added under description – this would include metadata to provide information on the process. Then click on *Create new layer* (red box). Once the new layer is complete, a green message displays (black oval) – *Band Arithmetic applied successfully*.

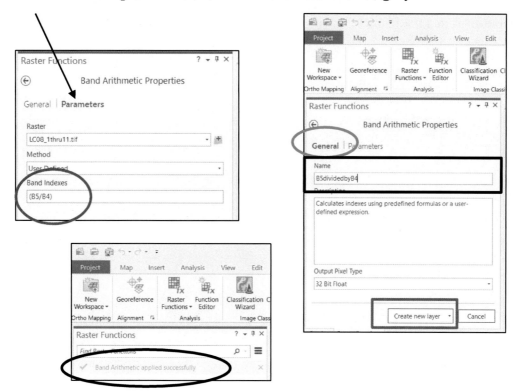

A new image layer is listed in *Contents* and displays in the map viewer. The brighter tones indicate the denser vegetation. The symbology in *Contents* shows the higher the value as the lighter color and the lower value as the darker color.

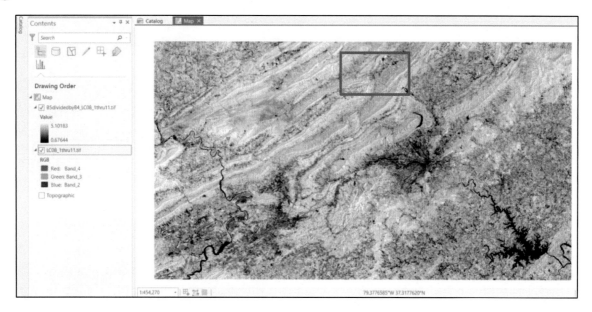

Can we confirm that the results showing brighter are denser vegetation? Use *Swipe* to compare the new image to the natural color composite.

The image on the top left is zoomed into the area in the red box (figure above). It contains forest and agricultural areas.

Natural color shows dense forest and the fields with vegetative growth. Both land covers are bright white.

When zoomed-in to the City of Roanoke (bottom left image), the roads and river in Roanoke appear very dark. No vegetation is present in the dark areas.

Please note – this process creates a new image. However, this new image is present only in the current map project. Once the tool has run successfully, the map project should be saved immediately. Tools in *Raster Functions* create an image useful for this map project only. This image cannot be used in another map project, and if the map project closes without being saved, the image will be lost.

Creating a Permanent Band Ratio Image using Geoprocessing Tools

We will repeat the process using a different method, which will create a new permanent file.

When using the *Geoprocessing* tools option under the *Analysis* tab, ArcGIS® Pro recognizes the pixel values for Landsat Imagery as integers (whole numbers). So, when performing math operations, the results are integers, usually rounded down. Results for band ratios must be real numbers (numbers with decimal points), otherwise our results will also be integers. This means we need to change our image values to floating point values. Go to the *Analysis* tab and select the *Tools*. Under *Find Tools,* type *Float*. Select *Float (Spatial Analyst Tool)*.

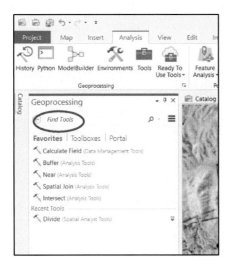 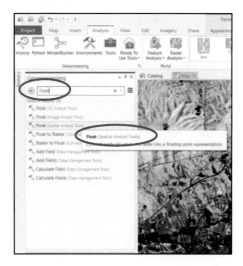

This tool uses the individual bands, not the composite image. So the tool needs to be run twice -- once for Band 5 and once for Band 4. Either add these individual bands to the project or navigate using the file folder at the end of the *Input Raster* line. Then, run the tool, twice, with the inputs shown below. The results will include new image layers in *Contents* and two new images in the map viewer.

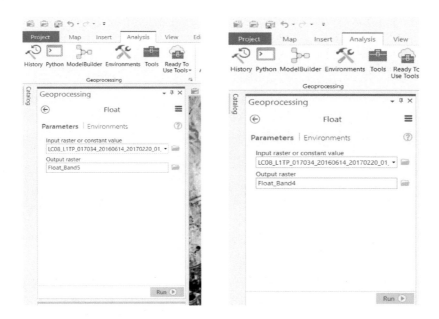

Now search for the *Divide - spatial analyst tool* (figure below on the far left), open it (middle figure below), and input the files as shown (figure below on the far right) – be sure to name the *Output Raster*. Click *Run*.

When the tool finishes, the *Completed successfully* message displays, hover the mouse over the message and a dialog box opens that provides information on the process.

A new imager layer is in the *Contents* and the map viewer, but since we used the original single bands, it is to the full extent of the Landsat scene. Additionally, it appears in *Contents* that the image is not the same as the values have a wider range. But again, this is the full scene and not the subset used in the *Raster Function* process.

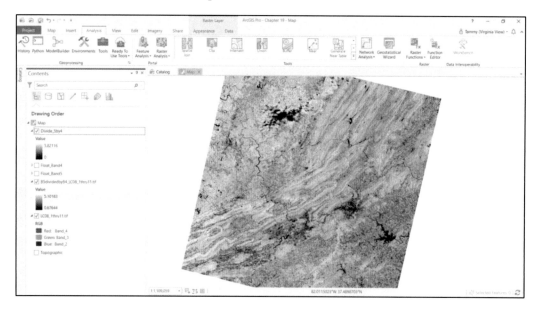

To verify that the results are the same, click on any pixel in the most recent new image. Examine the pixel value. Now click on that exact same pixel in the image created using *Raster Functions*.

The pixel values from both methods used to create the ratio images are the same.

We will generate another ratio image together - **4 / 7 Ratio** - (Red/MIR. This ratio is often used to identify differences in water turbidity. You can use either method outlined above, but if using the *Geoprocessing* tools, don't forget to modify the floating point image for each band. And remember, the *Geoprocessing* tools creates a new permanent file that can be used in other projects.

For demonstrations purposes, we are using the *Raster Functions > Band Arithmetic*:

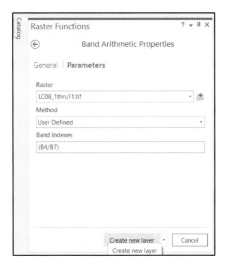

A new image layers is in *Contents* and in the map viewer.

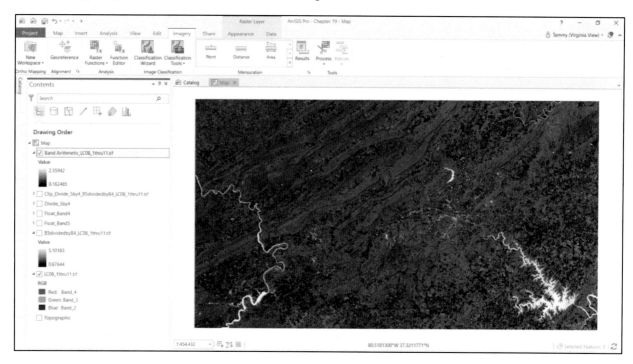

Areas of water are very bright. The New River located to the west (left), Smith Mountain Lake in the southeast and Carvin's Cover in the central portion of the image are very prominent, as are other individual water bodies scattered throughout the image. This band ratio is used to show water turbidity, so let's zoom into Smith Mountain Lake (located in the southeast corner of the image).

While most of the lake is very bright white, dark areas are apparent in the southeast where the lake drains into the river as well as in the northwest branch. Let's compare it to the natural color composite (using the *Swipe* tool).

What do you see? Why would areas leading into the lake be brighter? This river is running through a city and some agricultural areas, so is experiencing runoff, which makes the water more turbid and sediment-filled (so brighter pixel values in the natural color image). What about the dam area (red box)? The areas right above and right below the dam, are more turbid because the water is funneled through the turbines of the dam, thus is flowing more rapidly than the areas farther north and west.

Any simple ratio can be accomplished with these methods. More complex ratios can be accomplished using these tools, but ArcGIS® Pro also has some shortcut tools for some of these and *Raster calculator in Geoprocessing/Spatial Analyst* allows calculation in one step. We will explore these indices in the next section.

Vegetation Indices

Vegetation indices are another form of spectral enhancement. We discuss three (NIR/R, square root (NIR/R), and NDVI).

IR/R was already calculated above (5/4 ratio). For Landsat 8, Band 5 was NIR and Band 4 Red. This ratio can be calculated for other sensors, just make sure NIR and Red bands are used and not the band number. For example, for Landsat 7 ETM+, Band 4 is NIR and Band 3 is red.

Let's look at the square root of IR/R next. Since we already have NIR/Red, all we need to do is run a tool that calculates the square root.

We can do this two different ways, because we have already calculated the IR/R, so we just need to calculate the square root.

Go to Image tab, *Raster Functions > Arithmetic* and select *Square Root* (the tools are in alphabetical order).

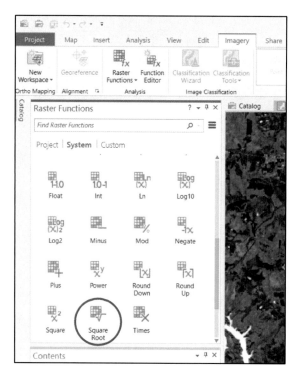

Open the tool. Choose one of the 5/4 ratio images created above. It does not matter which one – we selected the permanent one (the one created second using the *Geoprocessing* tools). Do not forget to name the new layer under *General* tab.

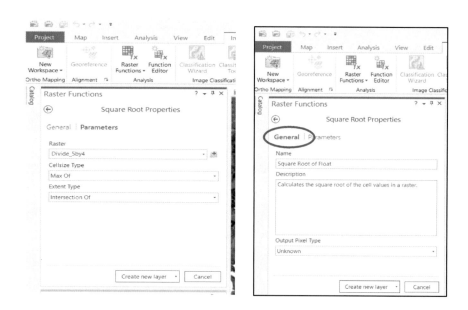

We have generated a new image. Because, we used the one created with the *Geoprocessing* tools, it reaches to the extent of the entire Landsat scene. But since we used *Raster Functions*, the image exists only for this map project.

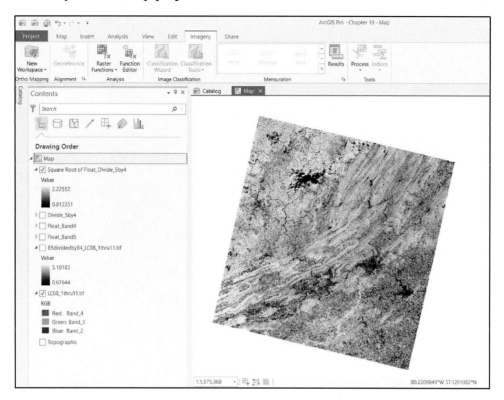

Now, run the process again, but go to *Analysis > Tools* and search for *Square Root (Spatial Analyst Tools)*. This time, we used the B5/B4 ratio image created with *Raster Functions*.

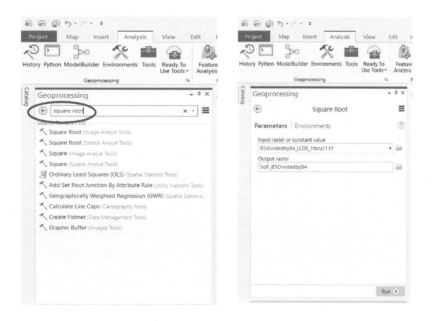

The resulting image displayed is the extent of the subset composite image (figure below)

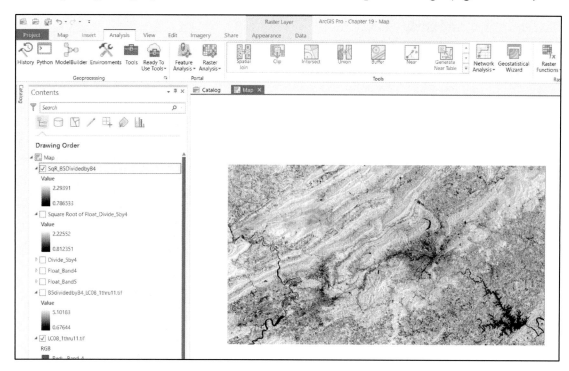

Looking at the *Contents* window, the image values are different. However, remember that they are not displayed at the same extent, so pixel value ranges will vary. Checking the values for any one pixel – they are the same.

The value of a very bright pixel near the airport runways

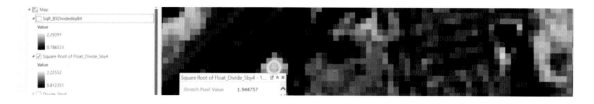

Now, what exactly did this index show? Zoom in on the mountain area around Carvin's Cove (figure below).

Adding the square root function (image above) makes the image a little brighter and provides a sharper distinction between features, as compared to just the B5/B4 ratio (figure below).

Above, we demonstrated a step-by-step method to do generate an enhanced image using an index. It is possible to do this using *Raster Calculator*, in just one equation. (Please note that within this single equation, float can also be calculated, but we will not do that since we already have the float images). Use of the *Raster Calculator* tool requires special attention to building the equation.

Go to the *Analysis* tab, *Tools* and search for the *Raster Calculator (Spatial Analyst Tool)*.

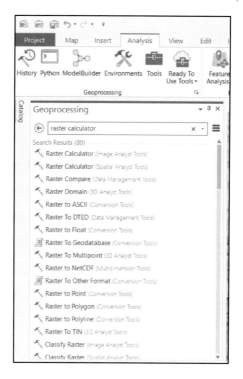

The tool should be populated as follows. Choose the image from the list on the left and the operator from the tools on the right.

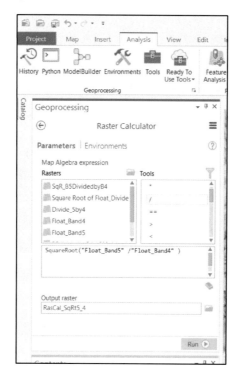

There is absolutely no difference between the two methods, except for the number of steps. Also, keep in mind that the image generated using the *Raster Calculator* is permanent and available for use in other map projects.

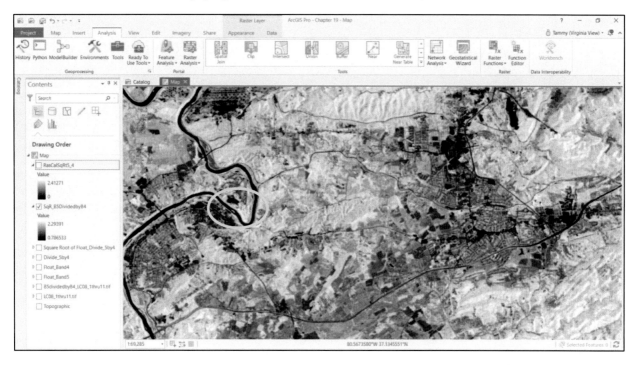

Again, to demonstrate that there is no difference in the results between the two methods, we will look at a pixel value from an island in the New River by Radford, Virginia (see yellow oval in above figure).

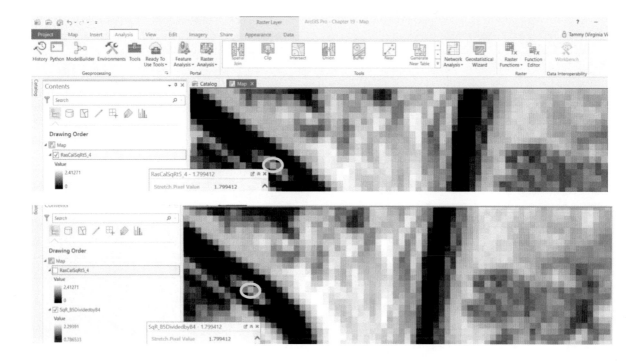

Calculating Normalized Difference Vegetation Index

The Normalized Difference Vegetation Index (NDVI) is a very important vegetative index, and the most commonly one used. Healthy green leaves have a higher reflectivity in the near infrared band, while stressed, dry, or diseased vegetation display lower levels of reflectivity. NDVI can therefore be useful an indicator of vegetation stress. It is a more complex calculation. The formula for NDVI is:

NIR-R/NIR+R   or (for Landsat 8) B5 – B4 / B5 + B4

Open *Raster Calculator*, if the original Landsat bands are not present in the map project, use the file folder and navigate to the computer's folder where they are stored. When selected, they are added as a choice in *Raster Calculator*, but not added to the map project.

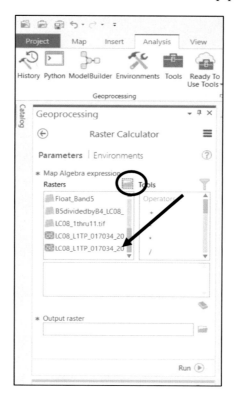

We now need to carefully build the equation. It is important to correctly place parentheses, otherwise the *Raster Calculator* tool will perform the operation step-by-step from left to right. The equation should look like this:

(Band 5 – Band 4)/(Band 5 + Band 4).

Do not type "Band 5", (etc.). Instead, select the specific image bands from the list on the left side of the *Geoprocessing* window.

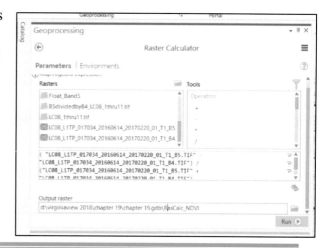

So, manually type an opening parenthesis - *(,* then select *Band 5* from the list (double click on it), then select the *minus sign* from the list on the right, then *select Band 4* from the list, then manually type a closing parenthesis - *).* Then select the division sign */,* then another parenthesis - *(,* then select Band 5, then select the plus sign, then select Band 4, and finally type the last parenthesis - *).*

Once the equation is written correctly, select *Run*.

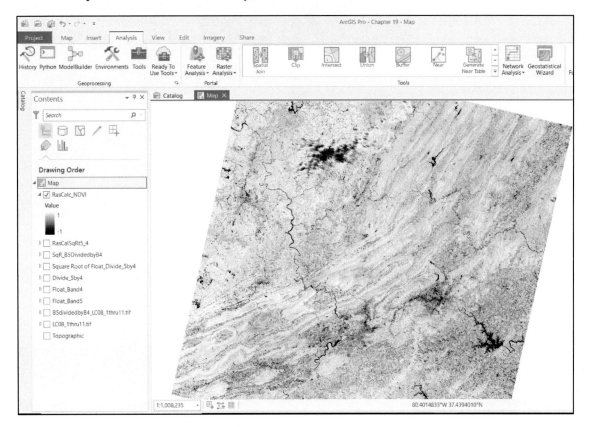

The NDVI result gives pixel values from -1 to +1. The closer to +1, the brighter the pixel. Higher values are associated with more vigorous (healthier) vegetation.

BUT-- guess what? There is an easier and much simpler way to generate an NDVI image in ArcGIS® Pro! But there is a catch -- the NDVI image created from two other options creates a new image that is only available in the current map project (*Raster Calculator* provides a permanent image).

The NDVI Short Cut in ArcGIS® Pro

Turn on the original *sub-set* composite image, then highlight it to enable the *Imagery* tab. Find at the last icon on the right – *Indices*. Select by clicking on the down arrow.

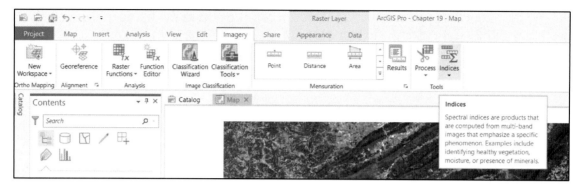

A list of a number of common indices are present, including *NDVI*.

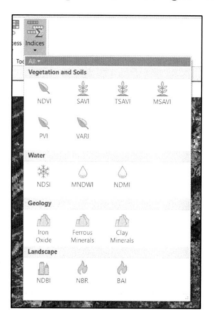

Select *NDVI*.

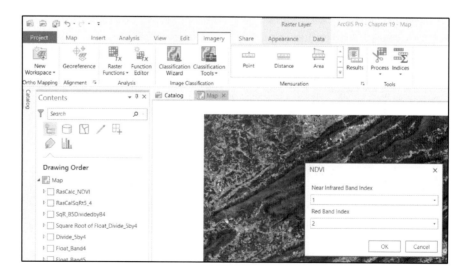

Enter the appropriate band number for Near Infrared and Red, for our 11 band composite Landsat 8 image – NIR is Band 5 and red is Band 4. Then select *OK*.

The results are shown in the figure below. The *Raster Calculator* generated image values that range from -1 to +1. Using the *Indices* tool, a different range of values were provided. What is the difference? Remember, the first NDVI image was created with the entire extent of the scene, this one was created from the sub-set multi-band image.

Additionally, the image created with this *Indices* tool is only available for use in this map project. So, quick, save the project so the image is not lost!

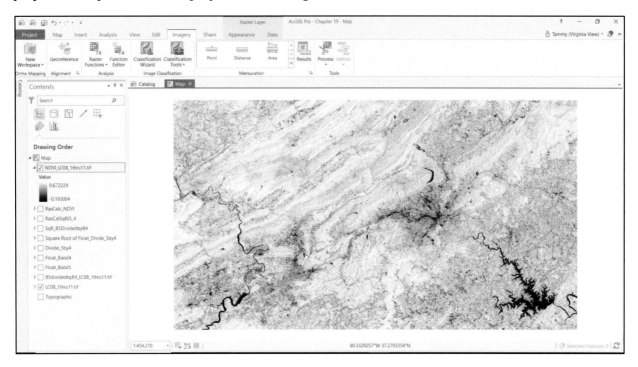

There is an additional option to generate NDVI -- *Raster Functions* (do you remember how to find it?). When you use the *Raster Functions* option, the *Raster* input is the composite image. From the dropdown arrows, select the appropriate band. Be careful, this tool has the visible red band as the first input. Be sure to check *Scientific Output* (red oval) - this option must be selected to get a real number result.

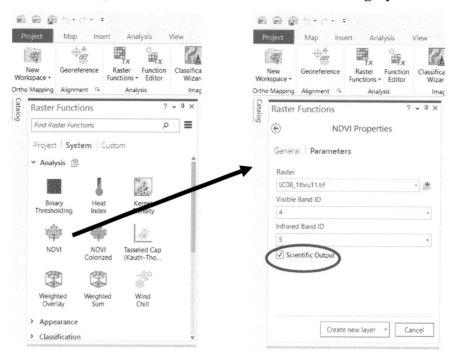

This process produces the exact same results as the *Indices* method and the *Raster Calculator* method.

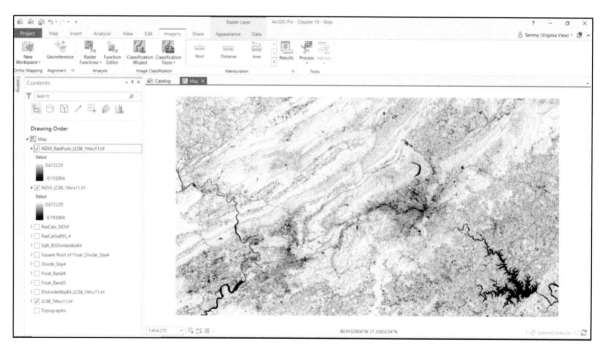

This is verified by comparing a pixel value for a selected pixel from each of the 3 methods (in the example below, an agricultural pixel is used for comparison).

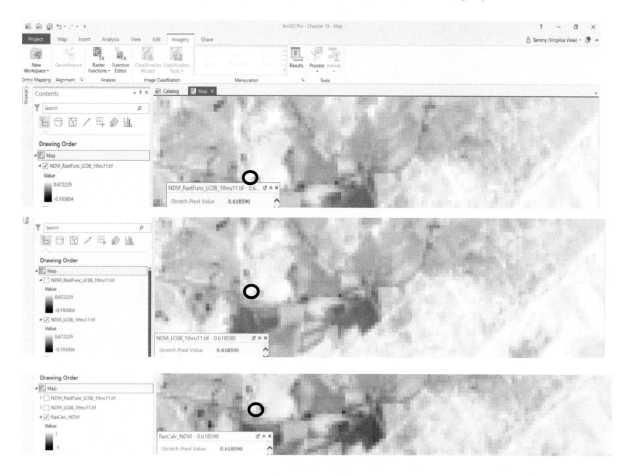

And a second comparison of pixel values using the 3 methods – of a water pixel in Smith Mountain Lake (figure below).

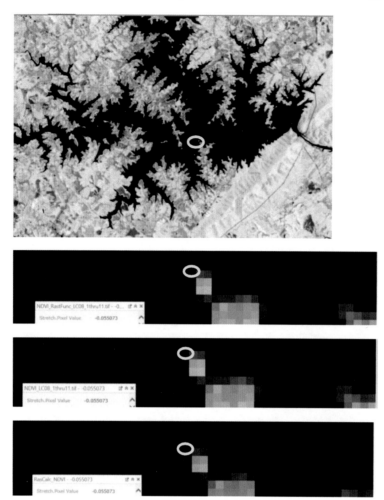

There is one additional method, but we do not recommend it. Notice that under *Raster Functions*, a *NDVI Colorized* option is available. Although ArcGIS® Pro help states *Scientific Output* is available (http://pro.arcgis.com/en/pro-app/help/data/imagery/ndvi-colorized-function.htm), using this method, the *Scientific Output* is not an available option at present.

Go back to *Raster Functions*, and open the *NDVI Colorized* tool. We will show the results from running this tool here. Please feel free to run the tool also, but then delete the results.

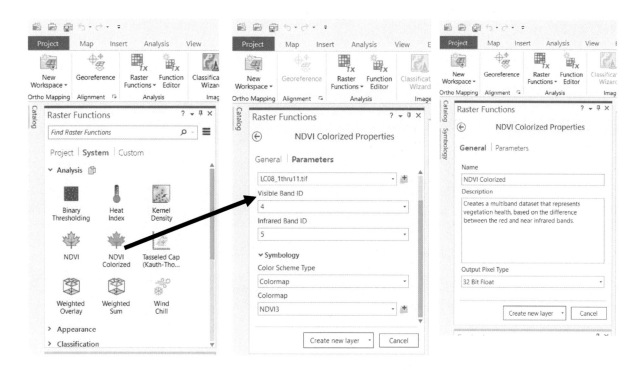

The figure below shows the results with colorized pixels and no *Scientific Output*. The image in the map viewer is colorized, but the pixel values in the *Contents* are integers, not real numbers – with NDVI, the values of the pixels should range from -1 to +1.

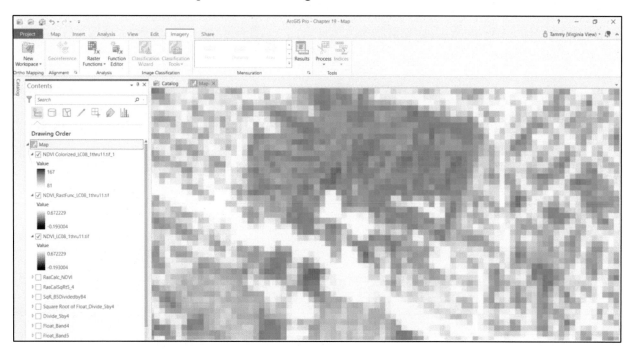

If a colorized NDVI image is preferred, then change the symbology on any NDVI image created above by following these steps:

    1. Go to *Symbology*, make sure *Stretched* is has been selected.

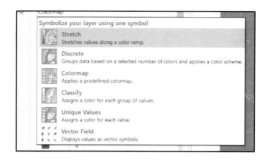

    2. Under *Stretched*, select *Yellow-Green continuous.*

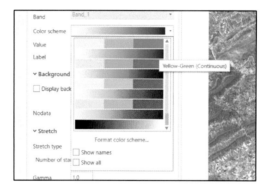

This symbology reflects what the human eye and brain would discern as healthy vegetation – the darkest green.

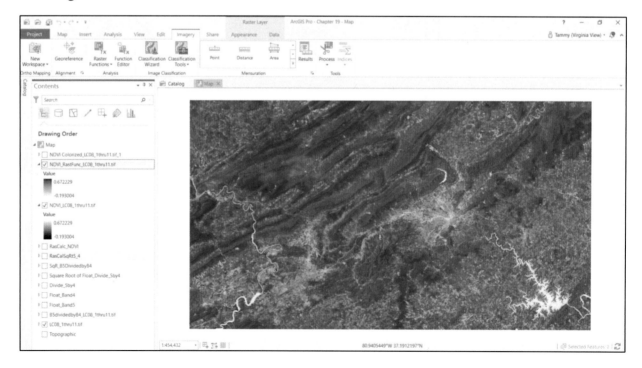

An alternative method to creating an NDVI image is available.

https://landsat.usgs.gov/landsat-surface-reflectance-high-level-data-products

Surface Reflectance products, including NDVI can be ordered (on-demand products but cannot be directly downloaded). Go to:

https://espa.cr.usgs.gov/login?next=https%3A%2F%2Fespa.cr.usgs.gov%2F.

The sign-in for the above is the same as for EarthExplorer.

The authors believe that there is tremendous value in learning how to generate image-derived products using *Spectral Enhancement* techniques and not solely rely on pre-processed products.

For definitions of the additional ratios available under Raster Functions Methods, see http://pro.arcgis.com/en/pro-app/help/data/imagery/band-arithmetic-function.htm

Within the last three chapters, we demonstrated the image enhancement processes. These processes are not only helpful for image analysis, but also for completing additional processing such as image classifications (discussed in Chapters 21 through 24).

The next chapter of this book, *Chapter 20 – Change Detection* will require downloading of two additional Landsat 8 scenes, so be prepared to review and utilize skills acquired in Chapters 11 – 13 and 15.

Introduction

Remotely sensed imagery is useful in detecting changes in features on the surface of the Earth. In order to detect changes in land use and land cover, imagery, usually from the same sensor and from two different dates, are required. The purpose of change detection is to identify changes in the spectral properties of specific features (pixels) associated with these two dates. The interval between dates can be as short as a few days (for example, to detect impacts of natural disasters), a few months (e.g., to assess growth in large agricultural fields), or a few to several years (such as monitoring changes in forest extent). Such analyses are called *Change Detection*.

Changing spectral properties of surface features provides information on effects such as land use changes (conversion from forest to urban), effects of natural disasters (such as hurricanes and wildland fires), or impacts of insect infestations on forest cover. Change detection applies algorithms, specifically designed to detect meaningful changes, in contrast to image differences originating in ephemeral, or superficial, features that do not signify meaningful differences over time.

A critical first step in a change detection analysis is the identification and selection of suitable pairs of images acquired over the same region. First, the two images must register either to each other, or to the surface of the Earth (e.g., the region they cover must match exactly when superimposed). Second, if used to track long-term changes, such as deforestation, the images need to be acquired during the same season. Finally, it is vital that no significant atmospheric effects have impacted an image. The two images must be compatible in almost every respect, including (but not limited to) − scale, geometry, and resolution. Otherwise, the change detection algorithm interprets incidental differences in image characteristics as genuine landscape changes.

Many alternative change detection algorithms exist and have been evaluated. There are two main change detection approaches: *pre-classification* and *post-classification* (image classification is discussed in Chapters 21 – 24). *Pre-classification change detection* examines differences in two images prior to any classification process. *Post-classification change detection* defines changes by comparing pixels in a pair of classified images (in which pixels have already been assigned to classes). Post-classification change detection typically reports changes as a summary (a difference in digital numbers) of the "from-to" changes of categories between the two dates.

This chapter introduces a simple procedure of pre-classification change detection – using one band from each date (note that the composite image created in Chapters 14 and 15 will NOT be used as an example) and calculating differences in pixel values between these two dates to evaluate changes. More complex approaches are available (such as those involving PCA analysis) but are beyond the scope of this book. This chapter also relies on knowledge gained from Chapters 11 and 13 through 19. This chapter does not review the processes learned in previous chapters but you will be expected to apply several of those processes. The specific chapter is referenced when a specific process is needed.

During our discussion of change detection analysis, two images acquired over southwestern Colorado will be used to evaluate landscape changes from drought and a wildland fire.

On June 1, 2018 a fire started in the San Juan National Forest of southwest Colorado. The cause of the fire remains unknown. This fire was named the *416 Fire*. As of June 21, 2018, the fire had destroyed more than 34,000 acres of forest and was only 35% contained (https://inciweb.nwcg.gov/incident/5822/). The extensive nature of the fire, and the inability to contain it, is directly related to recent drought conditions in Colorado (NOAA deemed this region to be in an exceptional drought). For additional information, refer to *https://www.drought.gov/drought/states/colorado*. A typical annual snowfall for this region is approximately 71 inches. However, in the 2017/2018 winter season, snowfall was 65% less than average. Local snowpack, typically present in June was gone by June in 2018 (*https://www.durangogov.org/Index.aspx?NID=288* and *https://howmuchwillitsnow.com/in/durango/co*).

Download two Landsat 8 images for this region before proceeding. The images are *Path 35, Row 34* with dates of June 15, 2017 and June 18, 2018. Follow the instructions in Chapters 11 and 13.

In EarthExplorer, the *Browse Overlay* for these two scenes will appear. EarthExplorer provides results in reverse chronological order (most recent dates are displayed first). So, as demonstrated in the figure below, the image on the left – June 18, 2018 will be listed first and then you will need to page through the results to the June 15, 2017 image (on the right).

Performing the Change Detection Process
As with processes demonstrated in Chapters 15, 18 and 19, ArcGIS® Pro provides multiple methods to conduct change detection. The section of this chapter will discuss using a change detection method step-by-step. Then, this chapter will provide the change detection results produced using two other

methods – *Raster Functions* and *Raster Calculator*. Students will need to refer to the prior chapters, if a refresher is needed for locating those methods.

Change detection means applying image differencing (i.e. subtracting corresponding pixels values at each pixel, and then displaying the differences as colors), so the areas that differ in brightness can be easily identified. To generate useful results, the analyst must apply an understanding of both the region represented on the image, as well as the subject of the analysis. Here, we will not use the composite image to calculate the differences, so it is important that you know which Landsat bands are best suited for distinguishing which features. Remember those bands that are useful for each analysis:

Landsat 8 Operational Land Imager (OLI) and Thermal Infrared Sensor (TIRS)

Reference

Barsi, J.A.; Lee, K.; Kvaran, G.; Markham, B.L.; Pedelty, J.A. The Spectral Response of the Landsat-8 Operational Land Imager. *Remote Sens.* **2014**, *6*, 10232-10251. doi:10.3390/rs61010232

Band	Wavelength	Useful for mapping
Band 1 – Coastal Aerosol	0.435 - 0.451	Coastal and aerosol studies
Band 2 – Blue	0.452 - 0.512	Bathymetric mapping, distinguishing soil from vegetation, and deciduous from coniferous vegetation
Band 3 - Green	0.533 - 0.590	Emphasizes peak vegetation, which is useful for assessing plant vigor
Band 4 - Red	0.636 - 0.673	Discriminates vegetation slopes
Band 5 - Near Infrared (NIR)	0.851 - 0.879	Emphasizes biomass content and shorelines
Band 6 - Short-wave Infrared (SWIR) 1	1.566 - 1.651	Discriminates moisture content of soil and vegetation; penetrates thin clouds
Band 7 - Short-wave Infrared (SWIR) 2	2.107 - 2.294	Improved moisture content of soil and vegetation and thin cloud penetration
Band 8 - Panchromatic	0.503 - 0.676	15 meter resolution, sharper image definition
Band 9 – Cirrus	1.363 - 1.384	Improved detection of cirrus cloud contamination
Band 10 – TIRS 1	10.60 – 11.19	100 meter resolution, thermal mapping and estimated soil moisture
Band 11 – TIRS 2	11.50 - 12.51	100 meter resolution, Improved thermal mapping and estimated soil moisture

Table from: https://landsat.usgs.gov/what-are-best-spectral-bands-use-my-study

We are going to use Band 5 from each image and will calculate pixel-by-pixel differences between the two images. Band 5, in the near-infrared, as noted in the table above, emphasizes biomass content (keep in mind that a fire will significantly lower biomass) and supports the identification of shorelines (shorelines discriminate between land and water – drought changes water body size, thus changes shorelines, and snow is just frozen water). Band 5, as an infrared band, will experience little, if any, atmospheric scattering.

Using the Imagery > Process > Difference Function

Open a new map project. Set the environments and workspaces, add Band 5 from each of the Colorado Landsat scenes, and then eliminate the background values. The June 18, 2018 should be the 1st layer listed in the *Contents* window.

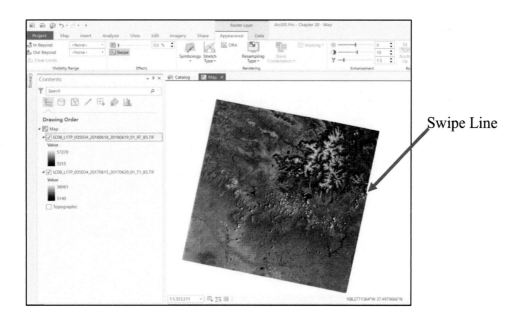

Swipe Line

First, highlight both layers in the *Contents* window – hold down *ctrl* on the keyboard and click on each layer. Then under the *Imagery* tab, locate *Difference* under the *Process* drop down arrow. Click on *Difference*.

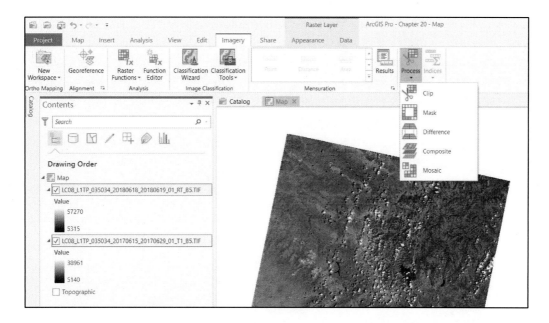

A new layer should be in *Contents* window called *Difference*. A new image should appear in the map viewer. If nothing happens, make sure that the two layers are highlighted, which is required for this function to process. Eliminate the background values for this new image.

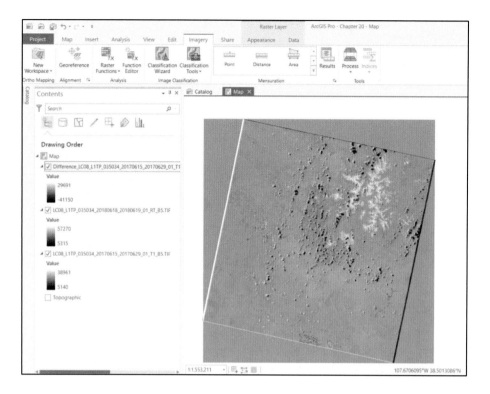

Don't forget to SAVE your project! This is a new layer that is only usable in the current map project, so if ArcGIS® Pro closes (prior to saving), this new image will be lost.

What does this new image, and the values in the Contents mean? The default symbology (*white*) represents an increase in a pixel's digital number, *black* means a decrease, *gray* means little or no change. But the image, in some ways, is hard to interpret using grayscale.

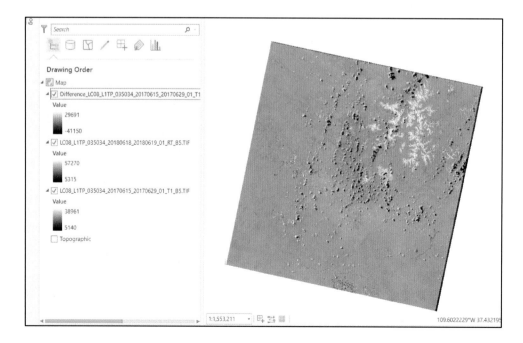

So, let's change the symbology to look different than the two grayscale Band 5s.

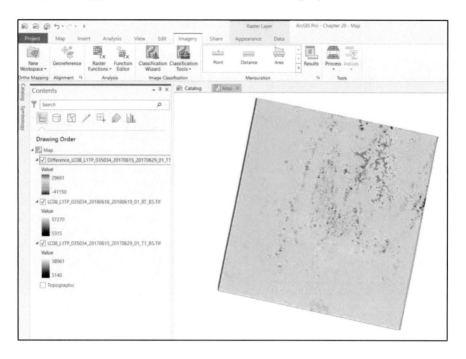

Even zoomed out to the full extent of the scene, what are the most obvious changes in the scene?

The June 18, 2018 image has clouds and the June 15, 2017 image was cloud-free. The clouds are shown as blue -- one of the most extremes in the change. Please note that when performing change detection, we recommend that clouds be eliminated. Change detection is used to monitor changes in the surface of the Earth. Clouds interfere with that process. For the purposes of this exercise, the presence versus absence of clouds provides an excellent example of the change detection process.

What is the second most obvious change? Snow cover. Snow was present in the mountains on June 15, 2017 but no snow was present in the June 18, 2018 image.

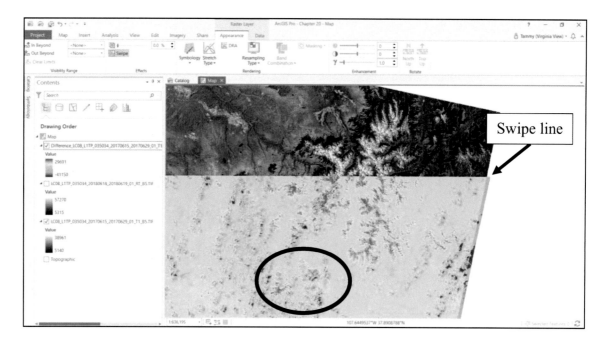

Let's take a closer look at the image for other changes. Zoom into the area of the black oval in the above figure.

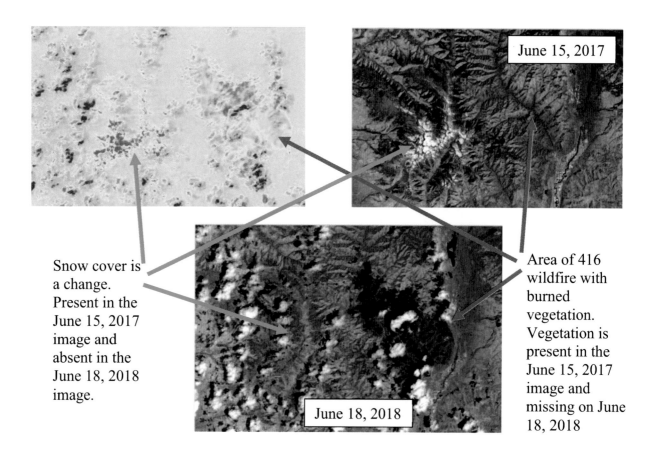

Snow cover is a change. Present in the June 15, 2017 image and absent in the June 18, 2018 image.

Area of 416 wildfire with burned vegetation. Vegetation is present in the June 15, 2017 image and missing on June 18, 2018

The lack of snow cover and the lack of vegetation both show a very high positive change in spectral values.

Let's look at one more area of change, just to the east of the 416 Wildfire are two lakes:

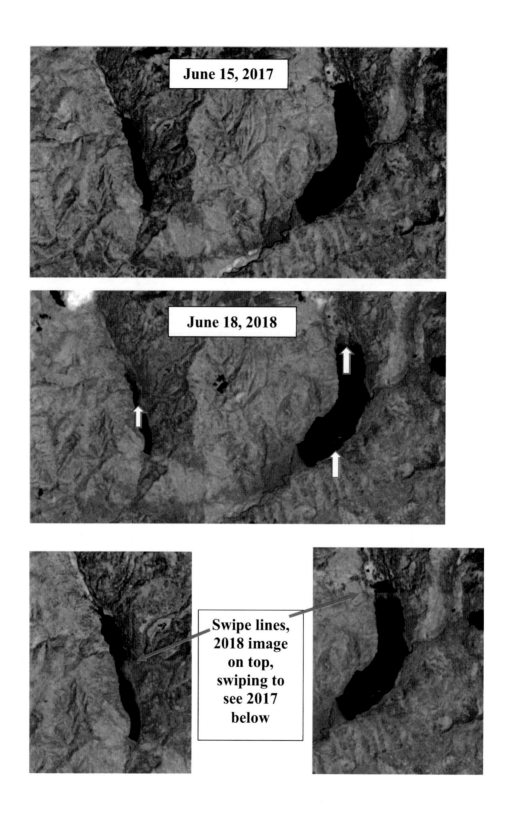

See the difference between the two Band 5 images in the figure above? The lakes in the June 18, 2018 image are not as large as the earlier June 15, 2017 image. (Further, the shallow water in 2018 exposes sediment deposits concealed below the surface in 2017, as indicated by the arrows).

Now, let's look at the change detection image in the figure below. Remember Band 5 is often used to discern shorelines.

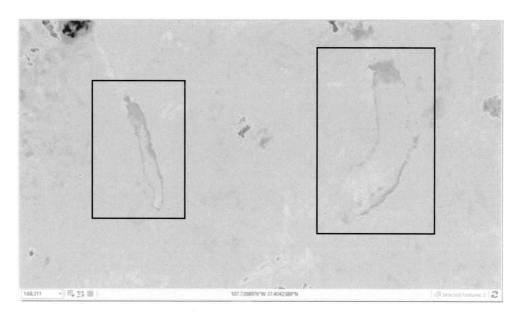

Change your *Stretch Method* to *Standard Deviation* (see figure below, review Chapter 17: Radiometric Enhancement of a Landsat 8 Image).

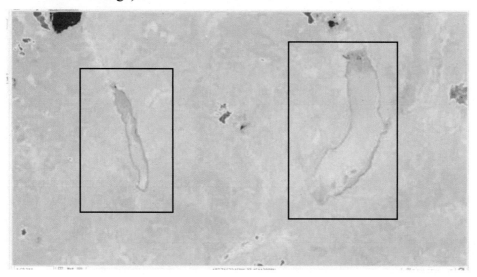

Once a change detection process has been completed within ArcGIS® Pro, it may be necessary to complete an image enhancement technique to discern the changes.

If you are unsure what the original features represent, when looking at a change detection image, it may be necessary to add a natural color or false-color composite image to the map project (reference Chapter 14: Creating a Composite Image for Landsat 8 Imagery).

In the following figures, we created a composite image from Bands 3, 4 and 5 of the June 15, 2017 scene, and then displayed the band combination as band 5 in Red, band 4 in Green and band 3 in Blue (Chapter 16: Band Combinations for Landsat 8 Imagery).

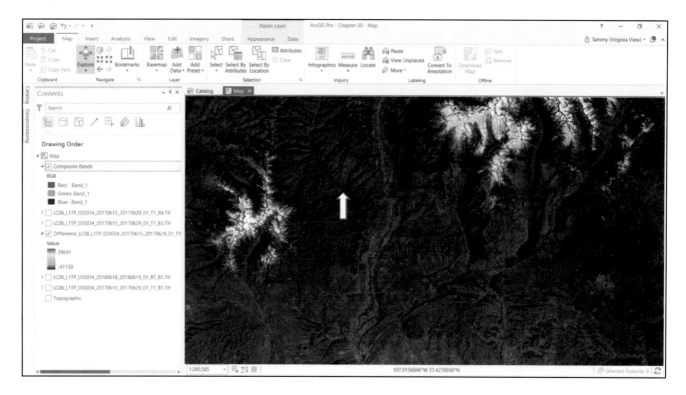

Recall from prior chapters on spectral properties of Landsat Bands, that this band combination reveals bright red as healthy vegetation. Now, complete the same steps for the June 18, 2018 image. See that the vegetation is clearly lacking (from the 416 Wildfire) and the lakes are visibly smaller (due to the drought).

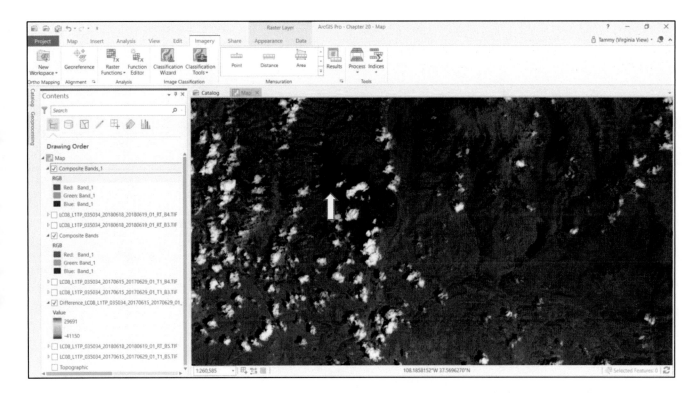

Thus far, we have completed a change detection analysis using the *Using the Imagery > Process > Difference Function*. Recall from prior chapters, ArcGIS® Pro provides several options to process functions.

Now, use the *Raster Functions > Math > Minus* found under *Raster Layer > Appearance*.

Our results are exactly the same. Remember, the *Stretch Method* in symbology needs to be the same in order for the images to display the same results.

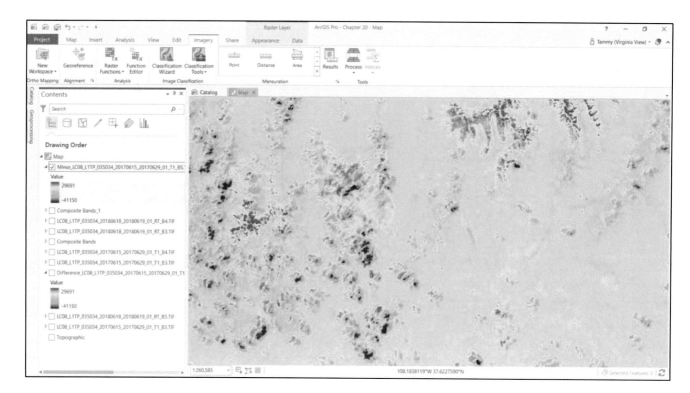

We now conclude the Change Detection process. Again, ArcGIS® Pro provides many options for this processing, including methods discussed here and using *Raster Calculator*.

Again, the band(s) selected for the change detection process will depend on the goal of the project, and the exact features preferred for evaluating the change. This chapter addresses change detection only. These images of southwestern Colorado will not be used in any other chapter.

Introduction:

Image classification is a process that sorts pixels (based on their spectral values) into informational classes or categories. A pixel is assigned to the class that corresponds to a specific set of criteria. Two methods to classify pixels are:

- *Unsupervised Classification (this chapter)*
- *Supervised Classification – (Chapters 22 - 24)*

With unsupervised classification, the pixels are clustered together based on *spectral homogeneity* and *spectral distance*. Spectral homogeneity is evaluated by the software program (in this book, ArcGIS® Pro). Spectral distance is measured using a variety of techniques, chosen by the analyst. Unsupervised classification produces classes of homogeneous spectral identities that may not exactly correspond to informational classes. While spectral classes denote pixels grouped by uniform brightness values, informational classes refer to groups that convey useful information (such designations as *land use*, *soil classes*, or *agricultural productivity*). When using unsupervised classification, the informational class may contain a variety of spectral identities. Therefore, a spectral class as identified by unsupervised classification seldom matches exactly to an informational class.

Objectives

The objectives associated with this chapter include:
- Complete an unsupervised classification on a Landsat 8 image;
- Determine the land use / landcover category associated within each spectral class;
- Create color-coded informational classes according to the following scheme:
  - ➢ Urban/built up/transportation = Class 1, assigned to red;
  - ➢ Mixed agriculture = Class 2, assigned to yellow;
  - ➢ Forest & Wetland = Class 3, assigned to green;
  - ➢ Open water = Class 4, assigned to blue; and
- Calculate the percentage of each informational class with respect to total area.

Conducting Unsupervised Classification

Open a new project, name it, save it and add the 11-band composite image created in Chapter 15 (the image clipped to the extent of the display). Set your workspaces and eliminate background values. To help discern features, set it to a natural color band combination.

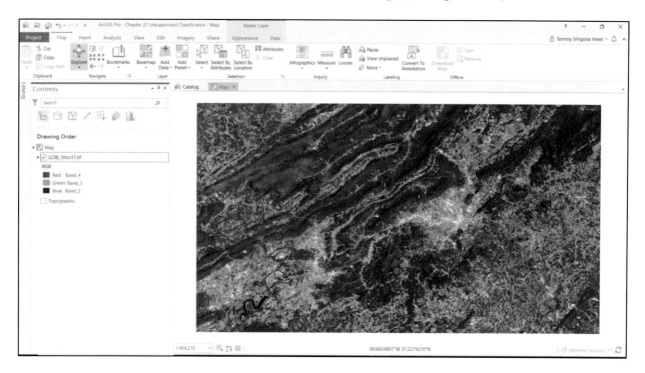

As with all other processes, multiple ways to complete the unsupervised classification exist. One way, is to select the *Imagery* tab and use the *Classification Wizard*. However, as with many other shortcut functions, this creates an image that is only usable in the current map document.

The method demonstrated within this chapter will create a permanent image, usable in other analyses, and we will use this image in the final chapter (Chapter 25: Accuracy Assessment). Go to the *Analysis* tab, *Tools* and search using the word *Classification*. We want ISO Cluster. Note that two ISO options are provided. Select the option that has a scrolled document as the icon (see figure below, red box).

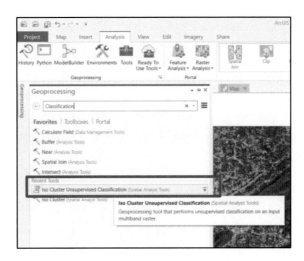

The following figure reveals the tool and the inputs required. Before we proceed, we will discuss some of the inputs.

Determining the Number of Classes (red arrow in prior figure)

Remember from above, for our final output, we want four different informational classes:

- Urban/built up/transportation = class #1, designated as red;
- Mixed agriculture = class #2, designated as yellow;
- Forest & Wetland = class #3, designated as green;
- Open water = class #4, designated as blue.

The number of classes in the *ISO Cluster Unsupervised Classification* dialog box refers to the number of spectral classes. Set this number to 25. Why? The image has over 65,000 different pixel values. Each category of features (or informational classes – water, agriculture, urban, forest) may consist of a range of spectral values. Unsupervised classification generates groups of pixels that form homogenous spectral identities. The number of spectral classes that should be used will depend on the number of informational classes, the complexity of the area of interest, employer (or government) requirements, and goals of the analysis. Determining the appropriate number of spectral classes may require running the *ISO Cluster Unsupervised Classification* tool multiple times using different numbers of spectral classes. Other parameters may also be required, but for our purposes, let's leave these parameters at their default settings.[1]

For the *Input raster bands*, chose the 11-band subset composite image. As noted above, set the *Number of classes* to 25 and leave all other parameters as default. Do not forget to name the new image something that is recognizable for the process (perhaps LC08_UnSup25). Be sure that the file is saved in the geodatabase for the project. Then select *Run* at the bottom.

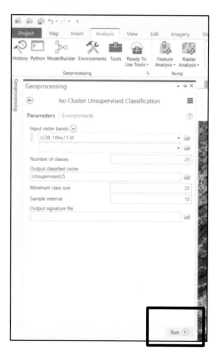

The classification process takes a few minutes. The current status of the process is visible in the bottom of the dialog box.

---

[1]For specifics on each of these options, refer to the ArcGIS® Pro help:http://pro.arcgis.com/en/pro-app/tool-reference/spatial-analyst/how-iso-cluster-works.htm

A new layer appears in the *Contents* and a new image will appear in the map viewer. There are 25 unique values. Colors have been randomly assigned to the new image (homogenous spectral classes, not informational classes).

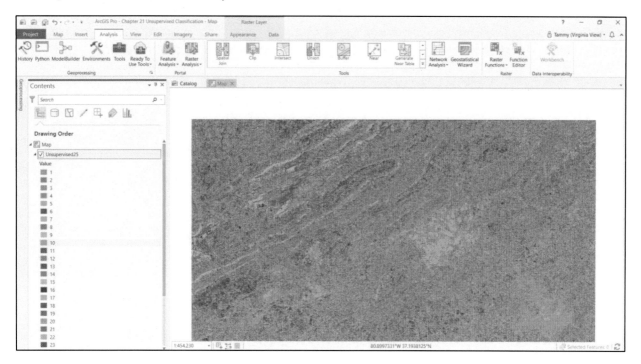

We will need to determine which spectral class(es) should be assigned to each informational class. Ultimately, all 25 spectral classes will be assigned to one of our 4 designed informational classes.

But before we do this, let's run the classification method once again to see what happens when the number of classes is changed. Set the number of classes to 50 and name the output raster and then select *Run*.

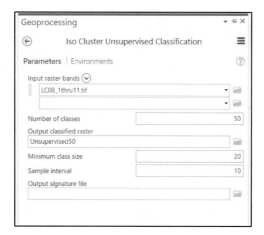

As before, a new layer appears in *Contents* and a new image in the map viewer. This time, 50 unique values and colors are assigned to the new image (again, these are homogenous spectral classes, not informational classes).

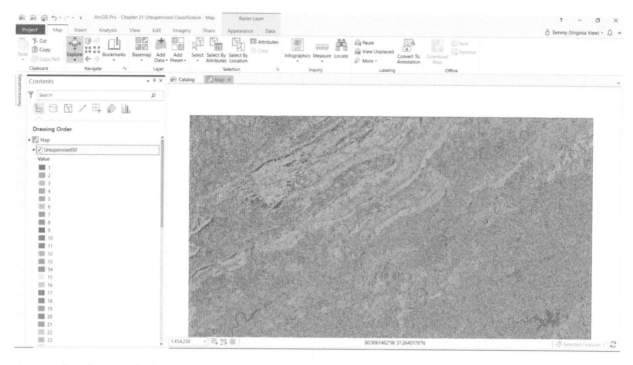

As previously noted, the number of spectral classes chosen is dependent upon many factors. For this image and its variation in land use, 50 classes are likely to be more appropriate than 25, but often the number of classes is contingent on the specific application.

Now we need to decide which informational class contains each spectral class. Which new image will we use?   We will use the Unsupervised_25 image (the image with 25 spectral classes) from here on, strictly for simplicity.

Remember the information class color scheme:

- Urban/built up/transportation = class #1, designated as red;
- Mixed agriculture = class #2, designated as yellow;
- Forest & Wetland = class #3, designated as green;
- Open water = class #4, designated as blue.

To help decide the spectral classes that belong to a particular information class, add a new basemap layer – an image. Remember from Chapter 4, go to the *Map* tab and *Basemap* – chose *Imagery*.

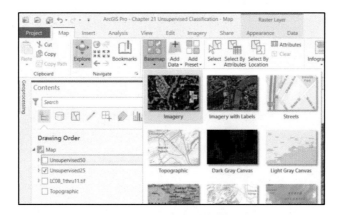

This basemap looks similar to our natural color composite.

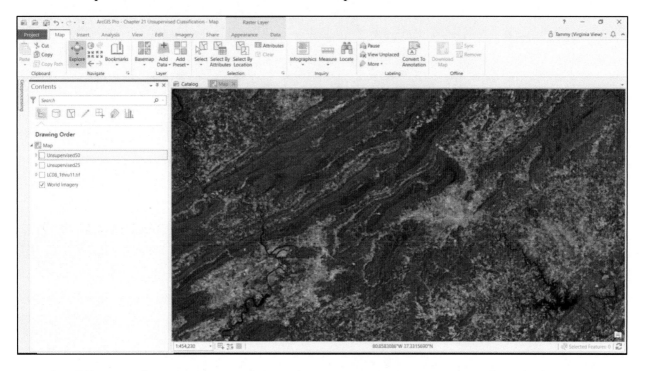

But, the differences between the two images become apparent as you zoom in. The basemap image changes to higher resolution aerial imagery, which will be needed to help determine the specific informational class:

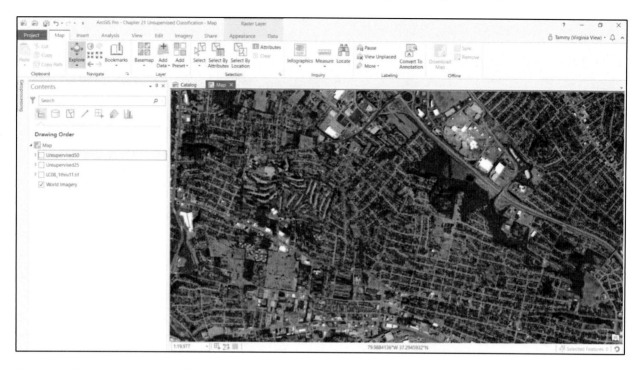

For your first step, change the color for any spectral class that already has any of our final informational color classes (red, yellow, green, blue) to any other color. This eliminates confusion if any spectral classes were colored by default to those colors. Or, you alternatively could begin by setting them to all the same color and then proceed.

The *Unsupervised 25* image overlaid on the imagery basemap will look something like this (see figure below. Note that the colors may vary). As an example, zoom into Roanoke and use the *Swipe tool* to view the aerial image underneath your unsupervised classification layer.

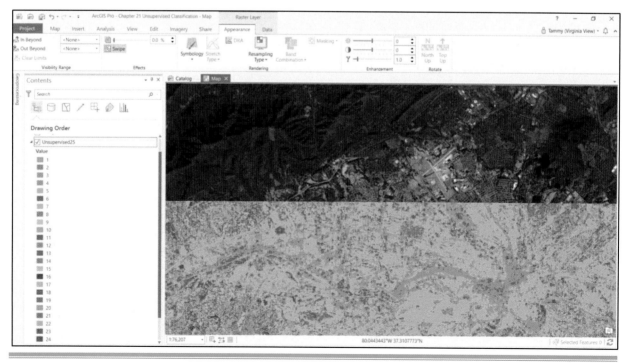

To change the spectral class color, start with water. Water is symbolized as blue, so zoom into Smith Mountain Lake to determine the pixel value and color. To check the pixel value, just click on a pixel. As a reminder, since this is a classified image, pixel values are not associated with brightness values, but have been assigned a classification value. The pixel value of your unsupervised classification (25 classes) will therefore range from 1-25.

In Contents, find that value under the layer name, right-click on the colored box and change it to blue. All water pixel spectral values will be assigned to blue.

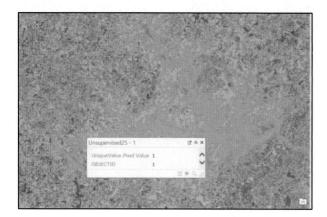
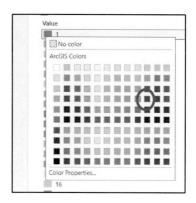

Then zoom to the rivers in the Roanoke and Radford areas, and change their colors to blue. To find the river in Roanoke, follow the blue water northwest out of Smith Mountain Lake. The river in Roanoke has a different color, so it will need to be changed. But be careful, since we only have 25 spectral classes -- mountain shadows can mimic water.

Continue with the other spectral classes – all 25 classed will need to evaluated and assigned to the appropriate color class. .

Associate agriculture fields as yellow:

Urban areas should be red. Should golf courses be classified as agriculture or urban (or, should you create a new category)? The same decisions have to be made for all classes, including the extensive tree canopy coverage in an urban area. For our purposes, we are classifying anything within the city as urban.

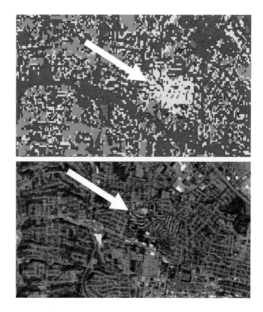

When finished with all 25 spectral classes, look at the overall image. Are the informational classes, generally correct? Do you have any blue areas within the mountains that are not water?

In *Contents*, the symbology lists 25 spectral values but only 4 colors – the colors pertaining to our informational classes.

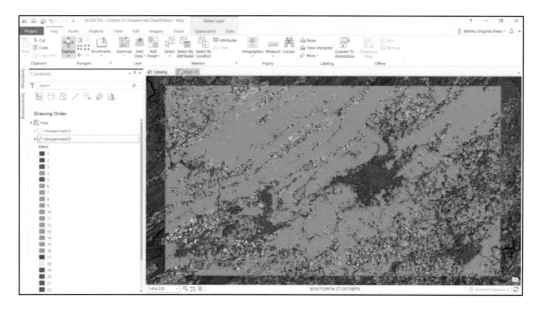

In the following figure, we zoomed to one of the blue areas in the mountains. The blue does correspond to a body of water. In addition, here are agricultural fields interspersed with forest and a road with a subdivision. Again, whether a subdivision should be designated as urban, agriculture, forest, etc. depends on project goals.

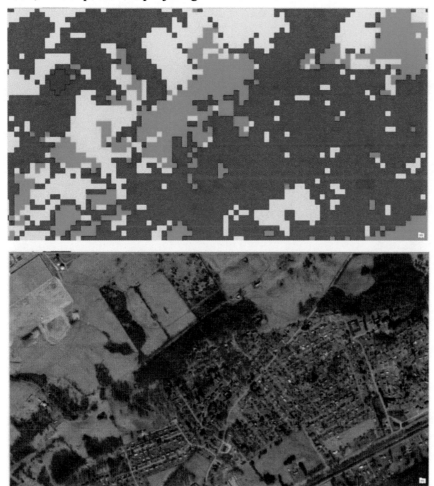

Continue to spot check the results – it is not necessary to do a complete accuracy assessment of all of the categories at this juncture. An accuracy assessment (the final step required in any image classification scheme) will be covered in the final chapter of this book (Chapter 25 – Accuracy Assessment). For now, we need to assign the spectral classes to informational classes.

Reclassifying Spectral Classes into Informational Classes

The 25 spectral classes are now colored to match the colors of the four informational classes. To change this to just four informational classes, select the *Analysis* tab and the *Tools*. Search using the word *Reclass*. Choose *Reclassify (Spatial Analyst Tools)*.

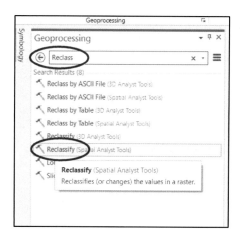

The *Input Raster* is the *Unsupervised 25* layer. Once that layer populates, the *Reclassification* table (black box in first figure) expands and lists all 25 values under the *Value* and *New* columns (red box in middle figure). Use the symbology under the Unsupervised 25 layer as a guide.

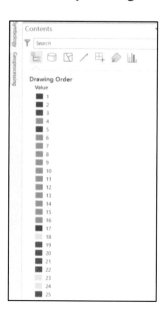

- All values coded as Red are Urban/built up/transportation, change to 1
- All values coded as Yellow are Mixed Agriculture, change to 2
- All values coded as Green are Forest & Wetland, change to 3
- All values coded as Blue are Open water, change to 4

Click in the row under *New* and make the change (see figure below). Do this for all of the 25 *Value*s (line by line).

Use the scroll bar on the right side of the *New* column to find and change each of the 25 values. Once all values are changed, do not forget to name the new file. Be sure to save it in the geodatabase. Click *Run*.

Once finished, the new layer will appear in the *Contents* and a new image will appear in the map viewer. The colors seen may not be the same as in the figure below as these are randomly assigned.

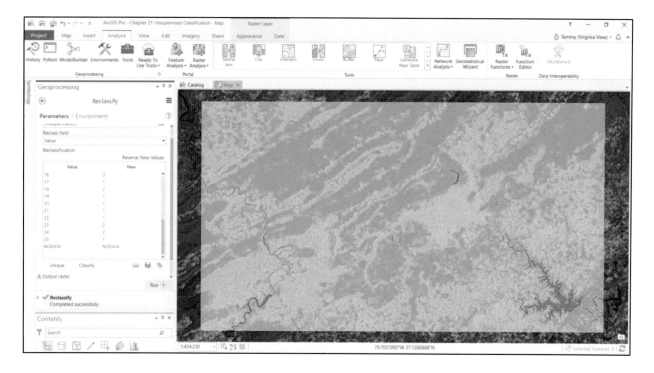

Go to *symbology* and change the color scheme. Under the *Label* column, type the informational class name. Just click in the box on the row for the correct color and type.

The two images (the spectral class image with the 25 values and the informational class image with 4 values) should look exactly the same if the *Reclass* process was completed correctly.

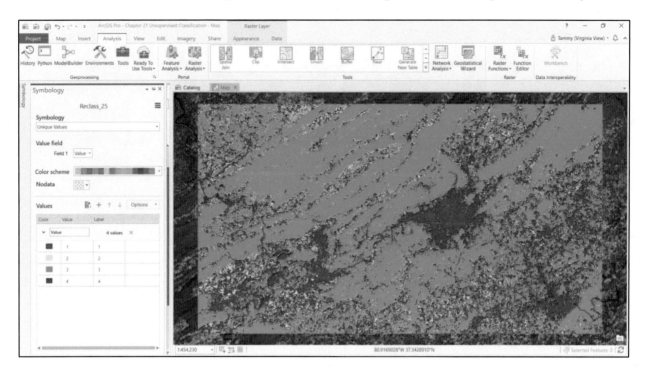

Calculating the Percent of Total Area for Each Informational Class

Once the pixels have been reclassified (to 4 classes), the total area of each class can be easily calculated. To do this, right click on the name of the *Reclass* file and open the *Attribute Table*. This table provides the number of cells (*Count*) in each informational class.

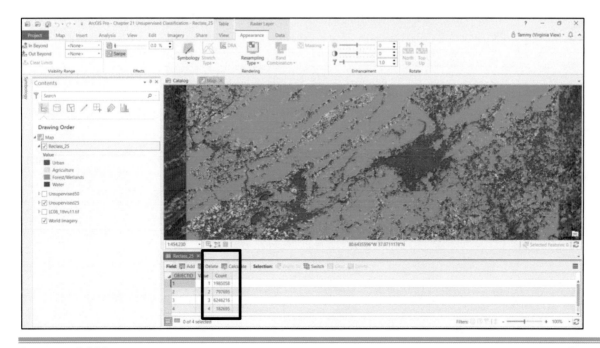

The percent of total area for each informational class can be calculated within the *Attribute Table*. First, select *Add* to add a field.

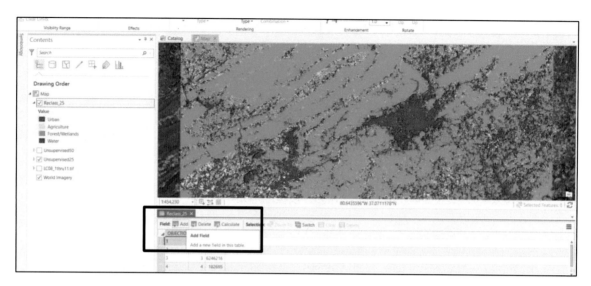

Then name the field – *percent* - and tab to each column in this new row to choose the individual parameters.

Under *Data type*, choose *Float* (the number will be a real number). The under *Number Format*, choose *Numeric*. (Again, as one column field is completed, just use the tab key to go to the next column.)

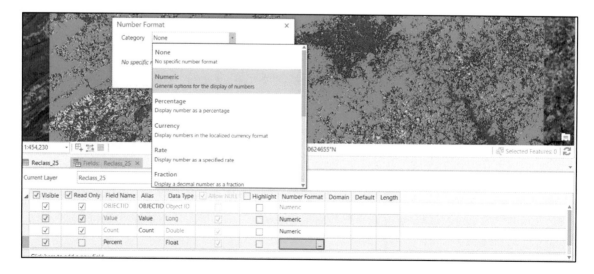

For *Numeric* under *Number Format*, select the options. For a percent, *2 Decimal places* should be sufficient. Then click *OK*.

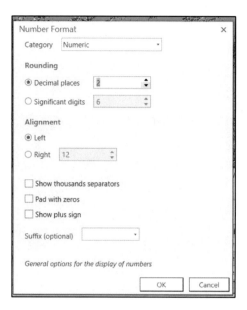

To save the new field, click on *Save* at the very top.

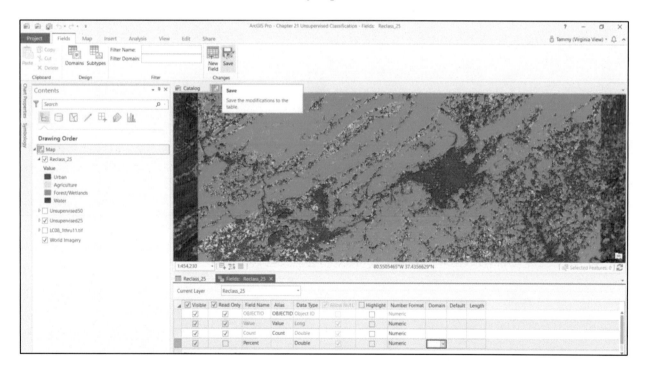

To calculate the value for the field, highlight the field name (*Percent* denoted in the figure below with a red arrow). Then click on the *Calculate* button (black box) and a dialog box opens in *Geoprocessing* (black arrow).

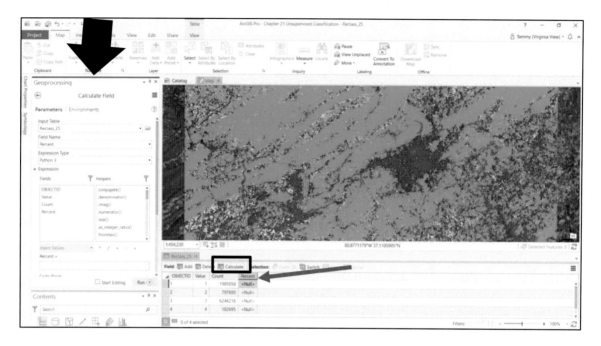

Fill in the dialog box under *Percent* = as follows:

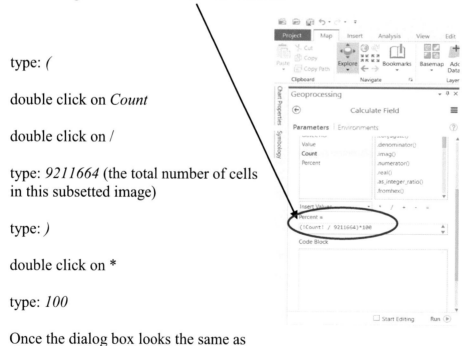

type: *(*

double click on *Count*

double click on */*

type: *9211664* (the total number of cells in this subsetted image)

type: *)*

double click on *

type: *100*

Once the dialog box looks the same as on the right, click *Run* on the bottom.

The new field now shows the percent of total for each informational class.

Can you add a new field (called area) and calculate the total number of hectares associated with each class?

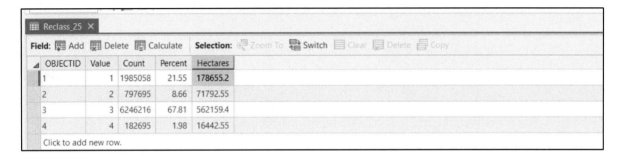

How accurate was the classification using the *ISO Cluster Unsupervised Classification* method and 25 classes? That is assessed in the last chapter of this book – Chapter 25: Accuracy Assessment. You may proceed directly to that chapter. But, we recommend that you complete the next three chapters, Chapter 22 – 24, which cover the supervised classification process.

Introduction

In comparison to software-controlled unsupervised classification process, an analyst has more control over the supervised classification process. Through supervised classification, the analyst selects pixels representing recognized landscape features/patterns, or pixels that can be identified from other sources, such as high resolution aerial photos. Knowledge of the data, the classes desired, and the algorithm to be used, is required before selecting training samples (samples of spectral values within the image and which pertain to specific features/patterns). By identifying patterns in the imagery, the analyst "trains" the software to identify pixels with similar characteristics. The analyst choses the spectral classes for the informational classes, thus, supervises the classification process.

Supervised training requires *a priori* (already known) information about the data, such as:

- the information needed to be extracted, for example, vegetation type, land use; and
- the classes most likely present in the image, e.g., types of land cover (forest, water, and bare earth or forest, agriculture and urban, or any combination thereof).

In supervised classification, the analyst relies on pattern recognition skills and *a priori* knowledge to direct the software in determining the spectral criteria (signatures) for data classification. The analyst selects training samples for each informational class by identification of either spatial or spectral characteristics about the pixels to be classified. For example, knowledge about a spatial characteristic may be known through field observations, analysis of high resolution aerial photography, personal experience, etc. Field data are considered to be the most accurate (correct) data about a study area. Field data should be collected for the same time period as the remotely sensed data, so that the data correspond as much as possible.

Nevertheless, all field data may not be completely accurate because of observation errors, instrument inaccuracies, and human shortcomings. ArcGIS® Pro calculates statistics from the training sample pixels to create a parametric signature for each class.

Every pixel value cannot be assigned to an informational class, but training data identifies many of the values. Then, for unassigned pixels, the analyst chooses the algorithm for the software to assign these unassigned pixels to specific classes. Additionally, some pixel values may fall into two classes – a situation discussed in Chapter 21 on unsupervised classification with respect to classification of water and the mountain shadows. In supervised classification, the analyst, likewise, chooses the method/algorithm that decides how to assign these pixels. Different algorithms include (but are not limited to minimum distance, maximum likelihood, Mahalanobis' Distance. Please see Campbell and Wynne (2011 – 5th edition, 6th edition forthcoming) for more information about supervised classification strategies.

Instructions on supervised classification are divided into three chapters. Chapter 22 (this chapter) introduces the different classification schemes available within ArcGIS® Pro, and then provides instruction on creating training samples to use in the classification.

Chapter 23 provides step-by-step instructions on how to evaluate the effectiveness of the training samples. Training samples must be evaluated prior to conducting the classification for many reasons, including:

- the spectral values for each class need to be independent of each other, without overlap;
- the full range of spectral values for a specific class must be included, to check for over training (e.g. too many training samples and they duplicate each other);
- the training samples represent a normal distribution of values; and
- the analyst should avoid selecting training data positioned near edges of parcels, to avoid introducing mixed pixels into the training data.

The final supervised classification chapter (24) provides instructions on creating a signature file for the classification scheme and conducting the actual supervised classification.

Objectives

The three chapters should be completed in sequent, Chapter 22 first, Chapter 23 second and then Chapter 24. Within these chapters (Chapters 22 – 24), you will:

- Create training samples (Chapter 22);
- Use histograms, scatterplots and statistics to evaluate normality, separability, and partitioning of training data (Chapter 23);
- Generate supervised signatures using training samples (Chapter 24); and
- Perform a supervised classification on a Landsat 8 image (Chapter 24).

This chapter uses the 11-band composite Landsat 8 image, subset to the extent of the map viewer that was created in Chapter 15. We will be using the same informational classes that we used in the chapter on unsupervised classification (Chapter 21), so as a reminder, the classes are:

- ➢ Urban/built up/transportation = class #1, designated as red
- ➢ Mixed agriculture = class #2, designated as yellow
- ➢ Forest and Wetland = class #3, designated as green
- ➢ Open water = class #4, designated as blue

Introduction to Classification Schemes and Methods Available in ArcGIS® Pro

Open a new blank map project, name it, save it, be sure to set your workspaces (as discussed in previous chapters) and add the 11-Band Composite image. Eliminate the background values, if necessary, and set the composite image to a natural color band combination.

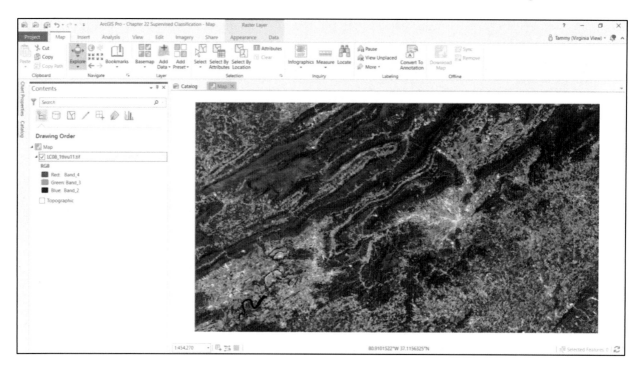

Before proceeding to the step-by-step process of supervised classification, we discuss alternative methods available in ArcGIS® Pro.

Image Classification Wizard

In Chapter 21, we briefly reviewed the *Image Classification Wizard* (under the *Imagery* tab). The *Image Classification Wizard* can also be used to perform a supervised classification. The *Image Classification Wizard* provides many shortcuts and avoids several steps in the supervised classification process. The Image Classification Wizard also bypasses many user prompts and decisions required with other software or other processes within ArcGIS® Pro.

Please note -- it is not necessary to follow along in ArcGIS® Pro at this juncture, we are just discussing methods available.

Within the *Image Classification Wizard*, the first choice is to select either unsupervised or supervised classification (see figure on left, below). When choosing supervised classification, the next choice is to select either *Pixel-based* or *Object-based* (middle figure). The on the next tab for the wizard is the choice for *Random Trees* or *Support Vector Machine* (figure on right).

These are only two of the many possible supervised classification methods within the *Image Classification Wizard*. Within the figures below are descriptions of these different methods. The *Image Classification Wizard* walks you through the classification process, step-by-step, but as noted in the prior chapter, the image generated is only useful within the map project where it was created. Additionally, the most frequently used supervised classification method -- maximum likelihood -- is not available with the *Image Classification Wizard*. We will demonstrate use of the wizard in Chapter 24: Conducting a Supervised Classification.

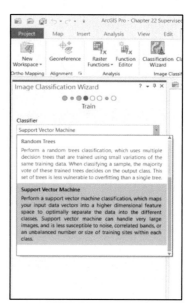

For more information on the *Image Classification Wizard*, refer to: https://pro.arcgis.com/en/pro-app/help/analysis/image-analyst/the-image-classification-wizard.htm.

Geoprocessing Tools

Geoprocessing tools provide additional options for classification. Under the *Analysis* tab, click on *Tools,* and search first using the word *classification* (results on the left in the figure below) and then search using the word *classify* (results on the right in the figure below).

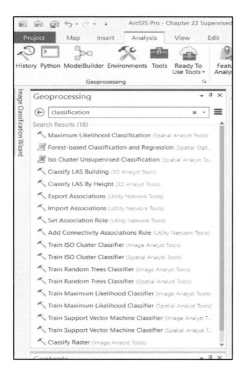

As demonstrated from the results above, additional classification methods are available, including *Maximum Likelihood, ISO* (used in Chapter 21 for unsupervised classification), and *Classify Raster*[1]. Within Chapter 24, we demonstrate both the *Maximum Likelihood* tool and the *Classify Raster* tool. These tools create a new permanent image usable in other map projects. But the use of these tools requires the use of other tools, including *Train Maximum Likelihood Classifie*r (this chapter) and *Create Signatures* (Chapter 24) – processes that are directly incorporated into the *Image Classification Wizard*. We will be demonstrating those tools also as it is important for students to understand the basics of supervised classification.

For more information on classification tools available in ArcGIS® Pro, refer to:
http://pro.arcgis.com/en/pro-app/tool-reference/spatial-analyst/an-overview-of-the-segmentation-and-classification-tools.htm.

Creating Training Samples

The first step associated with supervised classification is creating *training samples* – a sample of spectral values characterizing each informational class. The training sample shapefile is then used in supervised classification to evaluate the spectral values of all pixels in an image and to assign other pixels to a specific informational class.

There are multiple ways to create training samples – within the *Image Classification Wizard*, by using a specific tool for the method – *Train Maximum Likelihood, Train Random Tree Classifier*, etc., and under the *Imagery* tab > *Classification Tools*, an icon called *Training Samples Manager* (figure below).

Since we are going to demonstrate three different processes in ArcGIS® Pro, we want to create one training sample file for all three methods, we will use the *Training Samples Manager*.

Open the *Training Samples Manager* by clicking on the icon. An informational classification scheme is already built into the *Training Samples Manager* - NLCD 2011[2] (as seen in the figure below).

---

[1] LAS Classification refers to lidar data and beyond the scope of this book.
[2] For more information on the National Land Cover Database (NLCD 2011), refer to:
https://www.mrlc.gov/nlcd2011.php

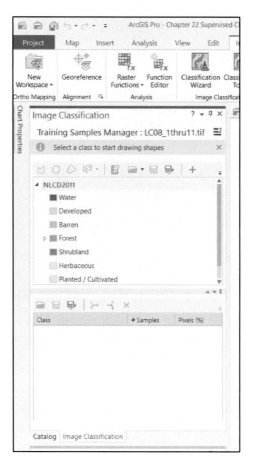

ArcGIS® Pro does not require that this informational class scheme be utilized.

If a new one is desired, just select the *Create New Schema* icon:

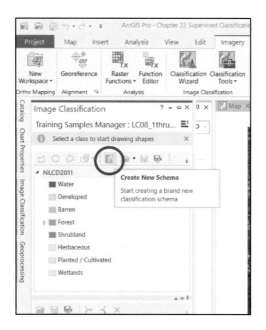

Or, if an informational class scheme already exists that you need to use, click on the file folder to navigate to that *Classification Schema*:

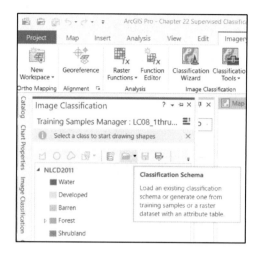

But, we can also start with the NLCD 2011 and modify it as needed. This will be demonstrated in this chapter, but we only need 4 informational classes as noted in the beginning of this chapter.

Right click on the name of any of the information classes listed under *NLCD 2011*. In the figure below, we right-clicked on *Shrubland*. As seen in the pop-up dialog box, classes can be added, removed or edited. Since we only use 4 informational class, we need to remove the others.

Highlight *Shrubland* and right-click and select *Remove Class*. *Don't worry*! As seen in the next figure, ArcGIS® Pro asks before it is removed. Select *Yes*.

Continue to remove other classes until only four classes remain – *Developed*, *Planted/cultivated*, *Forest and Water*. If you accidently removed too many, don't worry -- we will show how to add a class back again.

Once only 4 classes remain, rename them to correspond with the informational classes outlined on the second page of this Chapter. Right-click on *Developed*, select *Edit Properties*. The *Edit Class Properties* dialog box opens. Click in the *Name* line (box block in center figure below) and type *Urban*. Click *OK* at the bottom and ArcGIS® Pro confirms that the change was made (below figure on the right).

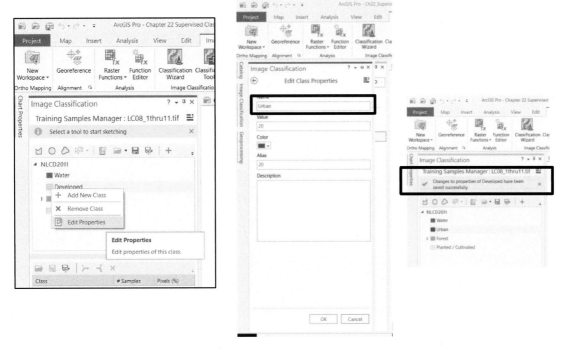

Do the same for *Planted/Cultivated* and rename this class to *Agriculture*. And now, there are only 4 classes:

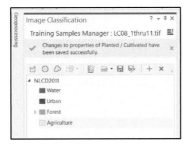

We will be working with these 4 informational classes. (If you removed an informational class by mistake, you can add a new class by selecting the + button to add a new class and name it for the one accidently deleted.)

Saving the Classification Schema

There are two ways to save the classification schema - either click on the *Save* button, or the *Save as*. We use the *Save As* (to save your classification schema as a new file) option, otherwise the NLCD 2011 schema will be overwritten with our changes. Click on *Save As*, name the new schema, and in *Output Location,* confirm that this file is saved in the correct folder.

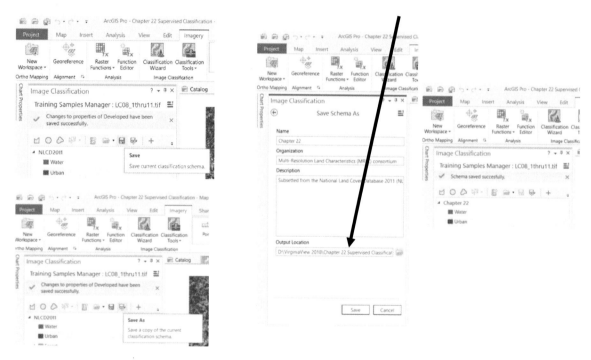

Now that the classification schema has been created, we need to create training samples.

Go to the bottom half of the window (figure below). (If a training sample already exists, it can be loaded by selecting the file folder – *Load Training Samples*.)

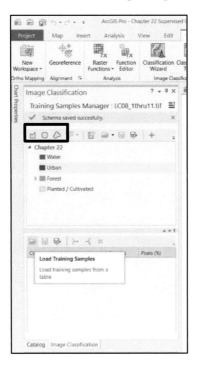

Since we do not have any existing training samples to load, we will create our own. We will create training samples by using the drawing tools at the top of the window (see black box in above figure).

Training samples can be created using several options, including: *Polygon*, *Circle* or *Freehand*. We found no difference between *Polygon* and *Freehand*, so we demonstrate *Polygon* and *Circle*.

Let's start with water. Zoom into Smith Mountain Lake, in the southeast portion of the image:

Highlight the word *Water* in the top box and then click on *Circle.*

 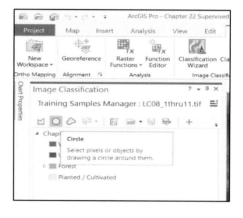

Place the mouse cursor anywhere in the lake's body. Be sure to stay away from shorelines -- we don't want to capture any of those as spectral values for water. Once an appropriate location is found, hold the left mouse button down (don't release it). Then, drag the mouse cursor outward to create the circle.

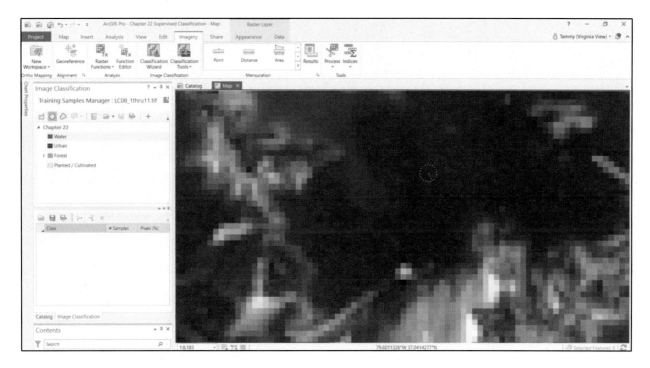

Again, stay away from the shore -- capture only water pixels.

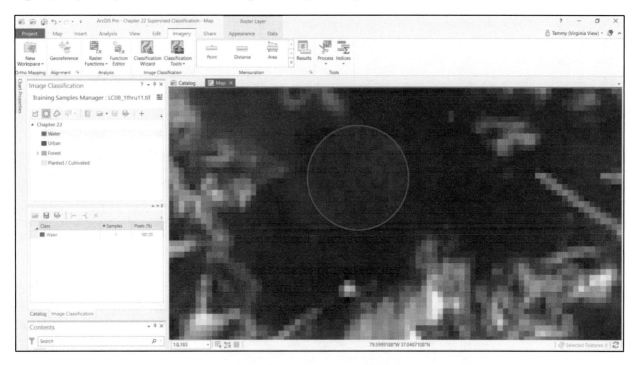

When you are satisfied with the pixels captured, then release the mouse button.

If you don't like the sample of pixels that you captured (either too many or too few), just highlight the Water sample listed in the bottom part of the window (red arrow), right-click and *Delete*. (Don't worry, sometimes it takes a few tries to get the hang of selecting samples.)

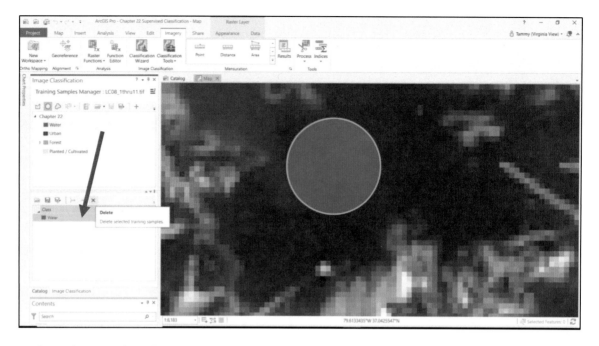

Zoom in and out and navigate around the scene to pick up additional water pixels for this lake.

If you are not comfortable with the *Circle* tool, then try the *Polygon* tool. The *Polygon* tool is most effective for non-symmetric areas. Note in the figure below that we also captured some of the water that is a bit turbulent. Remember, the point is to get samples of many different spectral values related to a specific feature.

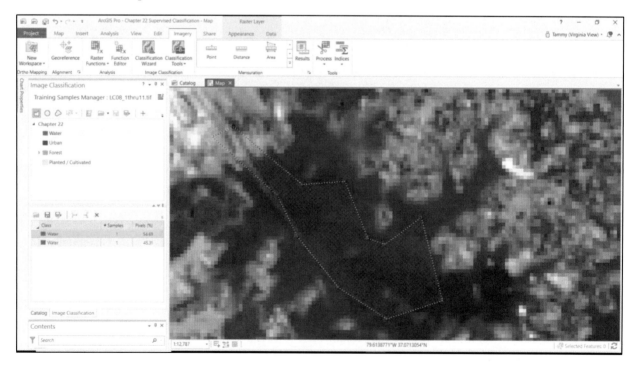

As training samples are added in the map viewer, each is separately listed in the *Training Sample Manager* – the bottom box. Don't just collect samples in the lake. Also, try collecting sample pixels in the rivers.

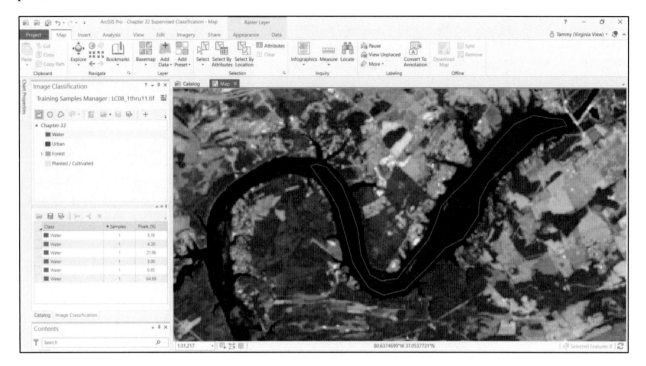

We recommend frequently saving your training samples. Select the *Save* icon. No, this is not the same file as the classification schema -- this is going to create a shapefile of the training samples. Name the training sample file so that you understand its purpose.

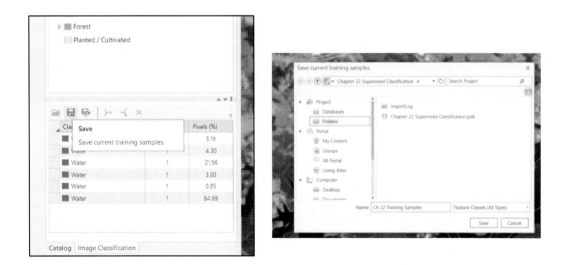

Save frequently so if ArcGIS® Pro closes, the work will not be lost.

Once finished with water, move on to training urban, forest and agriculture. Don't forget to highlight the class name in the top of the *Training Sample Manager* dialog box before training the next class.

The figure below illustrates an urban training sample. (As in Chapter 21 – Unsupervised Classification, we are not concerned with individual features within an urban area. For the purposes of this exercise, all streets, parks, golf courses, etc. within the urban area, will be classified as urban).

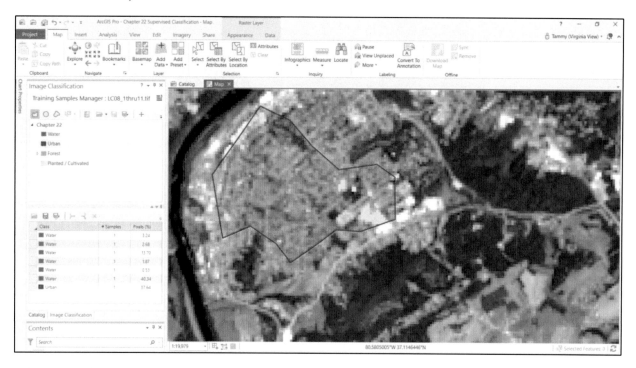

When complete, the image in the map viewer will display all the training samples. Collect samples across the entire geographic spread of the image, as is in the figure below. Avoid collecting any one class to a single location or region. In ArcGIS® Pro, the training samples for an individual informational class are color-coded according to the color scheme in the top of the *Training Sample Manager* dialog box – for example, forest training samples are green, urban are red, agriculture fields are yellow and water is blue. BE SURE TO SAVE!

When have you collected enough training samples? It depends on the area, the variation in spectral signatures of the land cover, and the project. Again, sample different areas of the image, different types of agriculture, forest, urban and water areas. In the next section, we evaluate the training samples to determine if we have collected sufficient training samples by evaluating the spectral coverage.

SAVE! Both your training samples and your project.

Please proceed to the next chapter, which provides the step-by-step process to evaluate the training samples. Training samples need to be evaluated before conducting the supervised classification (Chapter 24).

Introduction

In the prior section, we introduced the various classification methods available within ArcGIS® Pro and provided step-by-step instructions on creating training samples for each informational class.

Once training samples are created, the effectiveness of the training samples must be evaluated. This evaluation occurs for many reasons. Spectral values for each class should:

- be independent of each other, with no overlap;
- represent the full range of spectral values for a specific class;
- avoid over-training, (too many similar training samples will replicate information rather than depict variability within the class);
- represent a normal distribution of values (as best as may be feasible); and
- avoid selecting pixels that are positioned at the edges of land cover boundaries/tracts (to reduce the likelihood of mixed pixels, which can occur with mixed land-uses).

Objective

The objective of this chapter is to learn how to use histograms, scatterplots and statistics to evaluate normality, separability, and partitioning of training data.

This chapter uses the 11-band composite Landsat 8 image, subset to the extent of the map viewer created in Chapter 15, and the training sample shapefile created in the last section. We will also be creating an additional training sample shapefile, and additional subset images, for each of the training samples informational classes. We will be using the same informational classes:

- ➢ Urban/built up/transportation = Class #1, designated as red
- ➢ Mixed agriculture = Class #2, designated as yellow
- ➢ Forest and Wetland = Class #3, designated as green
- ➢ Open water = Class #4, designated as blue

Evaluating Training Samples Using Normality, Separability, and Partitioning

Before the evaluation starts, the shapefile created for training samples needs to be added to the current project in *Contents* as a map layer. The samples appear in the map viewer, but the actual shapefile is needed in the *Contents*. If you don't see the shapefile, initially, when navigating to the correct file folder, then you may need to refresh the connection (see the red circle in second figure below).

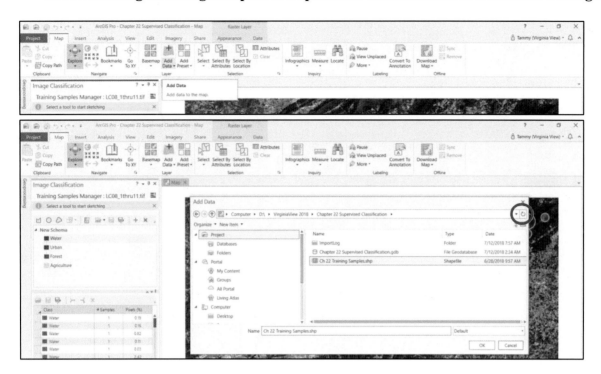

When the training sample shapefile is added, like any other polygon shapefile, the default symbology is single symbol.

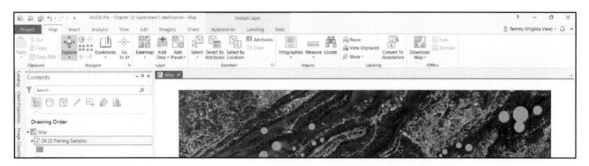

Go to *Symbology* and change to *Unique Values* and set the classification color scheme.

To begin evaluating the training samples, go to the *Raster Layer* tab and choose *Appearance*. Hover the mouse over the *Create Chart[1]* icon for three options – *Histogram*, *Scatter Plot* and *Spectral Profile*.

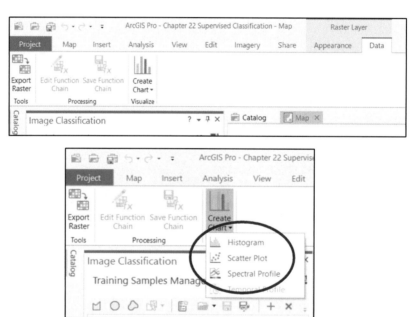

We will start with the 3rd option – *Spectral Profile*. The *Spectral Profile* graphs the spectral values of the pixels captured in the training samples (along the y-axis) for each band (along the x-axis) in the composite image. Graphing the spectral values provides information on whether multiple training samples, for a specific informational class, cover the same spectral values or a range of spectral values. If more than one training sample covers the same spectral values, we can eliminate one by deleting it or merging it with another training sample. We will evaluate each informational class, separately.

---

[1] Please note that this option is not available in any version of ArcGIS® Pro prior to 2.2.

Select *Create Spectral Profile*.

The *Chart Properties* dialog box opens and a new dialog box opens at the bottom of the map viewer. Please pay close attention to the next few instructions and the figures below, as you will need to toggle back and forth between the *Image Classification/Training Samples Manager* dialog box and the *Chart Properties* dialog box (it will become apparent as to why the training sample shapefile must be in *Contents*). We recommend that both dialog boxes are pinned so both dialog box names are at the top of the *Contents* dialog box (black box below), and thus easily accessed.

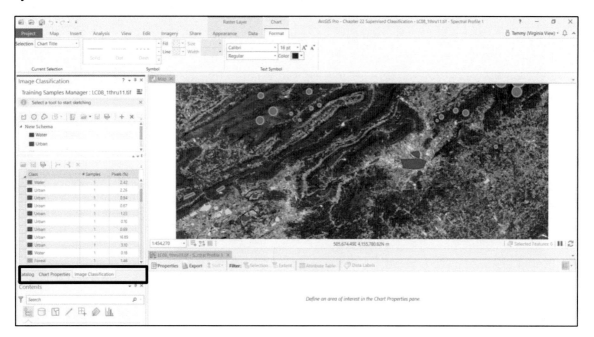

We will start with evaluating the *Urban* informational class. In the previous chapter, we created 8 training samples for the urban class.

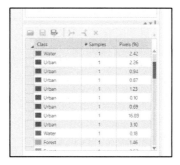

In *Chart Properties*, choose the *Feature Selector* icon.

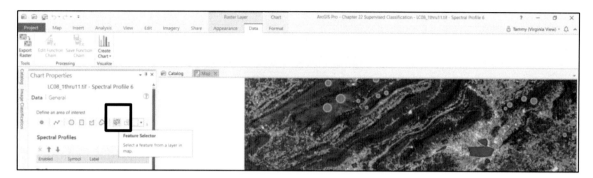

Now when you hover the mouse cursor in the map viewer, the cursor will now look like this:

This icon selects pixel values of all bands within the boundaries of that training sample and then graphs them. Do not select anything yet. We need to be careful that we know which sample is being selected in the *Training Sample Manager*. Please note that it may be necessary to zoom in to each sample in order to select it.

First, go back to the *Training Sample Manager* by clicking on the name of the dialog box – *Image Classification*.

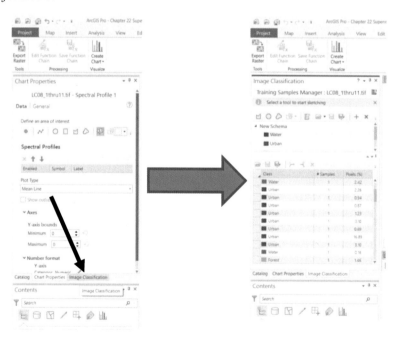

Then select the first *Urban* sample. It should be highlighted both in the dialog box and within the map viewer (in the figure below indicated by the black arrows).

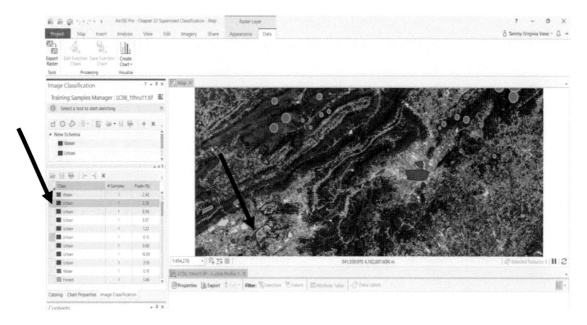

Now we know which training sample to select for graphing in *Chart Properties*.

Click on it with the left mouse button -- a spectral graph displays at the bottom of the map viewer.

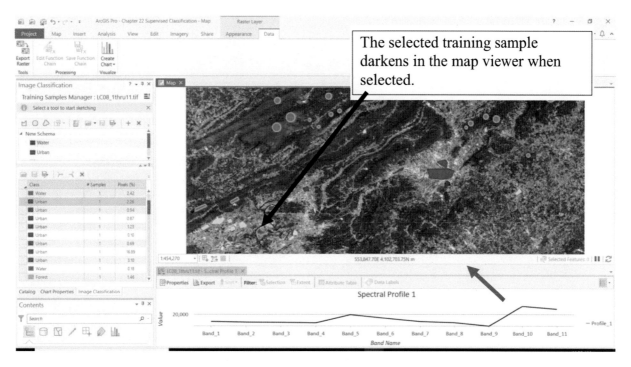

The selected training sample darkens in the map viewer when selected.

It does not appear to be associated with a wide range of values, but we need to expand the graph from top to bottom. Just click on it at the boundary between the graph and the map viewer (as indicated by the red arrow) to expand it.

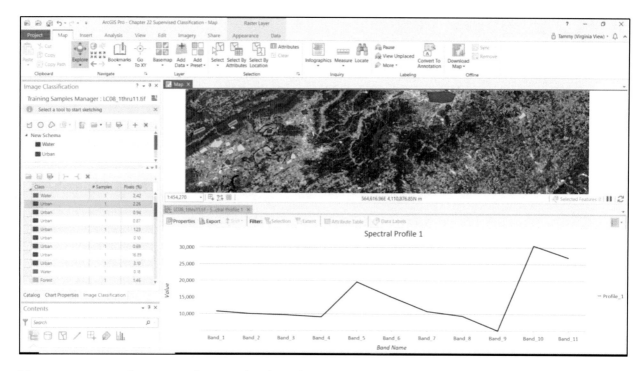

Now we can see the range of spectral values for each band for this one training sample. We need to add the second *Urban* training sample in order to conduct a comparison. In *Image Classification Training Manager*, select the 2nd training sample to know which one it is (it becomes highlighted in the map viewer), be sure that the *Feature Selector* icon is still enabled in *Chart Properties,* and select the same sample to add it to the *Spectral Profile* graph.

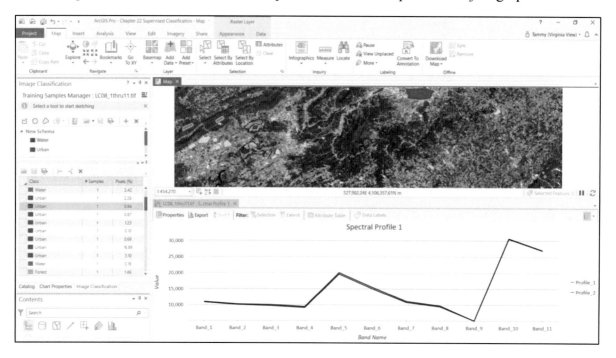

As seen, the profiles for these two training samples are very similar. Now, let's add a 3rd *Urban* training sample. This one is slightly different than the first two. It, again, may be necessary to expand the width of the graph to see differences.

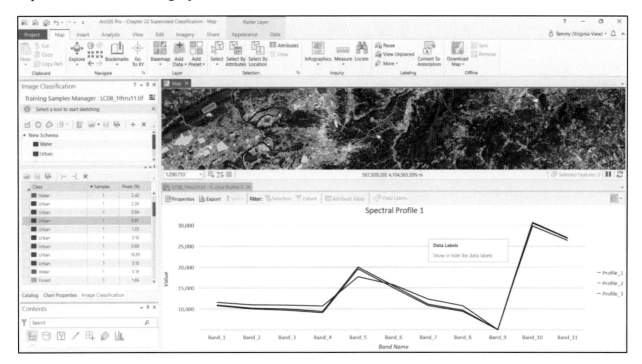

Continue to add additional *Urban* training samples, one by one and evaluate each histogram. If two are exactly the same, then these two samples should be combined into one. Be careful about combining dissimilar values into one sample. When merging training samples, some spectral values could be lost. Merging creates a new median, so values at the extreme may be lost. In the figure below, we have added all 8 samples for urban. Since we only have 8 urban samples, it is not hard to keep track of which sample belongs to which graph.

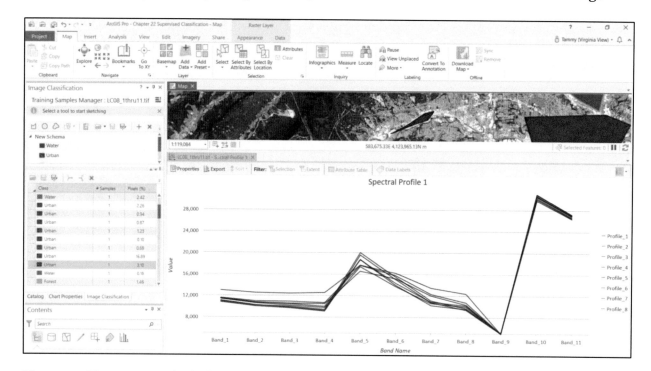

However, if necessary, the individual line colors can be changed to help with your spectral evaluation (see figure below) – just right click on the colored box and choose a new color.

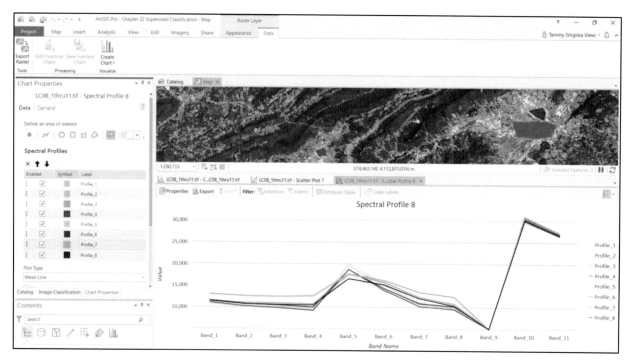

A note of caution.

When evaluating spectral values of the samples, do not look at the shape of the line, look at the range of values for individual bands (on the x-axis). Keep in mind that each individual band is useful for evaluating different features. In many instances, the values in Band 10, because Band

10 is not useful for urban environments, may have a small range, whereas the values for Bands 3 through 8 have much wider ranges:

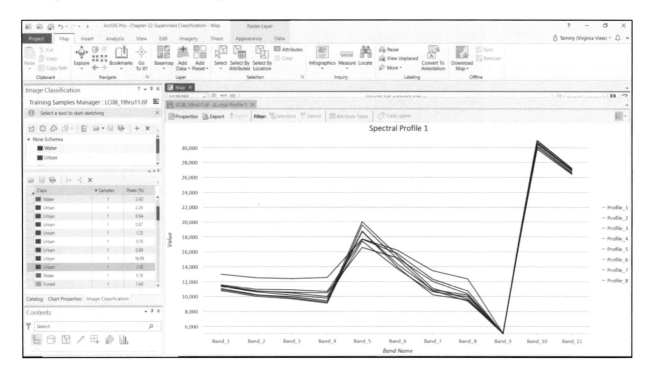

For the urban class, we are going to leave the 8 samples we created. You may make a different decision depending on how your graphs appear, the specific training samples chosen and your evaluation. Please note that, depending on what areas you trained, the graph will have a different look, and you may need to make different decisions.

So, now, let's evaluate the category - *water*. Then we will demonstrate how to merge training samples.

First, close the *Urban* graph. Then in *Create Chart*, choose *Create Spectral Profile*.

In *Chart Properties*, click on the *Feature Selector* icon. Go to *Image Classification/Training Sample Manager,* and select the first water sample to highlight it in the map viewer, and then select it in the map viewer. Follow the same procedure as in urban, just choose water samples.

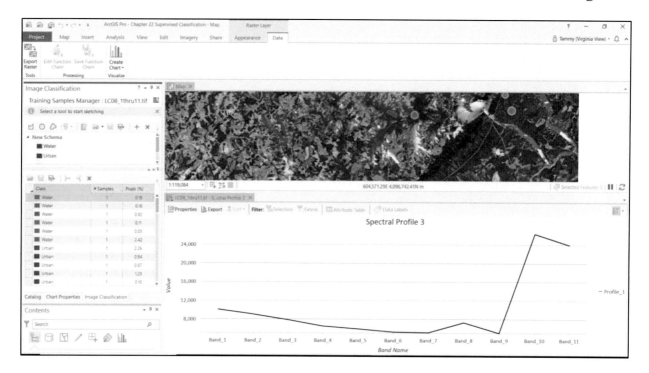

The spectral profile in the above graph (water) is very different from the urban spectral profiles. This is expected! Recall from prior chapters that spectral signatures should vary for different features (be sure to reference the Landsat 8 Band Sensitivities table that is included at the end of this chapter). Go ahead and add each training sample, evaluating each sample, and compare the samples to each other, as was just accomplished for the urban signatures.

The following graph shows the spectral properties for all water training samples (again, your graphs may look different).

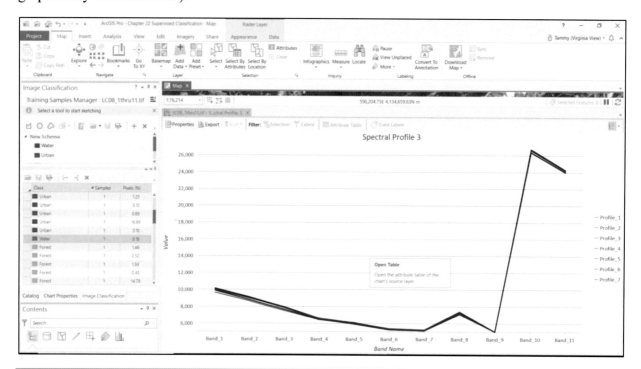

The water training samples show very few differences in spectral values between them, so we are going to combine them all into one sample to increase processing efficiency.

Within in the *Training Sample Manager*, highlight all of the water samples by holding down *ctrl* button on the computer's keyboard and then clicking on each sample. Note that when selecting more than one sample, the *Collapse* icon will become enabled.

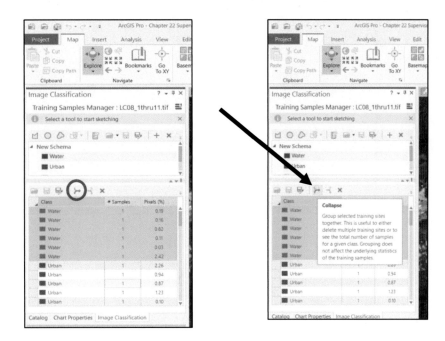

After you have selected all of the Water samples, select the *Collapse* icon. All of the water training samples have been collapsed (merged) into one sample (the blue figure below on the left). The new training sample now needs to be saved. Be sure to save this merged sample as a *new file* with a *new name*. We recommend that the original training sample shapefiles be maintained as separate files.

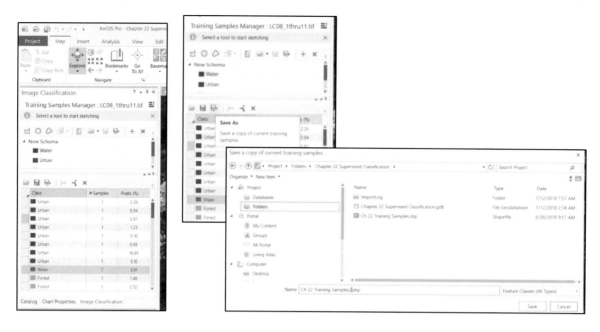

Now continue with the evaluation of training samples for the *Forest* class and then the *Agriculture* class.

All *Forest* spectral values are graphed in the below figure. Why is there a wider range of spectral values for forest in Band 5? (Answer – Band 5 is in the near infrared -- recall from prior chapters that vegetation has a greater range of spectral signatures in the near infrared.) Which of these training samples should be merged with each other? Please note that, although we do not show the process, we merged some samples. Don't forget to save frequently!

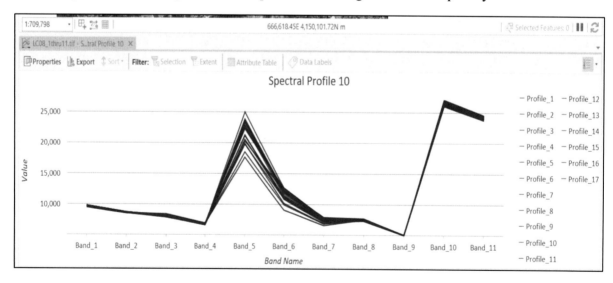

Now evaluate the training samples for *Agriculture* - complete each sample and graph them one by one. While the graph shows all samples, we have merged some samples as necessary. We are showing all samples to demonstrate that our agriculture samples contain spectral values that vary significantly. Agriculture spectral values vary much more and over many difference bands (relative to the samples from other informational classes). Can you speculate some reasons for this? (For your reference, we have included the Landsat 8 Band Sensitivities table at the end of this chapter). When evaluating the spectral values of the samples, evaluate all bands and all spectral values.

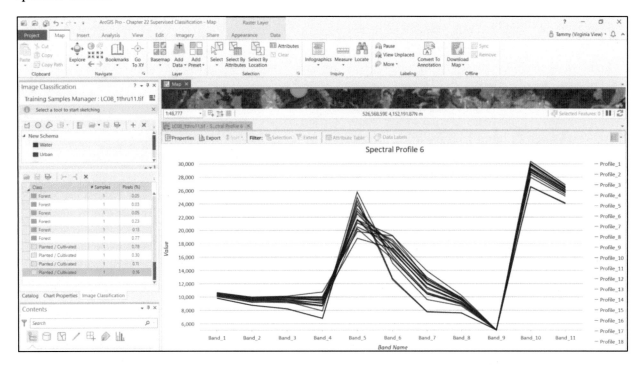

ArcGIS® Pro maintains a history of your steps and processes, so if you accidently merge training samples that you ultimately decide should not be merged, it is not necessary to start over. As long as you do not save, you can expand previously collapsed samples. If needed, highlight the merged sample in the list and the *Expand* icon is enabled. This icon only is enabled if you have highlighted a merged sample -- it does not enable for single samples. We will not demonstrate this capability-- we are just showing this option.

At this juncture, we have demonstrated how to evaluate the training samples to eliminate any significant overlap in spectral values. Leaving overlap within a class will not affect the results, it does, however, slow down the classification process. As an analyst becomes more knowledgeable and expert in the classification process, the number of training samples with overlapping spectral values will decrease.

Please now add the new training sample shapefile to the *Contents*.

Evaluating Separability using Scatterplots

Scatterplots plot the pixel values of the training data for two bands. One band is chosen for the x-axis and another band is chosen for the y-axis. When choosing the bands to plot, consideration must be given to which bands are best for identifying a specific feature (we have included Landsat 8 Band Sensitivities table at the end of this chapter). When viewing pixel values as scatterplots, points should not overlap if each classes' training samples' spectral values are separate from each other. If any overlapping exists, misclassification could occur.

To create scatterplots, select the *Raster Layer > Data* tab and under *Create Chart*, chose *Create Scatter Plot*.

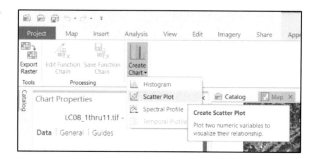

The *Chart Properties* dialog box opens along with a new blank window under the map viewer. This looks similar to the *Spectral Profile* discussed previously -- differences will become apparent as we proceed.

At the end of each axis line, click the dropdown arrow to choose the bands to plot. In the figure below, Band_2 is assigned to the *x-axis* and Band_5 is assigned to the *y-axis*.

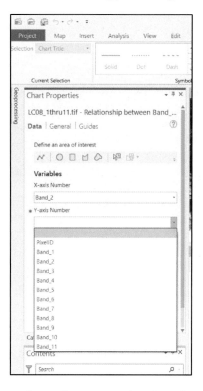

This results in the immediate generation of a scatterplot, but the scatterplot is for the entire composite image. Because we are only evaluating training samples, we need to make additional choices in *Chart Properties*.

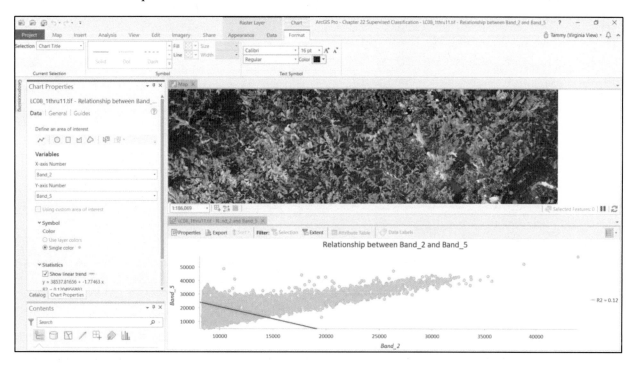

At the top of the *Chart Properties* window, click on *Feature Selector* (just as was required under *Spectral Profile* above).

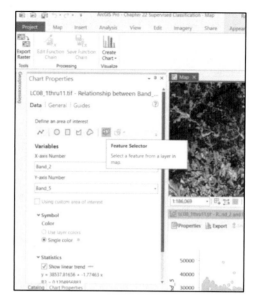

Next, click on one of the polygons in the map viewer – in this following figure, we chose one agriculture polygon. This selection plots the spectral values of every pixel within that specific polygon training sample. Note, this procedure does not plot the spectral values associated with all of the agriculture training sample polygons.

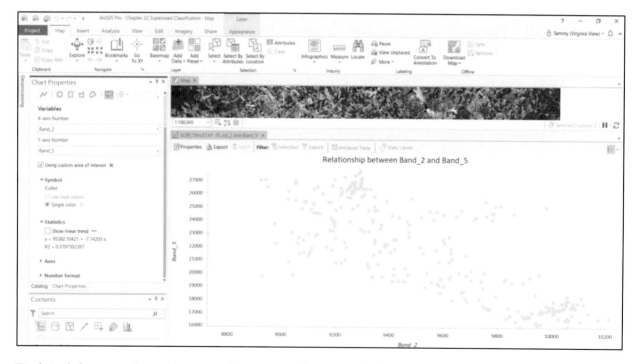

Each training sample polygon can be evaluated separately, but we wish to compare all pixel values from one class to another class across two bands. In order to do this, it will require that all training samples for each class be collapsed into one training sample for each class. Open the *Training Samples Manager* and be sure that the final training sample shapefile is loaded into the dialog box (the one completed after evaluating and merging in the previous section). Then, for each of the informational classes, collapse them into one training sample e.g. one for Water, one for Urban, one for Agriculture, and one for Forest. Then select *save as* and save it as a new shapefile.

Name it something simple, it will be used for scatterplots and later working with histograms. As seen below, here it was named *Ch 22 Training Samples3*.

Then add the new training sample shapefile to the *Contents,* and turn off any other training sample shapefiles, so that the newly added training sample is the only layer displayed on the composite image in the map viewer.

Now, go back to the *Image* tab, *Create Charts* and *Create Scatter Plot*. Use *Feature Selector* to select one of the agriculture polygons. Because we collapsed all the training samples for each class into one sample, all pixel values for all agriculture training sample locations will populate in the scatterplot window. We still need to change some of the other parameters.

Please note, at this juncture, *Use layer colors²* is not available for image scatterplots, so we cannot plot all 4 classes on the same graph at this time. We are going to compare the scatterplots with each other to make sure the spectral values are separated for each informational class (some overlap is okay). This can be accomplished by creating a scatterplot for each class. Be sure to set the minimum and maximum axis values the same for all 4 classes. What value range should be used? For Landsat 8, 65,536 possible values exist. But we have a subset of an entire scene. By checking the *Properties* of the composite image, it is possible to determine what the minimum and maximum values are. In the example below, we set the minimum value at 4500 (the smallest value present in our subset image is 4535) and the maximum value at 65000 (maximum value present is 64869):

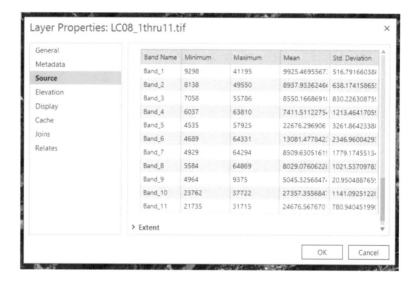

---

² Under Version 2.2, this option is not available but it may become available in future versions of ArcGIS® Pro.

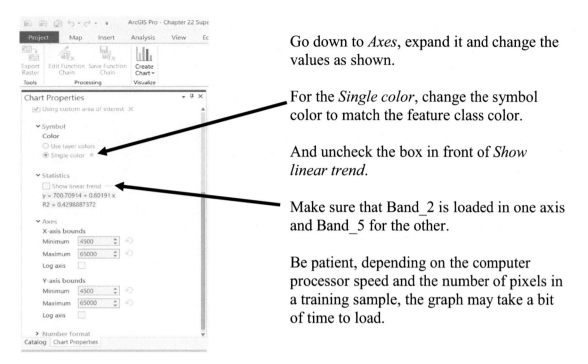

Go down to *Axes*, expand it and change the values as shown.

For the *Single color*, change the symbol color to match the feature class color.

And uncheck the box in front of *Show linear trend*.

Make sure that Band_2 is loaded in one axis and Band_5 for the other.

Be patient, depending on the computer processor speed and the number of pixels in a training sample, the graph may take a bit of time to load.

Results of graphing Band 2 and Band 5 with the Agriculture training samples (we will discuss in more detail after graphing all 4 training sample classes). As noted previously, in the spectral profile graph above, Agriculture has a wide variety of spectral values. This is again demonstrated in the Scatter Plot graph for Band 5 (Near Infrared) but demonstrates a small range in Band 2 (Blue visible):

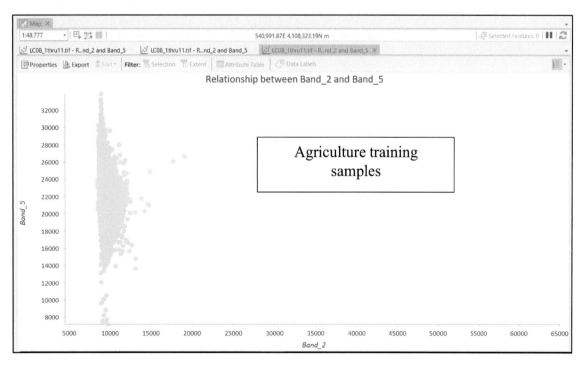

We recommend that you close the *Chart Properties* dialog box after creating the graph and then reopen *Chart Properties* to create the new graph. Closing and then reopening the dialog box for a new graph, keeps the prior graph(s) created (don't close the graph box, just the *Chart Properties* dialog box in the upper left corner).

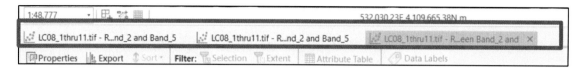

The figure below displays the results of graphing Band 2 and Band 5 with the water training samples (inset is an enlargement of the area of pixel values for the water training samples). Note that water absorbs most radiation so the spectral values have a very small range in both Band 2 (Blue Visible) and Band 5 (Near Infrared):

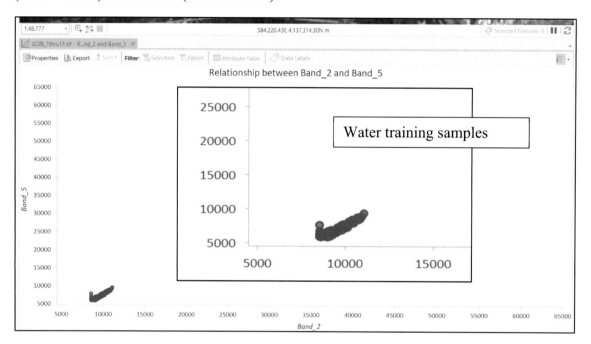

The figure below shows results of graphing Band 2 and Band 5 with the urban training samples. The urban samples show a wide range of values in both bands. Therefore the graph is much more scattered than the water example (above).

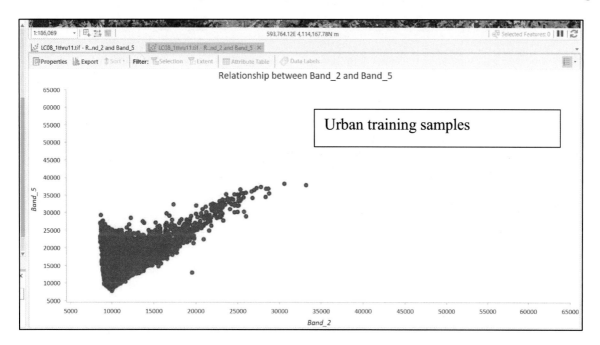

The figure below shows the results of graphing Band 2 and Band 5 with the forest training samples. Note that the pixel values have a wider range in Band 5 (Near Infrared) than in Band 2 (Blue Visible). Again, reference the *Band Sensitivities Chart* (at the end of this chapter) that summarizes the significance of different bands for different features.

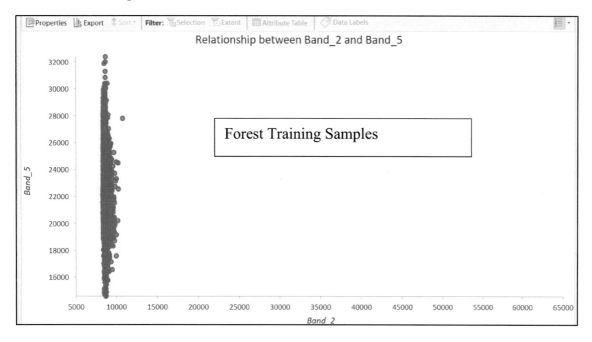

Because ArcGIS® Pro does not allow (with version 2.2) to graph all training samples, by symbology, in one graph, you must do a visual analysis and independent comparison for separability. Since each graph is saved within the window, you can toggle from graph to graph, looking for significant areas where the spectral values are overlapping the classes.

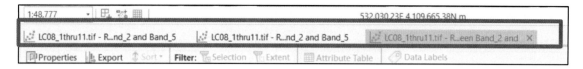

If such areas are located, training samples need to be reviewed to determine the class where they actually belong. This means going back to the training sample manager and adding training samples to one class and eliminating them from another. Again, many urban areas have parks with extensive tree canopy, mountain shadows may have spectral properties similar to water, etc. These variables need to be kept in mind when creating, and then, evaluating training samples.

Additionally, don't limit the analysis to just these two bands. As noted above, agriculture and forest do not show a very wide range of values in Band 2 (Blue Visible), so, it is necessary to continue the analysis, by graphing other bands. You will need to continue to do this for each band that's important for your analysis. You may also need to vary the axis values (as seen in the figures below). The first figure is agriculture in Band 3 (Green Visible) and Band 5 (Near Infrared).

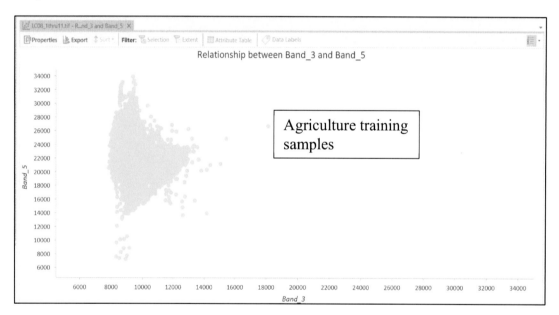

Below is the scatterplot for the urban class training samples in Bands 3 and 5. We are seeing significant overlap between areas of urban and agriculture. Many urban area greenspaces are interspersed with impervious surfaces (which can mimic bare earth). As we saw in Chapter 16: Band Combinations for Landsat 8 Imagery, the agriculture locations are in various stages of growth. (Don't forget to close the *Chart Properties* dialog box and then reopen it to make the next graph. If you just change the values in the open dialog box, the graph just created will be lost.)

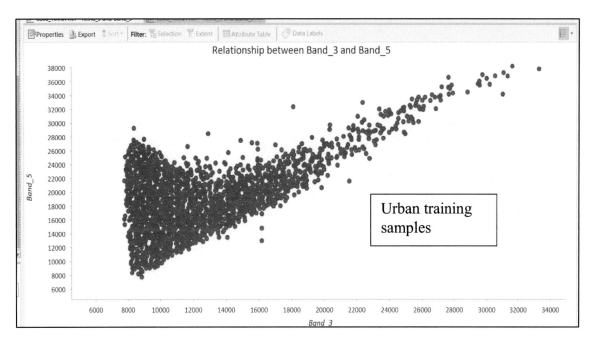

The figure below shows a scatterplot of water training samples for bands 3 and 5. This looks very similar to the water scatterplot for bands 2 and 5. Why does water cover such as small range of values? (Because clear, calm water absorbs most of the radiation.)

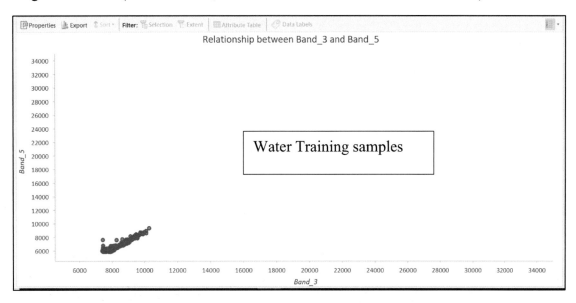

And, finally forest training samples, Band 5 (near-infrared) plotted against Band 3 (green visible). Because forest, like agriculture, is primarily plant life, we see much more range of values with this graph. Although, the graph is not as extensive as that of agriculture – do you know why? Agriculture will have a wider range of brightness values than forest in June because of the various stages of fields being planted for different crops and the variation in maturity rates.

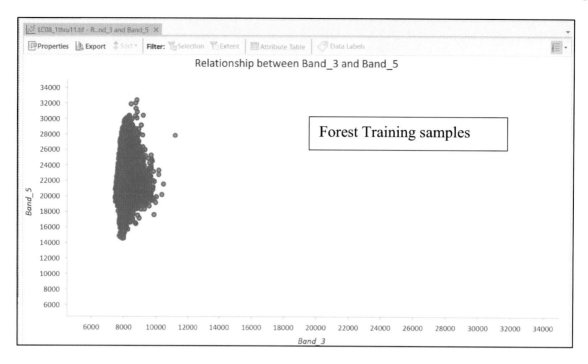

Evaluating Normality with Histograms

Recall from Chapter 17 (Radiometric Enhancement of Landsat 8 Imagery), that a histogram depicts the distribution of the numbers of pixels with respect to pixel values. We now need to evaluate pixel values within training data to assess their degree of normality. If pixel values within any one of the classes are not normally distributed (for example, they display a bimodal histogram) it is likely that a specific class has not been sufficiently trained. If this is the case, additional training samples are needed to cover missing spectral values. To evaluate a histogram, we need to use the 3rd training sample shapefile created – the one that collapsed all the training samples for each class into one training sample for each class. In order to create a histogram for training samples, we need to extract the pixel values for all bands of the composite image into a separate raster file for each informational class. We will be using the *Raster Functions* procedure demonstrated in Chapter 15 (*Subsetting a Composite Landsat 8 Image*).

We will evaluate each informational class separately, so we need to separately extract pixel values from the composite image for each of the training samples. We are also going to demonstrate how to select a feature from a vector shapefile and use that single feature as the clipping geometry in the *Raster Functions* tool.

To select an individual feature from a vector file, go to the *Map* tab and click on the *Select* icon – it is not necessary to click the down arrow and don't worry that it says *Select by Rectangle*, we just want the general *Select*.

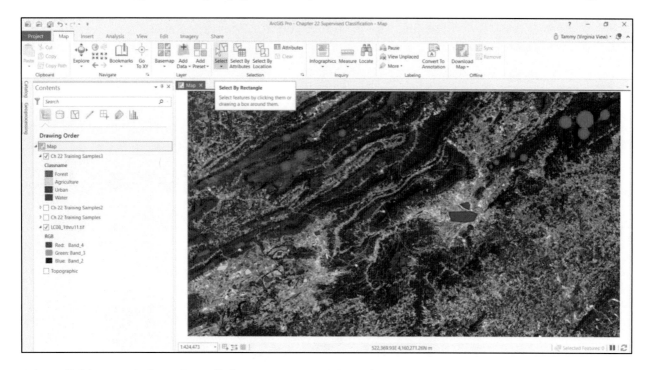

After clicking on *Select*, then click on any one of the polygons in the map viewer. In the figure below, we selected Forest and all Forest polygons became highlighted (remember, we collapsed all the separate training samples for Forest into one polygon when we started working with scatterplots).

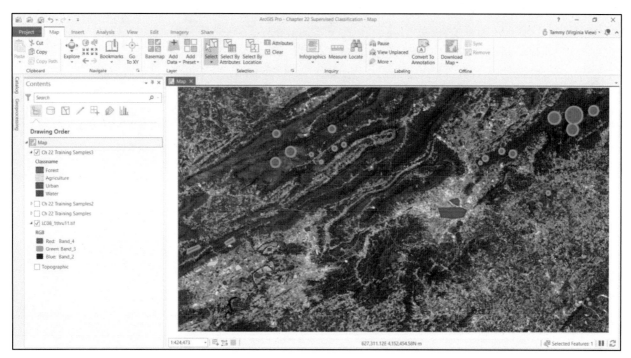

Now, make sure that the composite image is highlighted in *Contents*, go to the *Imagery* tab, then select *Raster Functions* (figure below).

Under the *Data Management* tools, select *Clip*.

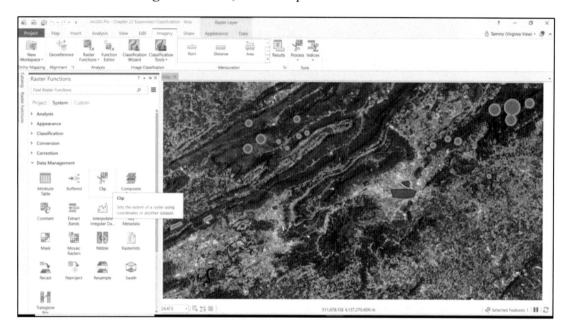

Again, this tool was used in Chapter 15. Be sure all the parameters are as shown below.

After selecting *Create New Layer*, the new layer appears in the *Contents*. If you check the *Properties* of this new layer, you will find that it is an 11 band composite image. It does not seem to be present in the map viewer.

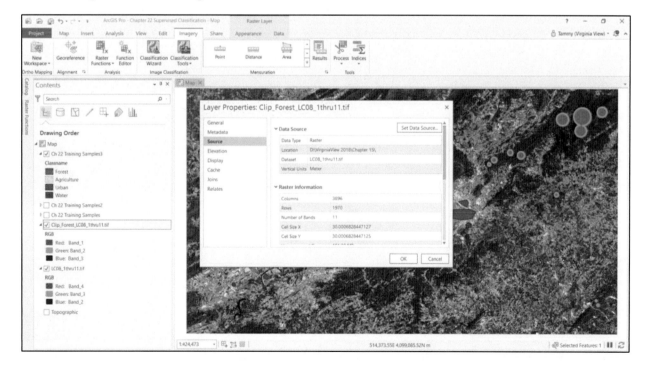

Turn off all layers except for the Clip_Forest. The 11 band composite image has been clipped to the extent of each of the forest training sample polygons.

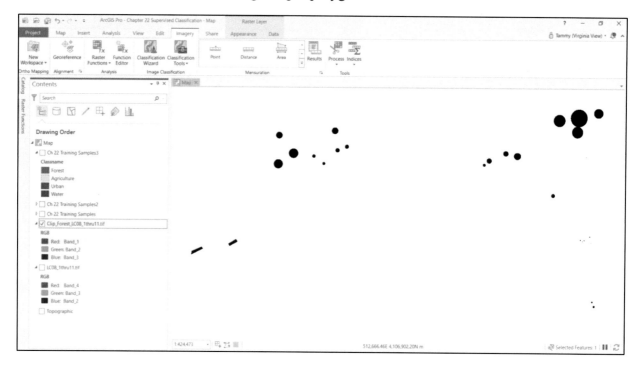

Set Band Combinations (See Chapter 16) for this new layer to Color Infrared (5-4-3).

Highlight this new layer in the *Contents*, go to *Raster Layer* tab, *Data, Create Chart*, and *Create Histogram*.

In *Chart Properties*, be sure that *Show Normal Distribution*, *Mean*, *Median* and *Std. Deviation* are all checked. Under *Variable*, choose Band_5 from the dropdown list.

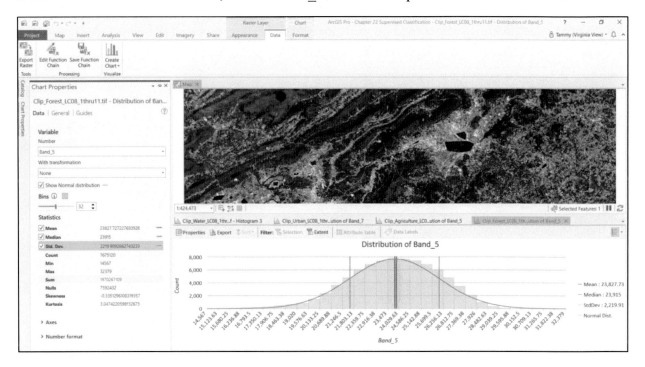

This distribution shows that our Forest Training Sample pixel values have a normal distribution in Band 5.

Do the same thing for each Band that is significant for the specific feature. For Forest, we also checked Band 3 (Green Visible).

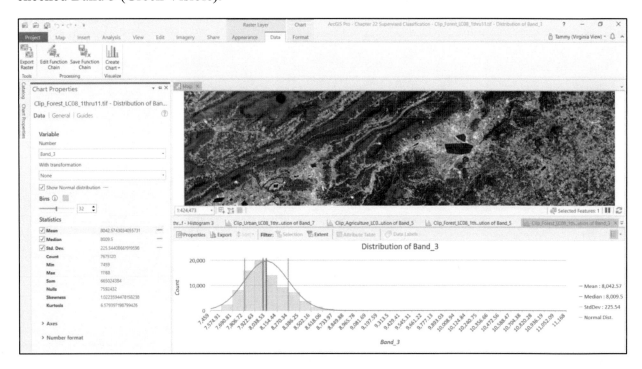

Now, do it for the other classes, setting the band combinations that best displays that specific feature and then looking at the histogram for those specific bands. As shown in the figure below, we have a separate clipped composite image (in *Contents*) for each of training sample classes. These layers are the only ones turned on, thus the only ones displayed in the map viewer.

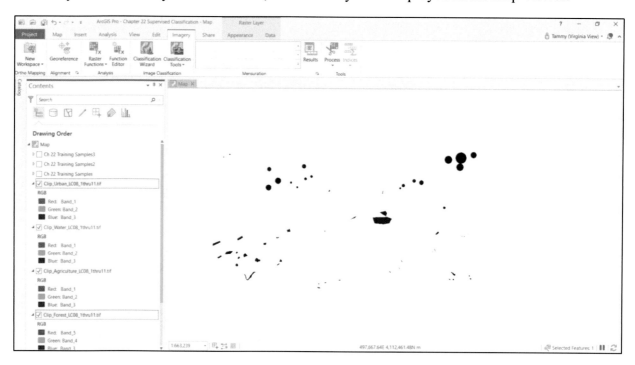

Agriculture's histogram for Band 5. Initially, it appears to be multi-modal, but this illustrates the importance of placing a check mark in *Show Normal distribution*.

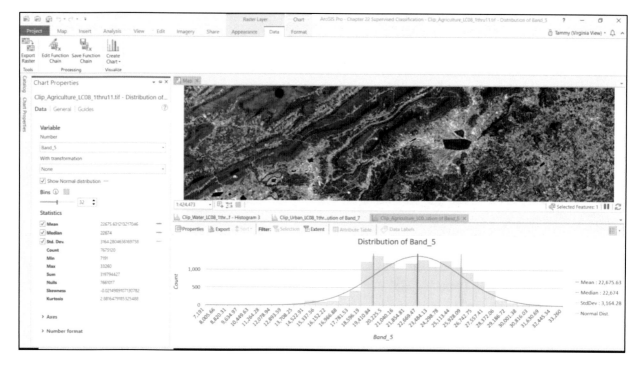

Urban in Band 7, still within a normal distribution.

The Water histogram displayed in Band 5. The distribution appears to be skewed to the left, but the majority of water pixel values are very low because clear, deep, water absorbs, and does not re-emit at most wavelengths.

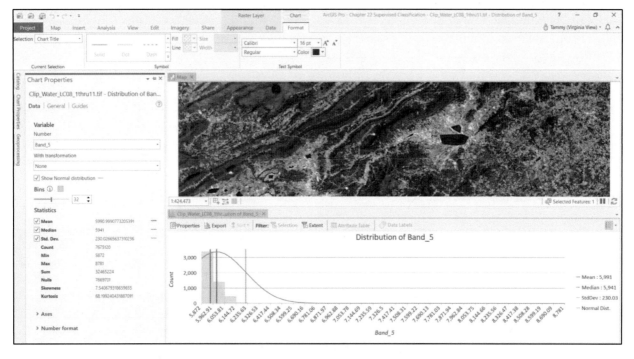

Again, examine each of the classes for normality in each of the significant bands. We state significant because, for our 11 band Landsat 8 image, Band 1 and Bands 10 and 11 are likely not significant for our analysis. Do you need to add any training data to any of the classes? Training data for each class may not cover the entire range of brightness values, as demonstrated for water.

Evaluation Co-Variance between Training Samples

Covariance evaluates the correlation of values between the different bands. Low values indicate that values in a pair of bands tend to increase and decrease independently. High values indicate that the values in the two bands tend to increase and decrease together — a high covariance. For effective classification, we prefer to see low covariances, indicating that the training data are providing independent information (i.e., data from training fields are not replicating each other).

To evaluate Covariance (and other statistics), go to the *Analysis* tab, *Tools* and search for *Band Collection Statistics*.

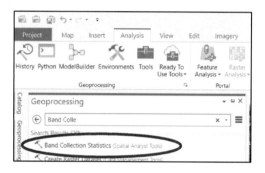

We will be using the new clipped images for each of our training samples in this tool. Open the tool. From the drop down arrow, choose the *Clip_Forest* (or any of the other files – we will be running the tool four times).

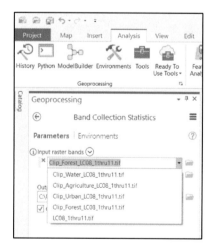

For *Output location*, leave the default location. (At the time of writing this chapter, navigating to the geodatabase for this project caused the tool to fail every time, whereas using the default location was successful.) Be sure to keep track of the name generated by ArcGIS® Pro.

Make sure that *Compute covariance and correlation matrices* is checked.

At the bottom, select *Run*.

Be patient while the tool runs.

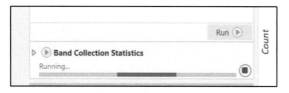

Once it is finished, a message displays – *Completed successfully*.

Now, re-run this tool for each of the training sample clipped composite images. Each time the tool finishes, you will see a new *Standalone Table* at the bottom of the *Contents* window.

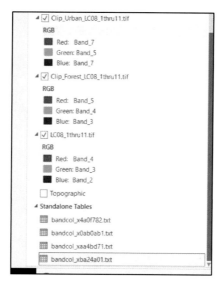

To view the results, highlight the first table, right click and select *Open*.

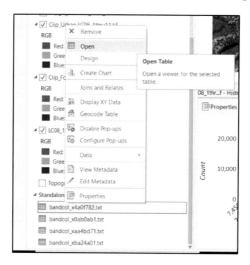

The table opens at the bottom of the map viewer. The following figure is a composite of the table using the scroll bar on the right. This table contains our Forest Training Samples.

#	Layer	MIN	MAX	MEAN	STD
		STATISTICS of INDIVIDUAL LAYERS			
	1	9341.0000	11575.0000	9559.6194	105.0798
	2	8292.0000	10755.0000	8514.3130	96.2518
	3	7459.0000	11168.0000	8042.5743	225.5441
	4	6385.0000	10601.0000	6679.0401	175.3642
	5	14567.0000	32379.0000	23827.7272	2219.9093
	6	8489.0000	21126.0000	11936.9243	863.1478
	7	6304.0000	14655.0000	7511.9609	385.3529
	8	6856.0000	13140.0000	7434.1000	201.8000
	9	4995.0000	5109.0000	5044.5517	10.7194
	10	25099.0000	28334.0000	26101.2784	405.2332
	11	23173.0000	25294.0000	23837.9751	281.3023

COVARIANCE MATRIX

# Layer	1	2	3	4	5	6	7	8	9	10	11
1	118.98045	97.69379	49.46034	99.68144	-841.14645	-19.47936	32.93868	80.44550	-2.89607	344.01088	219.38124
2	97.69379	99.78835	125.89118	144.82348	-589.70771	221.35653	163.18056	141.09903	-1.74251	326.49799	219.12180
3	49.46034	125.89118	547.69182	349.42530	1130.34015	1436.24391	741.46798	451.30993	0.73031	380.62847	294.82609
4	99.68144	144.82348	349.42530	331.13691	-506.33378	838.25359	539.10006	343.53167	-0.89235	390.88871	280.93344
5	-841.14645	-589.70771	1130.34015	-506.33378	53079.43259	13869.90671	3902.95393	281.10153	32.61354	-2610.01403	-1665.82095
6	-19.47936	221.35653	1436.24391	838.25359	13869.90671	8024.46675	3316.18896	1121.28157	10.03526	579.35294	514.80807
7	32.93868	163.18056	741.46798	539.10006	3902.95393	3316.18896	1599.33436	637.07873	3.56955	378.50201	320.23335
8	80.44550	141.09903	451.30993	343.53167	281.10153	1121.28157	637.07873	438.36169	-0.17626	389.71151	290.09678
9	-2.89607	-1.74251	0.73031	-0.89235	32.61354	10.03526	3.56955	-0.17626	1.24377	-7.69238	-4.68746
10	344.01088	326.49799	380.62847	390.88871	-2610.01403	579.35294	378.50201	389.71151	-7.69238	1769.61457	1213.19914
11	219.38124	219.12180	294.82609	280.93344	-1665.82095	514.80807	320.23335	290.09678	-4.68746	1213.19914	852.54580

CORRELATION MATRIX

# Layer	1	2	3	4	5	6	7	8	9	10	11
1	1.00000	0.89658	0.19375	0.50220	-0.33471	-0.01994	0.07551	0.35225	-0.23807	0.74971	0.68882
2	0.89658	1.00000	0.53850	0.79670	-0.25623	0.24737	0.40847	0.67463	-0.15641	0.77696	0.75125
3	0.19375	0.53850	1.00000	0.82051	0.20964	0.68510	0.79224	0.92107	0.02798	0.38663	0.43146
4	0.50220	0.79670	0.82051	1.00000	-0.12077	0.51424	0.74079	0.90167	-0.04397	0.51063	0.52874
5	-0.33471	-0.25623	0.20964	-0.12077	1.00000	0.67205	0.42360	0.05828	0.12693	-0.26930	-0.24763
6	-0.01994	0.24737	0.68510	0.51424	0.67205	1.00000	0.92568	0.59785	0.10045	0.15374	0.19682
7	0.07551	0.40847	0.79224	0.74079	0.42360	0.92568	1.00000	0.76086	0.08003	0.22499	0.27424
8	0.35225	0.67463	0.92107	0.90167	0.05828	0.59785	0.76086	1.00000	-0.00755	0.44247	0.47453
9	-0.23807	-0.15641	0.02798	-0.04397	0.12693	0.10045	0.08003	-0.00755	1.00000	-0.16396	-0.14395
10	0.74971	0.77696	0.38663	0.51063	-0.26930	0.15374	0.22499	0.44247	-0.16396	1.00000	0.98772
11	0.68882	0.75125	0.43146	0.52874	-0.24763	0.19682	0.27424	0.47453	-0.14395	0.98772	1.00000

The top chart presents statistics for each band's pixel values. Keep in mind that these values are just associated with our training samples. We have seen these values before, under histograms.

Next, let's look at the *correlation matrix* – bottom of the chart. Remember this analysis is to evaluate the bands and their similarities to each other. As such, when comparing Band 1 to Band 1, Band 2 to Band 2; the value is 1 – they are exactly alike. As values decrease from 1, the bands are more dissimilar.

Band 1 is next most closely correlated with Band 2 (0.89658). Review the Landsat 8 Band Sensitivities table (at the end of this chapter); the correlation makes some sense since Band 1 is used for Coastal areas and Band 1 (Blue Visible) is useful for Bathymetric mapping. Both of these bands involve some type of evaluation of water or water/land boundaries. Please examine each of these values to understand which bands are more closely correlated with one another.

Now let's take a look at the *covariance matrix* in the middle. Recall that low values indicate that the values in a pair of bands tend to increase and decrease independently. High values indicate that the values in the two bands tend to increase and decrease together— a high covariance. For effective classification, we prefer to see low covariances, indicating that the training data are providing independent information.

Now that we have finished evaluating our training samples and we have eliminated samples, merged samples, and created new samples, we are ready to proceed with classification.

Band Sensitivities for Landsat 8.

Reference

Barsi, J.A.; Lee, K.; Kvaran, G.; Markham, B.L.; Pedelty, J.A. The Spectral Response of the Landsat-8 Operational Land Imager. *Remote Sens.* **2014**, *6*, 10232-10251. doi:10.3390/rs61010232

Band	Wavelength	Useful for mapping
Band 1 – Coastal Aerosol	0.435 - 0.451	Coastal and aerosol studies
Band 2 – Blue	0.452 - 0.512	Bathymetric mapping, distinguishing soil from vegetation, and deciduous from coniferous vegetation
Band 3 - Green	0.533 - 0.590	Emphasizes peak vegetation, which is useful for assessing plant vigor
Band 4 - Red	0.636 - 0.673	Discriminates vegetation slopes
Band 5 - Near Infrared (NIR)	0.851 - 0.879	Emphasizes biomass content and shorelines
Band 6 - Short-wave Infrared (SWIR) 1	1.566 - 1.651	Discriminates moisture content of soil and vegetation; penetrates thin clouds
Band 7 - Short-wave Infrared (SWIR) 2	2.107 - 2.294	Improved moisture content of soil and vegetation and thin cloud penetration
Band 8 - Panchromatic	0.503 - 0.676	15 meter resolution, sharper image definition
Band 9 – Cirrus	1.363 - 1.384	Improved detection of cirrus cloud contamination
Band 10 – TIRS 1	10.60 – 11.19	100 meter resolution, thermal mapping and estimated soil moisture
Band 11 – TIRS 2	11.50 - 12.51	100 meter resolution, Improved thermal mapping and estimated soil moisture

Landsat 8 Bands and Associated Mapping Applications. Table from: https://landsat.usgs.gov/what-are-best-spectral-bands-use-my-study

Introduction

At this juncture, training samples have been created (Chapter 22) and evaluated (Chapter 23). In this, the final chapter on supervised classification, we provide details on completing a signature file and then conducting the supervised classification. We introduce three alternative procedures to conduct this classification (please note that there are many other techniques and algorithms, not mentioned here, to conduct a supervised classification).

Objectives
The objectives of this chapter are to:
- Generate supervised signatures using training samples;
- Perform a supervised classification on a Landsat 8 image using the maximum likelihood geoprocessing tool;
- Perform a supervised classification using the geoprocessing tool - *Classify Raster*; and
- Perform a supervised classification using the *Image Classification Wizard;*

This chapter uses the 11-band composite Landsat 8 image, subset to the extent of the map viewer created in Chapter 15. We will be using the same informational classes used in Chapters 21 - 23, so, as a reminder, the classes are:

- Urban/built up/transportation = class #1, designated as red
- Mixed agriculture = class #2, designated as yellow
- Forest and Wetland = class #3, designated as green
- Open water = class #4, designated as blue

Supervised Classification using Maximum Likelihood

If ArcGIS® Pro is not already open, open it and add the 11-band composite image (created in Chapter 15) and the training sample shapefile that was created in Chapter 23 – the one created while evaluating spectral signatures. (Do not use the shapefile with one training sample for each of the information classes). Set the image to a natural color (4-3-2) and the training sample shapefile to unique values for the informational class color symbology noted above. Do not forget to set the workspaces, etc.

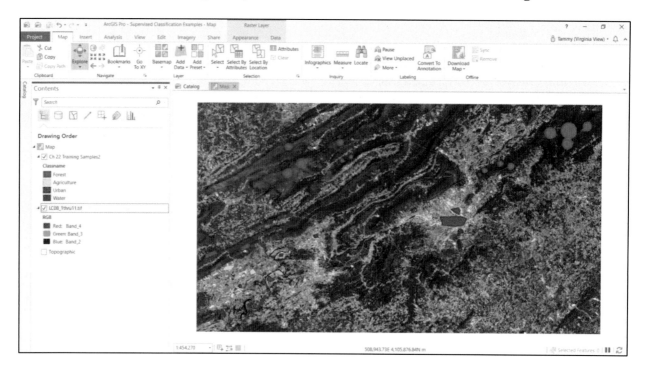

Creating a signature file

To use the maximum likelihood tool, we also need a signature file (a file with the spectral signatures for each informational class).

Go to the *Analysis* tab and select *Tools*. Search for *Create Signatures*. Open the tool.

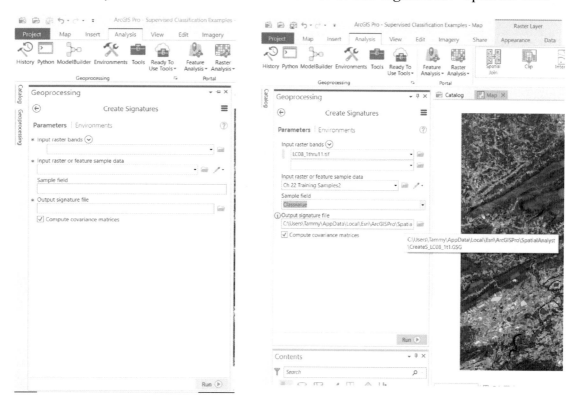

Your *Input raster bands* is the composite 11-band image. The *Input raster or feature sample data* is the training sample shapefile. *Sample field* should be *classvalue*. The output signature file – navigate to the project file folder, and save it in this location (however, at the time of writing this chapter, this step caused the tool to fail). If when creating the signature file, the tool fails to run the first time, use the default folder location. (Note that, when ArcGIS® Pro software was added, it automatically created a default workspace and geodatabase. Sometimes, when a tool fails to run, try to let it save in these default locations. For this particular tool, it solves the failure problem).

Once all parameters of the tool are populated, select *Run* at the bottom of the dialog box. As with other Geoprocessing operations, the status displays:

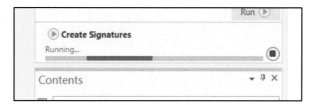

Once successful, a *Completed successfully* message displays.

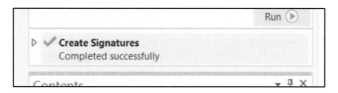

But, a new file does not show in *Contents* (figure below).

However, the new file will be listed in the appropriate folder location in the computer (again we note that the file created (.gsg) went into the default geodatabase and was automatically named by ArcGIS® Pro):

Geoprocessing Tools - Conducting a Maximum Likelihood Classification

Go to the *Analysis* tab, open *Tools* and search for *Maximum Likelihood Classification.*

Open the *Maximum Likelihood Classification* tool. For the *Input raster bands*, select the composite image. The *input signature file* is the file that we just created above (.gsg file extension). (If you are unable to navigate to the .gsg file from the file folder within the tool, see the next steps below).

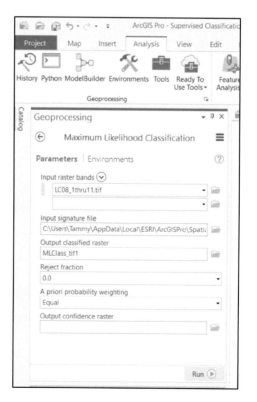

Within the Windows environment - navigate to the folder on C drive and open the folder to view the list of files. Place the window showing the file side by side with ArcGIS® Pro, highlight the .gsg file and drag the file into the field. (Yes! ArcGIS® Pro allows you to select and drag files into the program.)

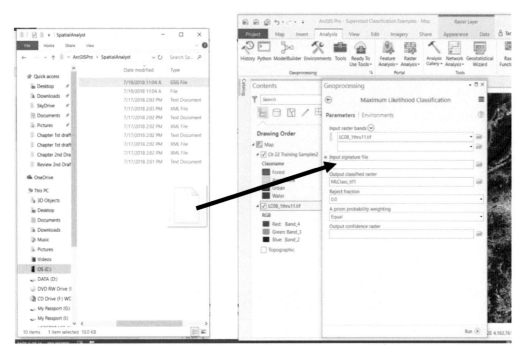

Rename the *Output classified raster*, if wanted. Leave *Reject fraction* at 0.0 because we want all cells to be classified.

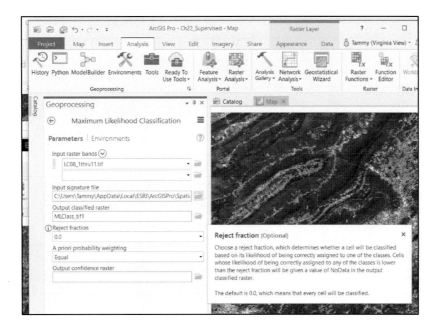

Under the *Environments* tab, do not change any settings. These settings can be changed, depending on needs of the final project.

Select *Run* at the bottom, the progress of the tool displays.

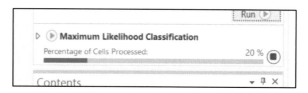

A *Completed successfully* message displays when the tool finishes.

Additionally, there is now a new layer in *Contents,* and a new image in the map viewer:

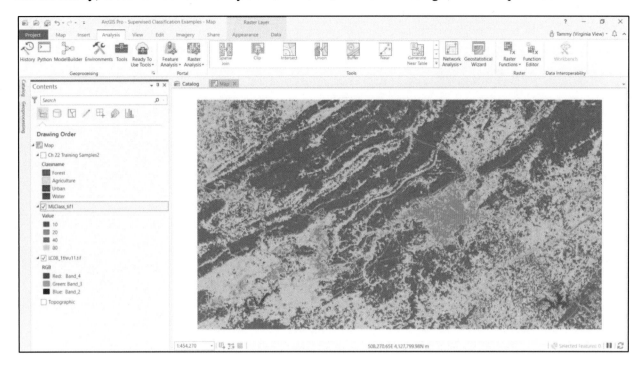

Again, the symbology is randomly selected, so correct by changing Water to blue, Urban to red; Forest to green; and Agriculture to yellow.

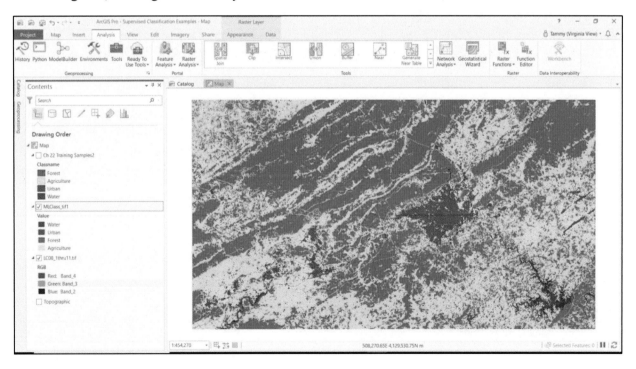

Calculating the Percent of Total Area for Each Informational Class. Now, calculate the number of hectares and the percent of total landcover for each informational class (just as accomplished in Chapter 21 – Unsupervised Classification). Do you remember how to do this?

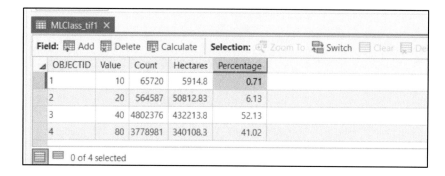

How accurate was your classification using the ***Maximum Likelihood Classification*** method? We will assess that in Chapter 25: Accuracy Assessment. We will use this maximum likelihood image and the percentages just calculated in that chapter. However, before proceeding to that chapter, we will demonstrate two additional classification processes available in ArcGIS® Pro. But, we also explain why we will be using this maximum likelihood image created with this specific geoprocessing tool in the accuracy assessment.

Geoprocessing Tools - the Classify Raster Tool

Geoprocessing tools provides additional options for classification. Under the *Analysis* tab, click on *Tools* and search for *Classify Raster*.

Open the *Classify Raster - Spatial Analyst Tool* (the second one in the list). As you can see from this tool, we need to specify an additional file – a definition file[1]. What is nice about this tool is that we do not actually have to use the maximum likelihood tool if we create a definition file based on the algorithm.

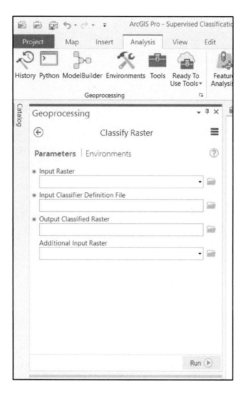

So, go back to search tools and find the *Train Maximum Likelihood Classifier*.

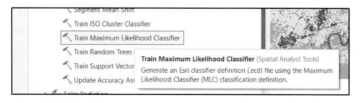

Open the tool (*Train Maximum Likelihood Classifier*), and enter the parameters as shown on the right. Leave everything else as default:

---

[1] A definition file is a .ecd file containing attribute statistics suitable for the appropriate classifier. For more information, refer to http://pro.arcgis.com/en/pro-app/tool-reference/spatial-analyst/classify-raster.htm. The *Raster Classify* tool can be used with any type of classification scheme (random trees, Support vector, etc.) with the appropriate definition file.

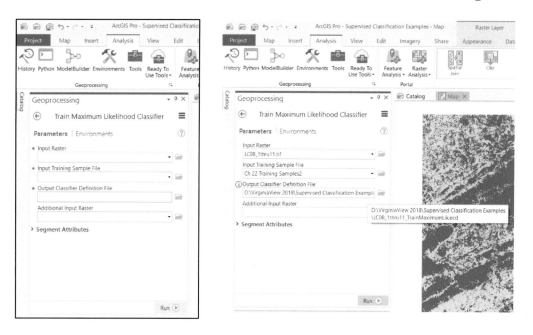

Select *Run*, and once complete, a *Completed successfully* message displays. No, it did not complete a new layer in the *Contents*.

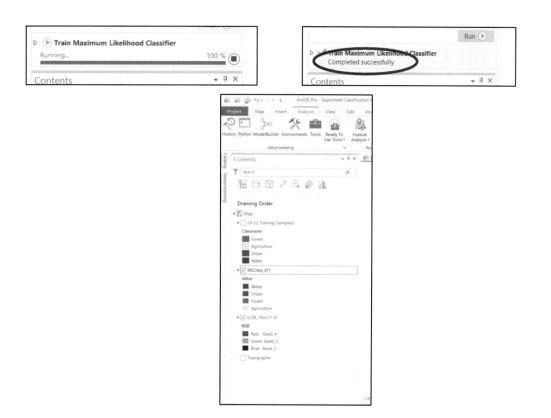

Now that we have a definition file, we can use *Classify Raster*. The inputs for this tool are outlined below. After these changes have been made, select *Run*:

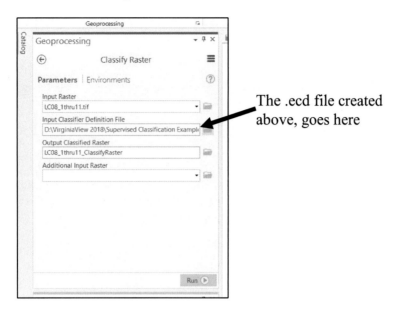

The .ecd file created above, goes here

Again, the progress of the processing can be monitored:

A message displays when completed:

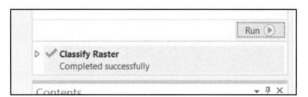

And, a new layer populates *Contents* with a new image in the *Map Viewer*. With this method, because the training sample shapefile was used in the creation of the definition file (.ecd), the symbology carried over to the new image.

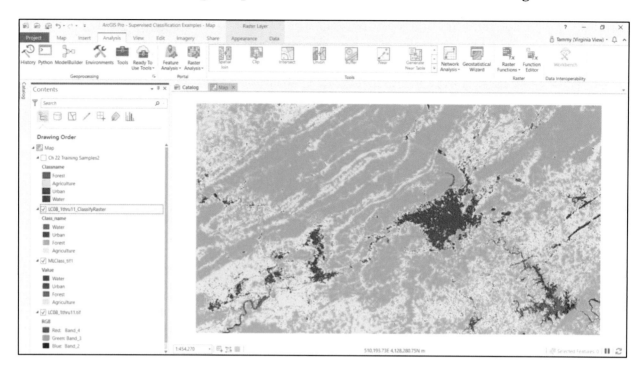

However, this method does not provide a cell count (see figure below), so calculating the number of hectares or the percent of landuse requires additional geoprocessing steps (we will demonstrate this process in the next section).

For more information on classification tools available in ArcGIS® Pro, refer to:
http://pro.arcgis.com/en/pro-app/tool-reference/spatial-analyst/an-overview-of-the-segmentation-and-classification-tools.htm.

Image Classification Wizard

In Chapter 21: Unsupervised Classification and Chapter 22: Introduction to Supervised Classification, we briefly reviewed the *Image Classification Wizard*. The *Image Classification Wizard* can also be used to do a supervised classification.

Go to *Imagery* tab, and select *Classification Wizard*.

In the wizard, in the first dialog box, under *Classification Method* - choose *Supervised* (figure below on left).

Then under *Classification Type*, choose *Pixel based* (middle figure).

Under *Classification Schema*, we have 4 choices (figure on right).

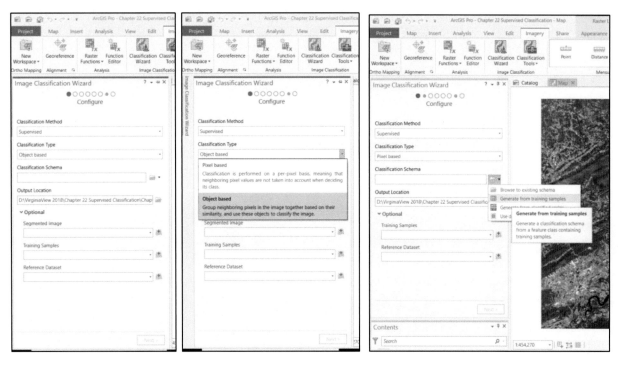

But, remember from Chapters 22 that we already created a classification schema based off of the NLCD 2011 schema, so browse to the location where the training sample schema was saved (.ecs) and add it.

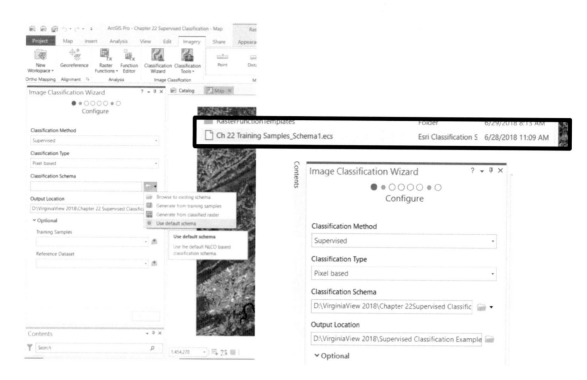

Under *Optional*, add the training samples shapefile:

Select *Next* at the bottom. Had we not already created the training samples, they can be created here. We chose to address them in Chapter 22, so you could better understand the process, so this step can be skipped here.

Select *Next* again. Maximum likelihood it not an option within the Image Classification Wizard. But, for demonstration purposes, select as the *Classifier – Support Vector Machine*. Then click *Run.*

As with all other *Geoprocessing*, a status is provided.

And a *Completed Successfully* message.

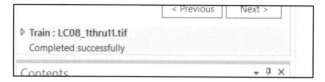

A new layer is in *Contents* and a new image in the map viewer. The new image has the appropriate symbology, because we again used the classification schema (.ecs). But, caution - the image is only available in this project. So, if completing an accuracy assessment with this image, the accuracy assessment must be accomplished within this project.

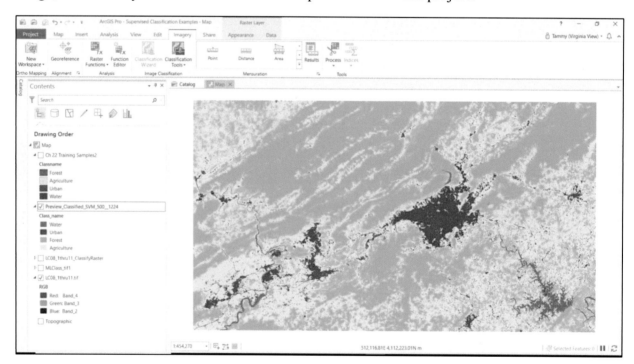

Or you can export it into a permanent file (figure below), by right-clicking on the file name and choosing *Data > Export Raster*. We will not demonstrate that step here.

Please note, that while this image file does have an attribute table, it does not have a count of the number of cells associated with each informational class (as happened with the *Classify Raster* method discussed in the prior section). From these results, the number of hectares and percent of landuse cannot be calculated based on the cell count without additional geoprocessing tools.

To calculate the number of cells per information class:

Go to *Analysis > Tools > Spatial Analyst Tools* (figure on left below) and open the tool - *Cell Statistics*.

The input is the *Preview_Classified_SVM_500_1224* generated from the *Image Classification Wizard*. Name the *Output Raster* and from the list of *Statistics*, choose *Sum* (figure on right below). Then choose *Run* at the bottom.

A new file is in the *Contents* and new image in the *map viewer*. Open the *Attribute Table* for this new file and a cell count is present (red circle below).

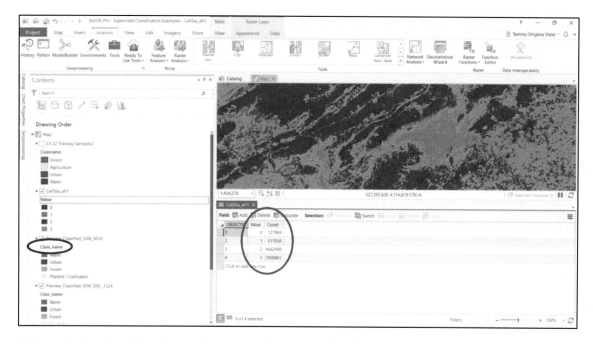

Although the classification scheme numbering (value field in the red oval above) has changed, the relationship of the value field to the informational class can easily be verified and corrected. Add a field and add the *Classname*:

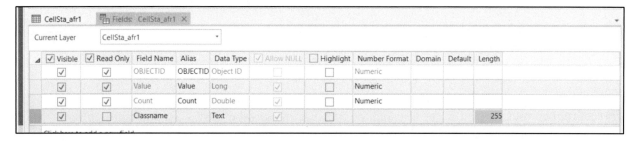

Then edit the field and manually type each *Classname*, verifying the correct information class is entered into the field (recall adding a new field in an attribute table from Chapter 21).

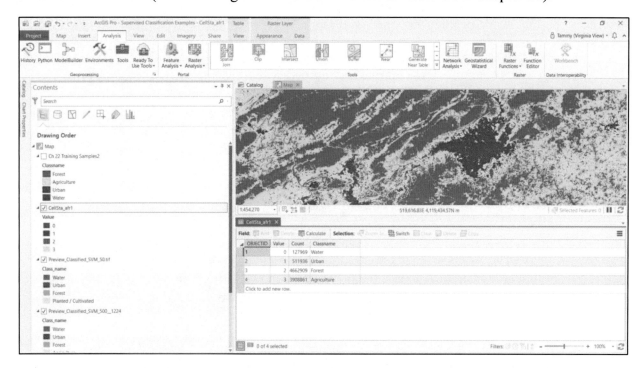

You can now, calculate the number of hectares and the percent of total landcover for each informational class (just as accomplished above and in Chapter 21 – Unsupervised Classification).

Again, we note that only two classification algorithms for supervised classification are available with the Wizard. For more information on the *Image Classification Wizard*, refer to: https://pro.arcgis.com/en/pro-app/help/analysis/image-analyst/the-image-classification-wizard.htm.

This concludes the chapter on supervised classification. We will use the file created using the Geoprocessing tool – Maximum Likelihood in the final chapter - Chapter 25 Accuracy Assessment.

Introduction

Accuracy Assessment compares a classified image to a reference image that matches the classified image with respect to scale, detail, categories, and projection. This is often conducted through a pixel-by-pixel comparison of a classified image to an image which is assumed to be a correct representation of the Earth's surface (such as an aerial photo). To determine how well a specific classification method performed, an *accuracy assessment* is conducted. Accuracy assessments are conducted for both unsupervised and supervised classifications and are always included in any project report. Although the pixel-by-pixel comparison is assessing *overall agreement* between the two images, in a remote sensing context, we typically regard the reference map to be an accuracy standard, and report disagreements between the two images as errors.[1]

In an accuracy assessment, an error matrix is compiled by comparing the two images pixel-by-pixel. Mismatches are regarded as errors, and are tabulated with respect to the number of incorrect matches, how the mismatched pixel was actually classified, and the percent of mismatched pixels. An *error matrix* consists of a table of values comparing the informational class code assigned to a specific pixel during the classification process to the actual informational class identified from an aerial photo. It is impossible to compare all of the pixels (which may number in the millions). Therefore, a sample of randomly selected pixels are used to generate the error matrix. Later in this chapter, we provide an example to illustrate calculation of the error matrix.

The final step of an accuracy assessment includes the calculation of Cohen's kappa co-efficient, derived from the error matrix. Kappa tells us how well the classification process performed as compared to a random assignment of values. For example, did we do better than if we had just randomly assigned the pixels to a specific informational class?

This chapter provides a step-by-step process for performing an accuracy assessment by completing an error matrix, then calculating Kappa.

The step-by-step process includes:

- A set of random points are generated in ArcGIS® Pro;
- For each point, the informational class associated with the pixel at that point is identified in an aerial photo;

---

[1] As a technicality: We note that the Accuracy Assessment strategy to be described here assesses the extent of agreement between two comparable maps, not always the "correctness" of a specific map. For example, we may wish to learn if several analysts provide interpretations that are consistent with one another, without necessarily deciding which interpretation is more accurate. Here, and most commonly throughout the practice of remote sensing, accuracy assessment is specifically applied to evaluate the match, and the degree of accuracy, in a comparison of two images.

- For each of these same points, the information class assigned during the classification process is identified;
- An error matrix is compiled;
- The percent of accuracy for each informational class is calculated;
- The percent of overall accuracy is calculated; and
- Kappa is calculated.

For more details on Accuracy Assessment and Kappa see Campbell and Wynne 5th edition (2011, 6th edition forthcoming in 2019), and (Congalton & Green, 2009)

As a reminder of our informational classes:

- Urban/built up/transportation = Class #1, assigned to red
- Mixed agriculture = Class #2, assigned to yellow
- Forest & Wetland = Class #3, assigned to green
- Open water = Class #4, assigned to blue

Classification Results from Prior Chapters

In Chapter 21, Classification of a Landsat 8 Image (Unsupervised) and Chapter 24: Conducting a Supervised Classification of a Landsat 8 Image, we calculated the number of pixels for each informational class and the percent of total land area represented by that class.

Table from Chapter 21: Classification of a Landsat 8 Image (Unsupervised):

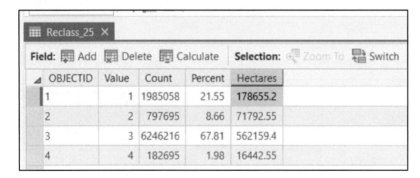

Table from Chapter 24: Conducting a Supervised Classification of a Landsat 8 Image:

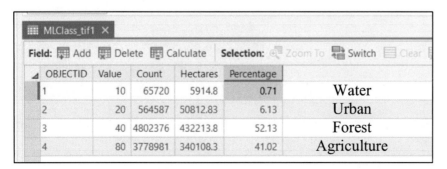

Comparing the results from the two tables:

Land Use	Hectares (unsupervised)	Percent (unsupervised)	Hectares (supervised)	Percent (supervised)	Difference*[2]
Urban	178,655.20	21.55	50,812.83	6.13	0.25%
Agriculture	71,792.55	8.66	340,108.30	41.02	-78.9%
Forest	562,159.40	67.81	432,213.80	52.13	30.1%
Water	16,442.55	1.98	5,914.80	0.71	178%

The two methods generated significantly different results. Remember from both chapters, we made different decisions when performing the classifications. For Chapter 21, we chose only 25 spectral classes (for efficiency in demonstrating the chapter, but noted that 50 classes was likely more appropriate). Which method performed best? An accuracy assessment can reveal if there is a difference.

Setting up ArcGIS Pro for an Accuracy Assessment

Open ArcGIS Pro, set up a new project. Add the *Reclass* of the unsupervised classified image created in Chapter 21 and the Maximum Likelihood classified image created in Chapter 24. Add the *Imagery* Basemap option. Set the workspaces. Be sure to set the symbology to the correct informational class values and colors.

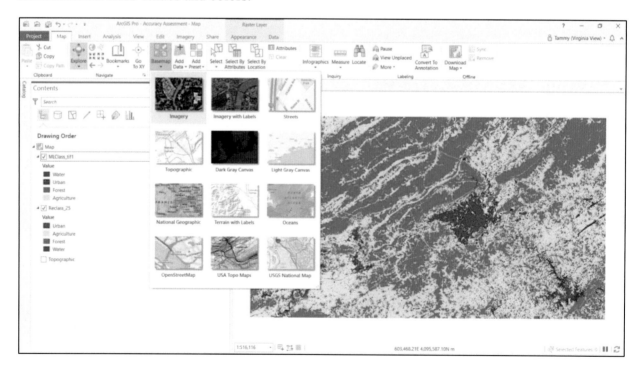

$$^2 \text{Difference} = \frac{\text{Hectares unsupervised} - \text{hectares supervised}}{\text{hectares supervised}} \times 100$$

Generating a Set of Random Points

To eliminate bias from an accuracy assessment (e.g. only choosing pixels that are known to be classified correctly), a random points file is first generated. Go to the *Analysis* tab, *Tools* and use the search word *Accuracy*. Choose *Create Accuracy Assessment Points (Spatial Analysis Tool)*.

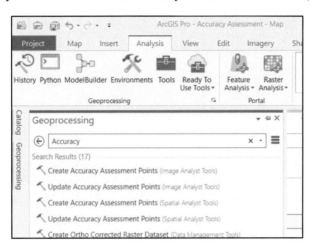

The tool opens and the first choice in *Input Raster*. Either of the classified images may be selected as the *Input Raster*. This choice will limit the areal extent within which the random points are generated and will automatically extract the class values when the new shapefile is created. We chose the unsupervised image.

Name the *Output Accuracy Assessment Points* shapefile and be sure that it is saving in the geodatabase.

The Target Field is *Classified*, this was automatically populated when the *Reclass* image was chosen (this is the name of the field within the Reclass_25 file that contains the informational class code).

The number of random points defaults to 500. The number of random points chosen depends on the extent of the area, the number of informational classes, and other considerations. For our purposes, demonstrating an accuracy assessment process, we have reduced the number of random points to 100.

Three sampling strategies are available, we strictly want *Random* choice, *no stratification.*

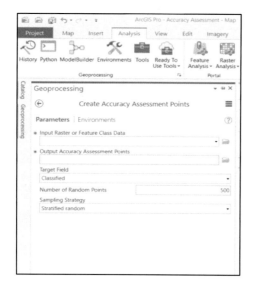

Once the fields are populated, click *Run* at the bottom. This tool runs quickly. A *Completed successfully* message displays in the bottom of the *Geoprocessing* dialog box, a new shapefile populates in the *Contents,* and displays in the map viewer. The symbology for the points is light purple and difficult to see.

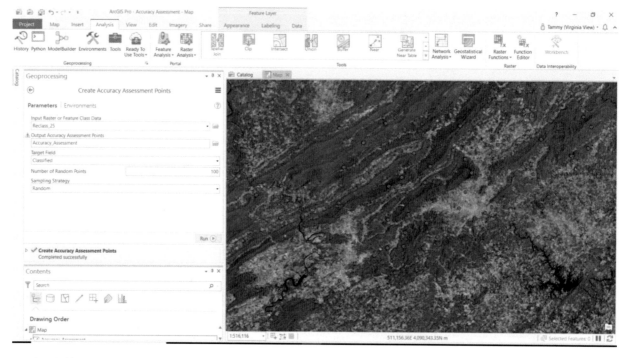

In the following figure, we changed the symbology of the random points layer to yellow to enhance their visibility and we opened the *Attribute Table.* As seen in the *Attribute Table,* the classified values for each point were automatically extracted. A second field that was added is called *GrndTruth (*ground truth is also known as field data in other usage). This field can be used if the true value for each of your points is going to be based on field evaluation.

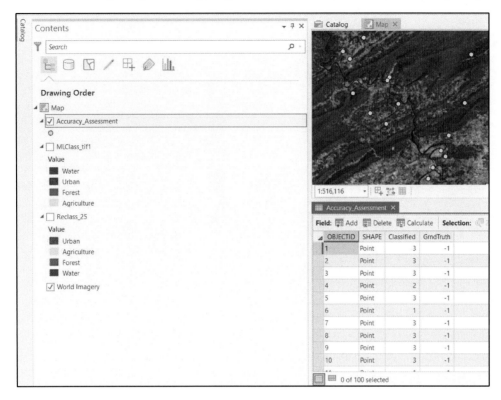

For our purposes, we are not verifying with ground truth, so we are deleting that field (*GrndTruth)*. Highlight the column and choose *Delete Field*:

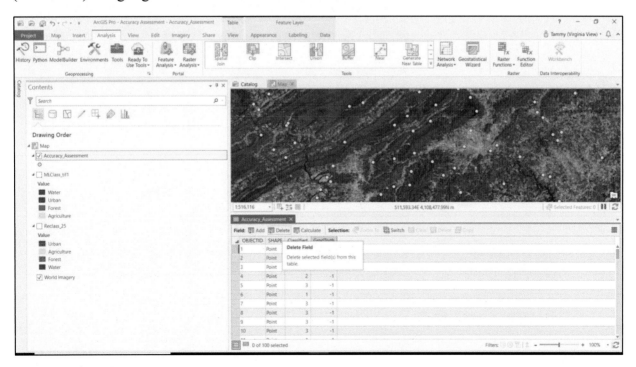

ArcGIS® Pro asks if you are sure, select *Yes*.

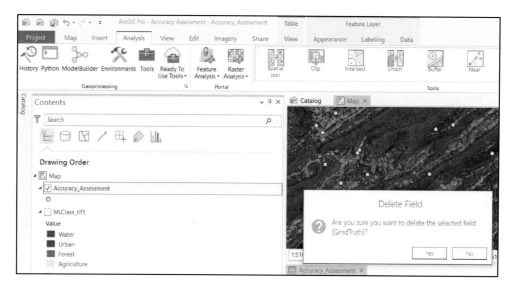

We want to add the values for the other classified raster to the same *Accuracy Assessment* (random points) shapefile. *Add a new field*-- we named the new field *ML_Class* since we are adding the maximum likelihood supervised classification results to each point. Don't forget to save!

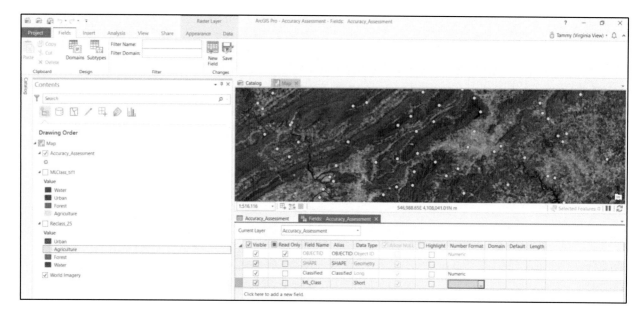

As you can see in the figure below, we now have columns (fields) associated with both of the classified images – one is already populated. Now we need to populate the other.

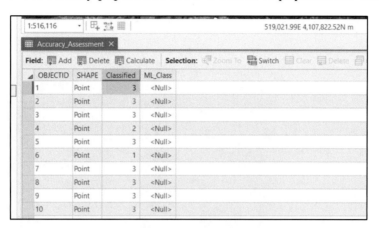

To add values from a raster file (the supervised classified image is a raster file) to a point shapefile, we will be using the *Extract Values to Points* tool.

Your *Input point features* is the Accuracy Assessment points shapefile created above.

The *Input Raster* is the second classified image (in our case, the maximum likelihood image).

This tool creates a new file, so be sure to name the *Output point features*. In this example, we named the new file *Accuracy_Assessment2*

Then select *Run.*

A new point shapefile (*Accuracy_Assessment2*) is added to *Contents* and the map viewer.

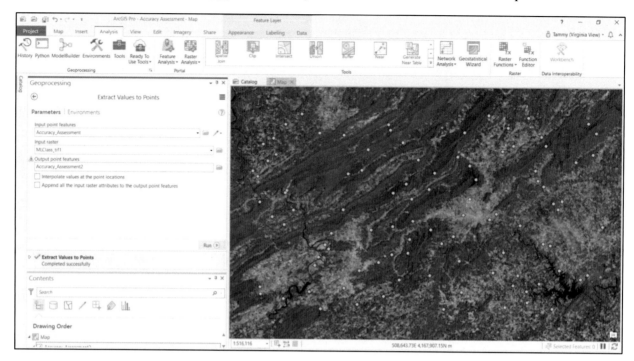

Open the *Attribute Table* for this new shapefile (*Accuracy_Assessment2*). As seen in the figure below, a new field is visible called *RasterValu*. This is the NLCD class value from the maximum likelihood classified image file. We need to calculate the information class value and populate it in the *ML_Class* field.

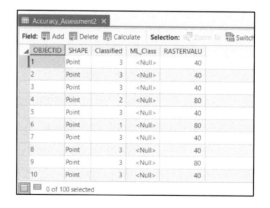

OBJECTID	SHAPE	Classified	ML_Class	RASTERVALU
1	Point	3	<Null>	40
2	Point	3	<Null>	40
3	Point	3	<Null>	40
4	Point	2	<Null>	80
5	Point	3	<Null>	40
6	Point	1	<Null>	80
7	Point	3	<Null>	40
8	Point	3	<Null>	40
9	Point	3	<Null>	80
10	Point	3	<Null>	40

0 of 100 selected

To verify which NLCD value belongs to which Informational Class, just look at the symbology:

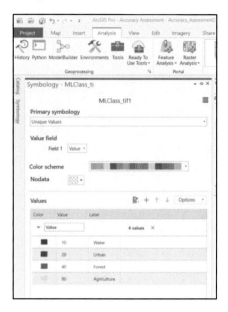

First, use *Select by Attributes* to open a geoprocessing window.

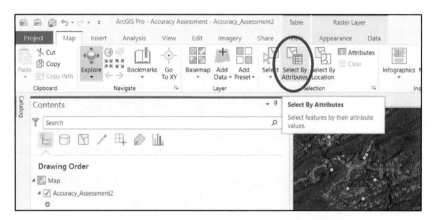

Within the *Select Layer by Attribute* geoprocessing window, make sure that the second accuracy assessment random point shapefile is populated under *Layer Name* or *Table View*. *Selection type* should be *New selection*. Under *Expression*, click on *Add Clause*.

As seen in the figure below, a new line opens – the expression to select one of the NLCD class is built here.

RasterValu for the *Field*.

Is Equal to

Then, from the dropdown arrow, choose one of the NLCD values, for this demonstration, we chose 40.

Select *Run*.

The tool runs and all those fields with NLCD value of 40 are highlighted. Remember from above, 40 is forest. So, we now need to change the ML Informational class to 3 for forest.

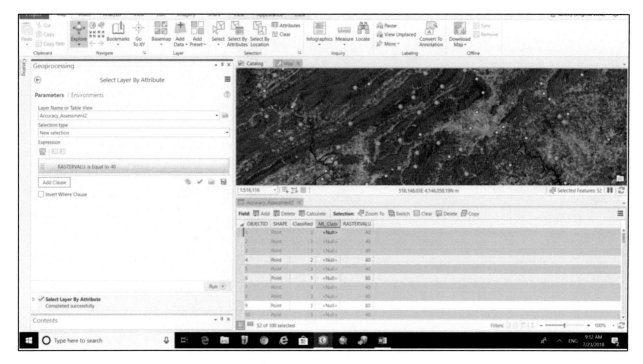

Highlight the column for ML_Class and select *Calculate Field*.

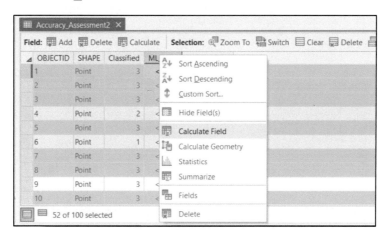

In the *Calculate Field* geoprocessing window, under *ML_Class* =, type 3 and then click on *Run*.

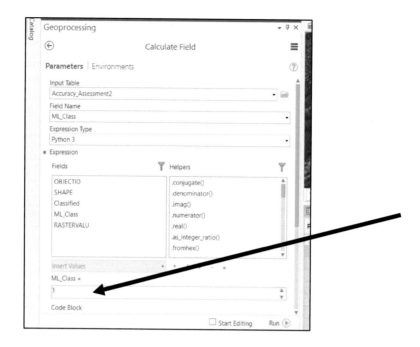

The *ML_Class* field for forest has updated to the informational class.

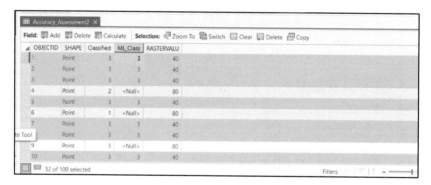

Do this for each of the 4 NLCD classes.

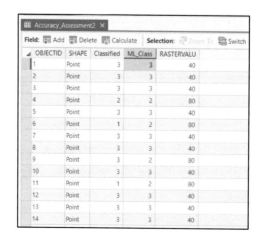

We no longer need the Rastervalu field, so it can be deleted. We need a field for the Aerial Imagery. We will be using the Aerial Imagery to populate the field we will use to compare our classified values (since we will not be using field data for ground truthing). Add a field for Aerial image. We will be using the imagery available from *Basemaps* in ArcGIS Pro. Note that when conducting an accuracy assessment, you need to use an aerial image that was acquired as close to the date of the original Landsat image as possible. For example, when examining the extent of urbanization, you do not compare an aerial image from the 1970's to a Landsat image acquired in 2018.

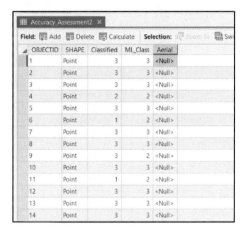

This new aerial field must be populated individually. First, make sure the only image turned on is the basemap. Right click on row in the *Attribute Table* and select *Zoom to*.

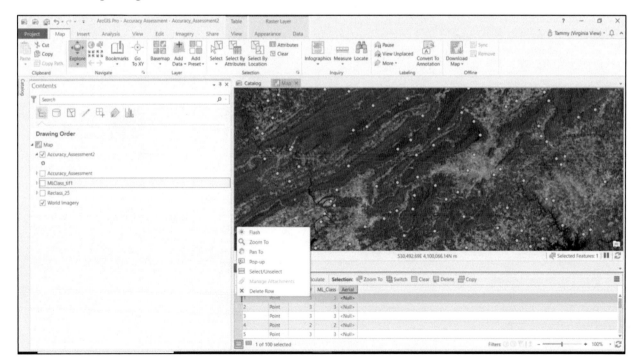

This zooms to the point and we can clearly see that this is forest (which is associated with Class 3):

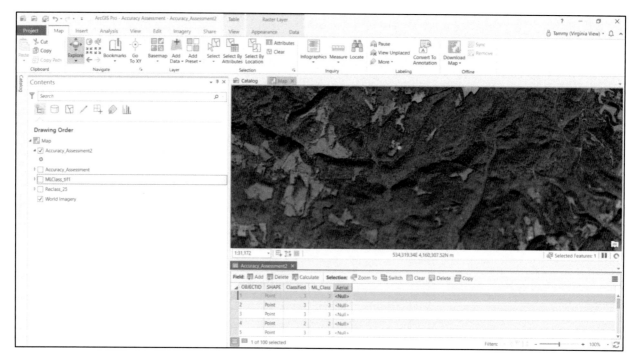

At the top of ArcGIS® Pro, go to *Edit* tab, choose *Attributes* and type in 3 under *Aerial*.

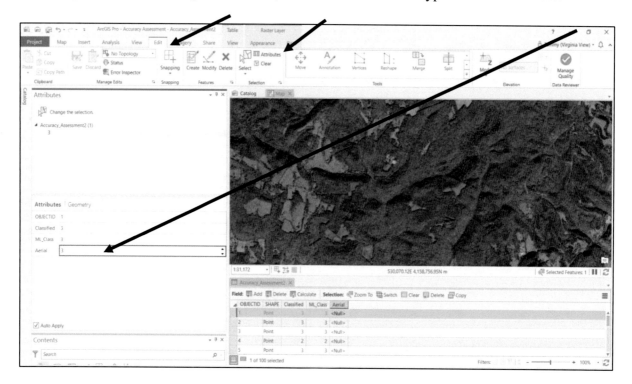

You must hit the *tab button* on the keyboard to change the value in the *Attribute Table*. Continue to follow this procedure for all 100 points until all points are classified based on the aerial photo. As seen in the figure below, sometimes, it might be necessary to zoom out to confirm the location because you may be zoomed in too far to make a determination, e.g. is the brown pixel a paved area or a bare agriculture field?

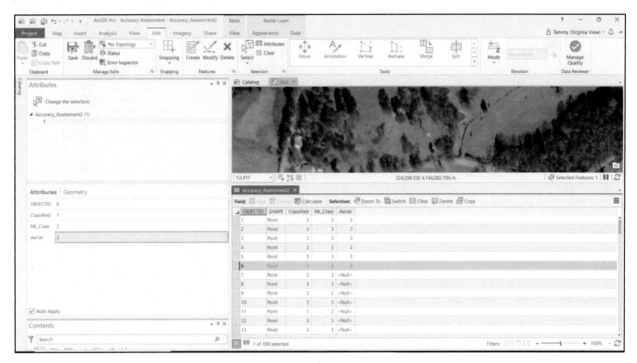

Save frequently – both the edits and the project!

Once all points are assigned to a class, close the *Attributes* edit window. Be sure that all 100 points were populated for Aerial values.

Summarizing the Results for the Error Matrix

With the *Attribute Table* open, right click on the column for *Aerial* and select *Summarize*.

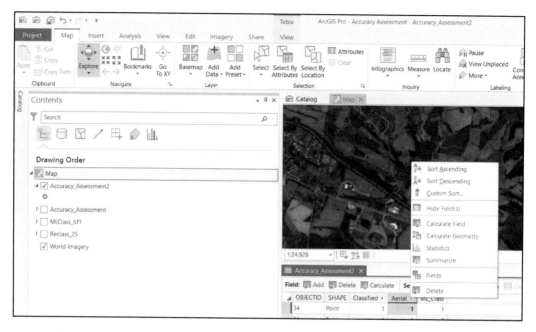

The *Summary Statistic* geoprocessing window opens. Please follow the next few steps very carefully.

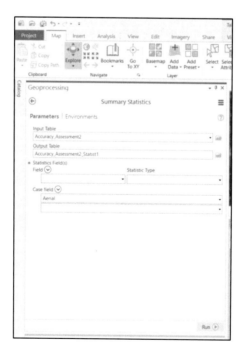

We are summarizing class values relative to Aerial, so choose *Aerial* for the first *Statistics Field*. We want a *Count* of the number of pixels for each informational class (1, 2, 3 and 4). We are comparing one of the classified images (we chose the unsupervised), so it gets populated in the second *Statistics Field*, again with the *Count* as the statistic. Under *Case field*, we want to list both again – *Aerial* in the first blank and then *Classified* in the second.

Once completely populated as shown above, select *Run* at the bottom. This tools runs very quickly and populated a *Standalone Table* in *Contents*.

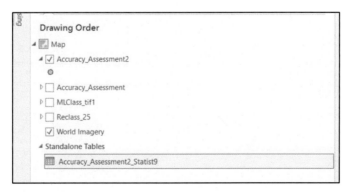

Right click on the table name and open the *Attribute Table*. We have a summary of Aerial classes and unsupervised classes for all 100 points.

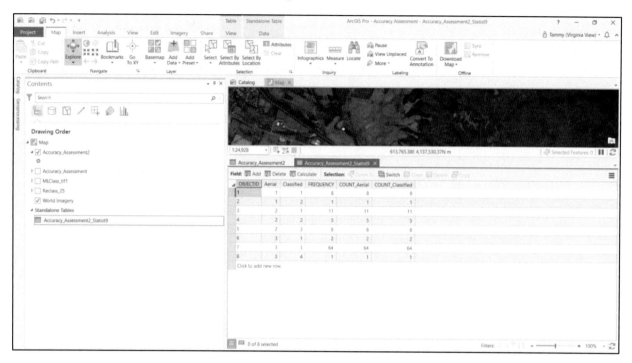

The following summary of the first 4 rows should help you to interpret the table:.

- *First Row* - The number of points identified as urban (1) in the aerial photo and also as urban (1) in the unsupervised classification equals 8.
- *Second Row* - The number of points identified as urban (1) in the aerial photo but as agriculture (2) in the unsupervised classification equals 1.
- *Third Row*- The number of points that are agriculture (2) in the aerial photo but classified as urban (1) in the unsupervised classification equals 11.
- *Fourth Row* - , The number of points that are agriculture (2) in the aerial photo and classified as agriculture (2) in the unsupervised classification equals 5.
- And, continue down for all 8 rows.

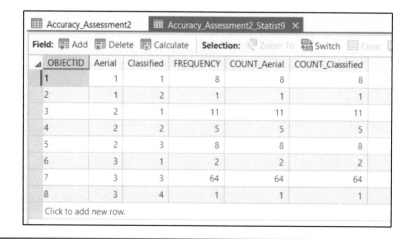

Now we can compile the *Error Matrix* and calculate *Kappa*.

Compiling the Error Matrix

Remember:

- Urban/built up/transportation = Class #1, assigned to red
- Mixed agriculture = Class #2, assigned to yellow
- Forest & Wetland = Class #3, assigned to green
- Open water = Class #4, assigned to blue

We are going to compile the matrix for the unsupervised classified image. From the tables above, the unsupervised image values were added to the random points file as *Classified*:

Error Matrix

	Water (4)	Urban (1)	Forest (3)	Agriculture (2)	
Water (4)	0 (a)	0 (b)	0 (c)	0 (d)	0 (e)
Urban (1)	0 (f)	8 (g)	0 (h)	1 (i)	9 (j)
Forest (3)	1 (k)	2 (l)	64 (m)	0 (n)	67 (o)
Agriculture (2)	0 (p)	11 (q)	8 (r)	5 (s)	24 (t)
	1 (u)	21 (v)	72 (w)	6 (x)	77 (y)

The values in the error matrix that you generate will not be the same as shown above, because your random set of points will be different from our example. But we will explain each field, so you can interpret your own matrix. Each of the fields in the above error matrix contains a letter within parenthesis. We will use each of those letters to explain the number that belongs in that field.

a – The number of random points that were identified as water in the aerial photo and classified as water in the unsupervised classified image

b – The number of random points that were identified as water in the aerial photo but classified as urban in the unsupervised classified image

c – The number of random points that were identified as water in the aerial photo but were classified as forest in the unsupervised classified image

d – The number of random points that were identified as water in the aerial photo but classified as agriculture in the unsupervised classified image

e – Total of the Row

f – The number of random points that were identified as urban in the aerial photo but were classified as water in the unsupervised classified image

g – The number of random points that were classified as urban in the aerial photo and urban in the unsupervised classified image

h – The number of random points that were classified as urban in the aerial photo but forest in the unsupervised classified image

i – The number of random points that were classified as urban in the aerial photo but agriculture in the unsupervised classified image

j – Total of the Row

k – The number of random points that were classified as forest in the aerial photo but water in the unsupervised classified image

l – The number of random points that were classified as forest in the aerial photo but urban in the unsupervised classified image

m – The number of random points that were classified as forest in the aerial photo and forest in the unsupervised classified image

n – The number of random points that were classified as forest in the aerial photo but agriculture in the unsupervised classified image

o – Total of the Row

p – The number of random points that were classified as agriculture in the aerial photo but water in the unsupervised classified image

q – The number of random points that were classified as agriculture in the aerial photo but urban in the unsupervised classified image

r – The number of random points that were classified as agriculture in the aerial photo but forest in the unsupervised classified image

s – The number of random points that were classified as agriculture in the aerial photo and agriculture in the unsupervised classified image

t – Total of the Row

u – Total of the Column

v – Total of the Column

w – Total of the Column

x – Total of the Column

y – Sum total of fields a, g, m and s

Calculating Overall Accuracy

Overall accuracy is the percentage of random points that are the same in both images. For our matrix above, that is 77 points (0 water, 8 urban, 64 forest and 5 agriculture). We have a total of 100 random points, so our overall accuracy is 77/100 or 77%.

User's accuracy, Producer's accuracy, errors of omission and errors of commission can also be calculated from the error matrix. We will not discuss these specific calculations or their use in this chapter. Once you have compiled the error matrix, these can be easily calculated. Please see Campbell and Wynne 5th edition, 2011 (6th edition forthcoming) for more information.

Calculation of Cohen's Kappa (k)

Kappa provides us with insight into our classification scheme and whether or not we achieved results better than we would have achieved strictly by chance. The formula for kappa is:

$$\frac{Observed - Expected}{1 - Expected}$$

Observed is overall accuracy. Expected is calculated from the rows and column totals above.

First, you calculate the product of the rows and columns.

	Water Column	Urban Column	Forest Column	Agriculture Column
Water Row	0 x 1 = 0	0 x 21 = 0	0 x 72 = 0	0 x 6 = 0
Urban Row	9 x 1 = 9	9 x 21 = 189	9 x 72 = 648	9 x 6 = 54
Forest Row	67 x 1 = 67	67 x 21 = 1407	67 x 72 = 4824	67 x 6 = 402
Agriculture Row	24 x 1 = 24	24 x 21 = 504	24 x 72 = 1728	24 x 6 = 144

Used to calculate product matrix

Then calculate what would be expected based on chance:

$$\frac{\text{Product matrix}}{\text{Cumulative sum of Product matrix}}$$

The product matrix is the sum of the diagonals: $0 + 189 + 4824 + 144 = 5157$

The Cumulative Sum is: $0 + 0 + 0 + 0 + 9 + 189 + 648 + 54 + 67 + 1407 + 4824 + 402 + 24 + 504 + 1728 + 144 = 10{,}000$

So, expected is 5157/10000 = 51.6%

$$k = \frac{0.77^3 - 0.516}{1 - 0.516}$$

$$k = .525$$

$$k = 52.5\%$$

The kappa coefficient for this classification is .525 which means that the classification is 52.5% better than would have occurred strictly by chance. Kappa can range from -1 to $+1$.

Remember, we only used 100 random points to conduct an accuracy assessment for this classification, and no water points were chosen. In this example, the number (of random points) is very low. When conducting an accuracy assessment to support your research project, the number of random points should be much higher. We used a small number of values for the accuracy assessment simply to illustrate the process using a practical example.

Now calculate your overall accuracy and Cohen's kappa for your supervised image.

Identifying Each Random Point's Value from Aerial Imagery in Google Earth

---

If using imagery in Google Earth as the reference image, once the first random points shapefile is generated, then convert the shapefile to KML using the *Layer To KML* geoprocessing tool.

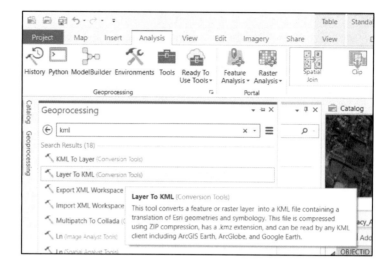

Open Google Earth. Once Google Earth has launched, go to *File/Open* and navigate to your workspace. Double-click on your .kml file and then click open to add it to Google Earth. Use the Google Earth Image date (using the historical image slider bar tool) that is closest to your Landsat date. You can then manually add the value to the attribute table of the random point shapefile using Edit as outlined above.

This concludes the chapter on accuracy assessment and the demonstration on remote sensing using ArcGIS® Pro. As noted, frequently, within each chapter, this book serves as a guide to using ArcGIS® Pro only, it does not provide sufficient information on making choices in remote sensing analysis specific to any individual project.

Made in the USA
Coppell, TX
30 December 2021

70430340R00247